Depends What You Mean By Extremist

John Safran is a writer and documentary maker.
His debut book, *Murder in Mississippi* (titled *God'll Cut You Down* in the US), won the 2014 Ned Kelly Award for Best True Crime and was a finalist in the 2015 Melbourne Prize for Literature Best Writing Award. His television work includes *John Safran vs God, Music Jamboree, Race Relations* and *The Goddam Election!*

johnsafran.com

ALSO BY JOHN SAFRAN

Murder in Mississippi

JOHN SAFRAN

Depends What You Mean By Extremist

Going Rogue with
Australian Deplorables

HAMISH HAMILTON
an imprint of
PENGUIN BOOKS

HAMISH HAMILTON

UK | USA | Canada | Ireland | Australia
India | New Zealand | South Africa | China

Penguin Books is part of the Penguin Random House group of companies
whose addresses can be found at global.penguinrandomhouse.com.

Penguin
Random House
Australia

First published by Penguin Random House Australia Pty Ltd, 2017

10 9 8 7 6 5 4 3 2 1

Text copyright © John Safran 2017

Cover design by Alex Ross © Penguin Random House Australia Pty Ltd.
Cover photograph by Noah Erlich
Typeset in Adobe Caslon Pro 11.5/18 by Samantha Jayaweera,
Penguin Random House Australia Pty Ltd.
Colour separation by Splitting Image Colour Studio, Clayton, Victoria
Printed and bound in Australia by Griffin Press, an accredited ISO AS/NZS 14001
Environmental Management Systems printer.

National Library of Australia
Cataloguing-in-Publication data:

Safran, John.
Depends what you mean by extremist: going rogue with
Australian deplorables / John Safran.
9781926428772 (paperback)
Radicalism – Australia. Radicalism – Religious aspects – Islam.
Islamic fundamentalism – Australia.

penguin.com.au

I have been a stranger in a strange land

MOSES, EXODUS 2:22

CONTENTS

INTRODUCTION

A photo rolls into my Facebook feed. A skinhead with a swastika inked on his noggin and a cool-as-fuck black dude are staring each other down. The photo was snapped at the first rally of Reclaim Australia, a group 'fighting back against Islam and multiculturalism'.

The black dude is part of No Room for Racism. These guys sprung up in response to Reclaim Australia. And No Room for Racism has turned this photo into an advertisement, to encourage its supporters to rock up to the next Reclaim Australia versus No Room for Racism showdown.

It's mid-2015 and this is all happening in Melbourne. Thrilled that there's something as exciting as skinheads roaming around my home town – I've been into racists since high school – I scribble down the date of the upcoming rally.

A woman, blond and white, climbs onto the back of a ute outside Parliament House in Melbourne. She is the first Reclaim Australia speaker to address the rally.

'First I'd like to pay respect to the Wurundjeri people, the traditional owners of the land,' she says.

Strange way to start your rally against multiculturalism, I think to myself. I pull out my phone and report this to my Facebook followers. (More about that later.)

A couple of hundred people have turned up to support Reclaim Australia, which is in fact a loose collective of different groups. The supporters are protected by a double line of police, who are holding back over a thousand folks from No Room for Racism. STAND WITH MUSLIMS AGAINST RACISM reads one of their huge banners.

Back here, with the guys against multiculturalism, Pastor Daniel Nalliah from Catch The Fire Ministries climbs onto the ute and begins the chant: 'Aussie, Aussie, Aussie! Oi! Oi! Oi!'

Pastor Daniel looks nothing like the skinhead in the photo. In fact he is a Sri Lankan immigrant. He warns that back where he used to live, Muslims caused grief, and they're going to do the same here. They're moving in and not assimilating.

What a tangle! If assimilating is about leaving your ethnic grievances behind when you immigrate, maybe he's the one not assimilating.

Next onto the ute is another immigrant – a young man of Cook Islands heritage – who starts belting out 'Amazing Grace' like he's auditioning for *The Voice*. Many in the crowd sing and sway along. About half of these Reclaim Australia people are from Pastor Daniel's Catch The Fire Ministries, and most of them are Asian, Indian or African.

I upload a collage of this very multicultural anti-multicultural rally to my Facebook page. Immediately, progressives start psychoanalysing: 'These brown people are victims of racist Australia! They want to be accepted by the dominant white-supremacy culture, so they debase themselves this way!'

That's not where my mind goes, though, because I grew up among the devout. In my experience, Australian intellectuals – you know, the folks on *Q&A* who tell you what's going on – just don't get religion. How scripture and faith can channel a person's life. I'll have to find out more, but maybe religion trumps skin colour for these guys at the rally.

Finally a white man climbs onto the ute. He even wears an akubra. This is more like a 'classic Aussie', to be expected at a rally against multiculturalism. He grabs the microphone and starts talking about how much he loves his Thai wife. The crowd seems to be taking all this in its stride.

But Catch The Fire Ministries is not the only gang here supporting Reclaim Australia. In search of the racists I was promised in that photo of the skinhead, I drift from the ute deeper into the crowd, where big red flags cast shadows. This is the territory of the far-right United Patriots Front. Here are white Australians who look like bikies.

'Turn on the gas!' a leather-clad man shouts at Jewish John Safran.

'Is that a joke?' I ask.

'No, no,' he mumbles, immediately backing down.

I've met Holocaust deniers before, but this is the first Holocaust-joke denier I've come across.

An emo-Nazi, lanky, dressed in black with a Korean-boy-band haircut, just stares and stares at me.

'You Jewish parasite,' he hisses eventually. 'Write about me and see what happens!' He informs me I've only had a book published because of the Jewish puppetmasters who control everything. 'Fuck off, you're not wanted here!' he wraps up, motioning me over to those on the other side of the police line. He tells me he'll come after me if I write anything funny about him. Think I'll still leave in the Korean-boy-band haircut bit.

Someone who seems to be a United Patriots Front leader tries to settle the angry young man down. He doesn't want his group to be seen as neo-Nazis. Earlier, a tubby man with a swastika tattooed on his head (a different skinhead to the one in the photo) was chased off. Now this UPF leader climbs onto the ute and stands next to Pastor Daniel. He tells us his name is Blair Cottrell and gives a rousing speech about the dangers of Islam, punching his Popeye arms into the air. He says he's fed up with multiculturalism too. I look around to see if anyone else thinks it's odd he's sharing a ute with a Sri Lankan immigrant. Seems not.

Afterwards, like my friends in the theatre, Blair hangs around fishing for positive feedback on his performance.

When I pull my phone from my pocket I'm surprised to see my

sarcastic Facebook posts have gone viral. A small group of young activists – a couple of Muslims, a couple of Asian Australians – are furious. I am a white man taking up space in this discussion that belongs to people of colour.

I know that for some, history only goes as far back as last week's BuzzFeed listicle, but still. Strange that they can't understand why a Jew is curious about a far-right rally in his home town. Hey, BuzzFeed, maybe you can help educate them on this matter. I even have the headline: Schindler's Listicle.

The next day, one of the other UPF leaders who spoke at the rally posts a video on Facebook. Shermon Burgess had sprung youthfully up onto the back of the ute, and while Blair Cottrell had huffed and puffed into the microphone until his face turned beetroot, Shermon twanged out his opposition to Islam like he was Paul Hogan.

In the video, Shermon is wearing an akubra and a flannel shirt. His hands are tucked behind his back. 'Patriots, we have been through so much together,' he begins. He lists the three rallies the UPF have helped organise so far: Federation Square, Richmond town hall, and the most recent one, the one I rocked up to, at Parliament House. It occurs to me that these all happened along my train line. The train line that threads through inner-city Melbourne – the home of smug bastards who sneer at Far North Queensland for harvesting bigots.

Shermon promises that the UPF have a lot more in store. 'Get ready, patriots, it's gonna be big.' His hands rise from behind his back, revealing an Australian flag, like a kid showing off his Batman cape. He clucks and winks.

That same day, a stranger called Rebecca vibrates in my pocket. 'You probably won't see this,' she writes in a Facebook message. 'But anyway, I saw you at the rally yesterday and was like Hey it's John Safran. I was with the United Patriots Front. I liked a few of your Facebook posts. But some of them were a tad judgemental. Like the *heil* one.'

(I'd posted: 'I'm at the Reclaim Australia rally in Melbourne this morning. If you see me come over and say heil.')

'Anyway,' Rebecca goes on, 'I hope you gained an open mind about the rally cos it seemed like you were against it. My dad's side has Jewish heritage so I'm half Jewish in a way. And there were two other Jewish girls on the UPF bus with me from Sydney.'

So it turns out I wasn't the only Jew at the rally. There were two and a half more. Not protesting against the UPF, but supporting them? That clinches it. Skinheads side by side with Jews; immigrants against immigrants; Shermon's promise of a far-right hajj – this is a case for John Safran, Jew Detective.

I ask Rebecca the Half-Jewess if she'll catch up with me when I'm next in Sydney. She says yes.

CAST

The wrong immigrant story

A large porcelain doll is creeping me out from the corner of the motel reception, like a toy in a horror film. That the motel owner no doubt thinks it's adorable reminds me that two people can see the same thing very differently. I've driven six hours to Mildura, the fruit-picking capital of regional Victoria.

Pastor Daniel Nalliah, the Sri Lankan on the back of the ute, has booked the small conference room here. Books and CDs are for sale on a table, a coffee urn bubbles next to a tray of biscuits. Most folks in the small crowd are old and wearing jumpers. Everyone's white.

The pastor has come to pitch his political party, Rise Up Australia. Like his church, it has become part of the sprawl that

7

makes up Reclaim Australia. 'My first SBS radio interview,' Pastor Daniel begins, 'the guy, he said, "Today Australia has a brand new political party. Nothing but another Pauline Hanson One Nation. This is another white Australia supremacist party!"'

We chuckle.

'Well, I'm cracking up laughing on the other side of the phone. I said, "Mate, you obviously have not done your homework. I am not a white man. I'm a black fellow, mate!"'

We burst out laughing. This is like a Chris Rock concert.

'The SBS guy says, "Something's really wrong here. How can a black fellow lead a white Australia party?"' Pastor Daniel scans the crowd with his big brown eyes. 'I just love my country.'

Pastor Daniel insists his party, and the broader Reclaim movement, support a 'multiracial' and 'multiethnic' Australia – that's a society where immigrants assimilate. He says they only oppose multiculturalism, where immigrants stick to their old ways.

Pastor Daniel sways and flops while speaking, needing the support of the podium. He's afflicted with an injured ankle. His eyes squint from pain, so you warm to him like you would a wounded wombat.

He rolls into a Bible story. The walls of Jerusalem had broken down. Those inside the city were complacent. But one man, Jeremiah, who lived outside the city, could see it was vulnerable to attack. Jeremiah had the outsider's perspective. Pastor Daniel says that when he arrived in Australia in 1997, he felt like Jeremiah. The walls of Australia were down. He had just come from Saudi Arabia where he witnessed three beheadings. Why wouldn't anyone listen to him about the dangers of Islam? Then, four years later, aeroplanes ploughed into the World Trade Center. Now, he tells us, Australians wanted to listen to him. He even had meetings with Prime Minister John Howard. He likes Mr Howard and Mr Abbott but he's not that crash-hot on Mr Turnbull, who has just knifed Mr Abbott.

Prime Minister Turnbull has betrayed Tony Abbott, the pastor argues, as Judas did Jesus. So, he tells the audience, his church's political party is their only choice in the fight against the Islamisation of Australia.

Pastor Daniel wanders over to me after his speech. 'Just take a seat,' he says. 'I want to pray for you, man.'

He presses his hand on my head. 'Father, I pray for John. Lord, I remember the time he did a documentary and I watched it on TV. When he was in a church, he had the touch from you. I pray that you will connect him back into your hands.'

I repeat after him: 'Dear Lord Jesus, forgive me for any wrong I have done. Come into my heart and show me who you are.'

He pats my head goodbye and I tell him I'll see him tomorrow morning at the local church.

A bloke by the biscuit tray explains that Mildura is a violent place and race is to blame. The Tongans and other Islanders all want to fight each other here. And the local Aboriginal people are from different tribes, so they all fight each other too. I ask if the white people fight anyone.

'Well, that's a good point . . . I hadn't . . . I suppose they do.'

The church where Pastor Daniel is appearing this morning was once the clubhouse for Mildura's sailing enthusiasts. But drought dried up the lake, so the sailing club moved on. The church leaders have found that the locals most receptive to their message are the new Chinese immigrants, many not fluent in English.

That explains the presence of Jiang, a young local Chinese man acting as translator. He stands next to Pastor Daniel in front of a largely Chinese congregation.

'I'm a walking miracle! I should have been beheaded!' is Pastor Daniel's strong opener. He's referring to his dangerous past, preaching in Saudi Arabia.

'我是一个行走的奇迹! 有人应该斩首我的!' Jiang says.

'Today,' the pastor continues, 'we live in a society where the Bible is being removed in many parts of Europe, and guess what is replacing it? The Qur'an.'

Jiang squints at Pastor Daniel. 'Kooran?' he asks.

'Qur'an!'

Jiang still doesn't understand. He's never heard the word before.

'The Muslim holy book,' Pastor Daniel elaborates. 'Or rather, respectfully, the unholy book!'

'Ooooh,' says Jiang. '穆斯林圣或者邪的.'

'That book,' Pastor Daniel says, 'actually tells the Muslim to lie for the cause of promoting Islam. It's known as *taqiyya*.'

Jiang begins to struggle out a translation. His aunt is seated in the congregation. She raises her arm and snaps her fingers, like a tiger mum, and corrects a translation error. Jiang looks ashamed.

Pastor Daniel moves on from Islam, clicking a button on a remote control. A photo of a girl in a hospital bed pops up behind him. He reveals how he prayed for this girl the night her life support was to be turned off. She was healed. The Melbourne hospital staff were so impressed they said he didn't have to pay for parking.

Later, outside the church, a white couple are slowly and loudly explaining something to Jiang.

'It's okay to lie?' Jiang asks.

'That's what they're taught,' the woman says. 'That's what they live for!'

'I never knew.' Jiang's eyebrows rise as he takes this in, and I see the exact moment a new concept is chalked onto his mind. He says he's grateful Pastor Daniel came, because most of the Chinese people here haven't had a chance to learn about Muslims before.

Pastor Daniel, meanwhile, is sipping water on the balcony of the former sailing clubhouse. I ask if he can show me which parts of the Qur'an cause him concern. He tells me he's not the best person to ask.

'I can introduce you to a guy – I wouldn't call myself a scholarly person on Islam.'

Strange response, considering his travelling roadshow routine.

His conversation curls back to witnessing violence in Saudi Arabia and narrowly avoiding it himself. Once, he was baptising people in the sea when a military jeep pulled up. He dropped the man he was dunking and everyone swam around, convincing the soldiers they were just having a fun day at the beach.

What made him take that risk of baptising people in the sea?

'I hear from God,' Pastor Daniel explains. 'Either I'm a nutcase or I hear from God.'

I tell Pastor Daniel that some people on Twitter say he jumped onto the ute and spoke at the rally in order to pander to white Australia.

But he insists that God directs him, 'through dreams and visions', to work with Reclaim. The National Party's Barnaby Joyce has mocked Pastor Daniel for calling bottle shops 'Satan's stronghold'. It occurs to me that if Pastor Daniel's motivation is to suck up to white Australia, he wouldn't be denouncing beer.

The pastor knows that the concept of Satan would be a laugh for the average Aussie, but he says he won't budge. 'I can't lie to be somebody. I have to be who I am. If they accept me, they accept me as a Christian. If not, tough luck.'

(Later it strikes me the pastor has basically said, 'I will not assimilate.')

There have been consequences to his fiery preaching. In 2002 three Muslim men, feeling that Pastor Daniel and his fellow preacher, also an immigrant, had vilified Muslims at a church workshop, filed a complaint under the Racial and Religious Tolerance Act of Victoria. The preachers spent five years, on and off, in court, first losing the case then winning in an appeal.

At the time, journalist David Marr wrote a piece in which he mistakenly assumed the two 'hellfire Christian preachers' were white. But I've made my own flub. I assumed the three Muslim complainants were non-white. Not so, the pastor tells me. They were three Anglo-Aussies. Converts.

Strolling back to my car I message a friend about Pastor Daniel and his court case: 'Three white Australians try to shut up a brown immigrant. #CheckYourPrivilege #WhiteTears.'

The Gharqad tree

Rebecca, the Half-Jewess, sits across the table at a Hungarian cafe in Surry Hills, Sydney, nibbling a cake. She's as pale as I am.

Rebecca became obsessed with her Jewish roots – something that hardly ever came up in her family – ten years ago, when she was sixteen.

'What triggered that?' I ask. 'Were you into Anne Frank or something?'

'My grandpa was going through Alzheimer's,' she says. 'And he started telling me stories I'd never heard – when he was a kid and his family, they'd always have Shabbos every Friday.'

At nineteen she met a handsome man at a party. He was Muslim but not practising, and a few months later he threaded an engagement ring on her finger. Three months after that she was pregnant.

'I was happy until . . . I had my dog living with us and as soon as he found out that his mum was coming from India it just all changed. He was like, "I want your dog gone."'

'He wanted the dog gone?'

'Yeah, and all of the sudden my dog got really sick and the vet thinks that she was poisoned.'

'Why did he say he wanted the dog gone?'

'Because they just don't like dogs.'

'Sort of like an Islamic thing?'

'Yeah. Muslims don't like dogs. They only like cats.'

She told him the dog was staying.

Just as her sick grandfather had awoken the Jew in her, his mother's impending visit seemed to have woken up the Muslim in him.

'He started reading the Qur'an more and buying all these books on hadiths.'

A hadith is a narration of things the prophet Mohammed said or did. The couple would lie in bed and instead of fidgeting with their iPhones like they used to, they'd be nose-deep in Qur'ans.

Unlike Pastor Daniel, Rebecca has some specifics. She pushes two loose-leaf pages across the cafe table, handwritten passages from the Qur'an and Hadith: 'The most vehement of mankind in hostility are the Jews . . . They will spare no pain to corrupt you. They desire nothing but your ruin . . . Those [Jews] who incurred the curse of Allah and his wrath, those whom some He transformed into apes and swine . . .'

Rebecca's grandfather had been rolling through her mind as she read them. 'I was just writing all the verses that I didn't quite understand. And I took it to the imam at Wollongong, with my fiancé with me. I'm asking him all these questions and he's basically just going, "It doesn't matter. It doesn't matter. It doesn't matter." I'm like, "I'm asking you what does it mean? Do you believe that everyone's an enemy or that you should wage war against them?" He's just like, "Next one. Next one. Next one."'

Her fiancé's mother didn't end up visiting Australia, but he flew to India. He met a woman and dumped the Half-Jewess. Their son goes to a Christian school – because two religions worked out so well, why not chuck in a third?

Years later she found the Facebook pages for the United Patriots Front and Reclaim Australia. To her they seemed to get it. She edged into private messages with the people behind the pages. Soon she was gliding down the highway on the UPF bus to the Melbourne Reclaim rally.

Also on the bus sat an old bald man with Coke bottle glasses who started muttering about Jewish bankers. One of the UPF organisers told him to shut up and started making phone calls. The bus pulled up in a small town. The old man was thrown off to waiting police. It turned out he was an infamous neo-Nazi named The Skull. Rebecca says the UPF's prompt removal of him proves the group is not anti-Semitic.

I brush a crumb off the two loose-leaf pages. One item has caught my eye and I read it aloud. '"The last hour will not come," according to Mohammed, '"unless the Muslims will fight against the Jews and the Muslims would kill them until the Jews would hide themselves behind a stone or a tree. And a stone or a tree would say 'Muslim, or the servant of Allah, there is a Jew behind me; come kill him." One type of tree will keep quiet, though, something called the Gharqad tree, "for it is the tree of the Jews."

'Talking trees and talking stones,' I say to Rebecca. 'That's like *The Wizard of Oz*.'

'I know,' she says.

I fold up the sheets of paper and slide them into my pocket.

Walking from the Hungarian cafe, I remember a young man and his dog at the Reclaim rally. Distressed, he flapped his smartphone at me, pointing at a jpg with violent Qur'an quotes he'd seen on Facebook. That's why he'd come down to join with Reclaim.

How weird. Across the country there are people reading the Qur'an and becoming radicalised. But these particular readers aren't Muslim.

If Rebecca is taking old stories too seriously, she's not the only one. My fellow Melburnian Jake Bilardi, a 'white jihadi', was planning a killing spree here, should he be unable to get to Iraq. But he did make it there, blowing up himself (and possibly others, although reports differ) in 2015. On his blog he had written about the massacre at the kosher deli in Paris that followed the massacre at the *Charlie Hebdo* offices.

The Jews, he wrote, are becoming so terrified 'that they are looking towards Israel as a safe haven. They don't realise though that no matter where they are we will fight them until the trees and stones speak and say: "O Muslim, there is a Jew hiding behind me, come and kill him."'

All this has got me thinking of the young activists griping about me online that day of the Reclaim rally. It was very important to these people that I was 'white' and not 'Jewish' – or else things stopped being neat. One complained that I was a 'white saviour' and that people should stop reading my tweets and follow Muslim comedian Aamer Rahman instead. An academic, shitty with me, tweeted that Jewishness has dissolved into whiteness and is no longer an ethnic identity that makes you 'the other'.

But Jake Bilardi certainly felt Jews were 'the other'. And if Rebecca's notes are true (I'll have to snoop further), so does the Qur'an.

One more thing. The Qur'an wasn't the only book to awaken Jake Bilardi. In the same way the Qur'an had freaked out Rebecca, the Jewish scriptures had freaked out Jake. He said they proved that Jews thought they were 'superior to all other races'. Another Australian radicalised by a holy book not their own.

No Leni Riefenstahl

Shermon Burgess, the UPF leader, stands in a park gripping a Muslim newspaper. He doesn't say where he's filming this video. Maybe it's his home town of Cooma, a four-hour drive south of Sydney. He tells his Facebook audience that the front-page story is an attack on his group. The newspaper is unhappy about a UPF rally to be held this weekend in the Victorian town of Bendigo. The council there has approved blueprints for a mosque, and UPF want the decision reversed.

'What do we think of this, patriots?' Shermon says with a huge grin, waving the newspaper. He produces a cigarette lighter. He clicks for a while; the cigarette lighter won't light. He's no longer grinning. He creates a sort of tepee with his arms to block the wind. A minute later a corner of the paper catches alight, although it's a weak flame. 'That's what we think of the *Australasian Muslim Times!*' he declares, throwing it to the ground. The flame goes out.

I forward a few of Shermon's videos to a friend.

'Why's there smudge on the lens?' she writes back.

'Nationalists can be really bad with production values,' I tell her. 'A cursory look at YouTube shows that most teenagers – many not members of the Master Race – can put out high-quality videos with the same general equipment.'

On the day of the anti-mosque rally I park ten minutes' walk from the Bendigo town hall, the advertised location. It's cool how you don't need Google Maps for these protests, you just stroll towards the distant shouts of 'Nazi scum off our streets!' The UPF have organised this one alone, without Reclaim Australia, so Pastor Daniel probably won't be here. I'm interested to see the kind of crowd the UPF pulls by itself.

I knew the lay of the land at the Melbourne rally. I could see how the police kept No Room for Racism and the far right apart, blocking off laneways and plugging other holes. But here, along this shopping strip in regional Victoria, I haven't a clue if the cops have things covered.

'Oh Jesus!' I squeak outside a cafe. A swarm of black-hooded kids has jumped a UPF supporter and a chair flies overhead.

(In the coming months I see this footage on the news several times. Sometimes it's implied that the kids in black hoodies are the right-wingers, other times the left-wingers, depending on what the news story wants to say.)

Bad production values or not, Shermon's videos – plus other far-right promotional material – must be working. There were fewer than two hundred people at the Melbourne rally; here, over four hundred far-right supporters are squeezed into the square in front of the town hall. I hear one 'patriot' ask another if Shermon is speaking today. Another gushes over Blair Cottrell's latest online rant. In the age where anyone can be Instagram- and Facebook-famous, that's what the leaders are becoming.

No Room for Racism is run by socialists. And folks from different socialist and anarchist groups are the ones who rock up to protest these far-right rallies. They don't have blossoming celebs, equivalent to Blair and Shermon. (The rising star posted on their Facebook pages is an old American man, Bernie Sanders.) No Room for Racism's numbers are down. They pulled over a thousand in Melbourne, a couple of hundred today.

On the steps of the town hall, a man with medals pinned to

his chest bounces on his toes next to several well-dressed men and women. The anti-Islam speakers weren't looking this sharp at the last rally. When it's their turn at the microphone, they all use the expression 'this is a family day', like they've been briefed by a PR company: our market research shows your brand is associated with bogan Nazi bikies, so try to be less bogan Nazi bikie-like.

An emotional man with bushy eyebrows tells us that if the proposed mosque is built in Bendigo 'the foundation of Australia will be lost forever'. His first example: Muslims sometimes pray on the street outside the mosque.

'They block off the entire street!' he shouts. 'And I ask you today, if you've got a child at home with an egg or nut allergy and they go into anaphylactic shock, how is the ambulance care going to get to that child?'

The dastardly Muslims–peanut allergy connection!

You really can reverse-park anything into your belief system.

A woman in the crowd solves the conundrum of how to get the ambulance past the praying Muslims. 'Run 'em over!' she screams.

The next bloke thanks the police here because 'they're good men and women even though they sometimes stick a "yellow canary" on our cars'.

I point my camera at the stairs of the town hall. A man with a shorn head strides over, bumping his chest into my lens. I look around. Everyone else is free to take photos.

'Is something wrong?' I ask.

He remains silent and smirks without meeting my eyes. At 'family days', I think to myself, there aren't usually people threatening you. He drifts off but returns when I raise my camera again. I note the UPF logo on his shirt. So they've had merch printed up since the last rally.

Blair grabs the microphone. He's a fitness fanatic who uploads videos of his weightlifting sessions to Facebook. He's as big as a person and a half. This is his first public appearance since an anarchist dug up comments he posted before his UPF days. Under a photograph of Adolf Hitler, he had written, 'There should be a picture of this man in every classroom and every school, and his book should be issued to every student annually.'

'Identity cannot be bought from supermarkets and milk bars,' Blair blares. 'Identity cannot be purchased through credit cards and eBay!'

A few minutes into his speech it occurs to me that he doesn't talk much about Islam. He briefly mentions it's 'a symptom of a bigger problem' and moves on.

'Strength and honour exists inside your hearts, you need to feel it!'

'You are a racist!' sing the socialists and anarchists from the other side of the police line. 'You are a racist!'

'You need to feel it in people around you,' Blair continues, unfazed. 'You need to feel it in the person next to you and understand this is my brother, this is my countryman, and I know this person will not let me down!'

'You are a wanker!' sing the socialists and anarchists. 'You are a wanker!'

'Ever . . . in ever . . . in . . .'

Blair has lost focus and fumbled his line. This is Australia. He can stand being called a racist, but being called a wanker has hit him.

A woman with platinum-blond hair speaks next. 'Mohammed, you picked the wrong country!' she snarls. She talks about ISIS throwing gay people off buildings. Why don't the 'caring lefties' care about that?

'By the look of them,' she adds, glancing over the police line, 'if ISIS took over, about two-thirds of them would be thrown off the building!'

The crowd laughs at her poofter joke.

An anarchist climbs up a lightpole and sets an Australian flag alight.

'No! No! No!' cry the UPF supporters, rushing towards the police line. The police shoot capsicum spray at them and they retreat with scrunched-up faces. Blair has slid to the side of the town hall and is pouring water in his eyes.

The next speaker doesn't mention the spraying at all, let alone complain about the cops. It wouldn't fit the far right's brand. They want to position themselves as normal Australians, not radicals like the socialists and the anarchists. But if they're not radicals, why did the police spray them?

And for those on the other side of the police line, having the cops protect them doesn't serve their brand either.

I join a woman under a tree. She has a posh tinge to her accent. She says she's travelled to Sudan and seen how horribly Christians are treated in an Islamic country. She fears Australia could become like that if things aren't kept in check.

'There's a lot of sort of snobbery around this,' she says. 'Like my sister, for instance, would never come to a thing like this because she thinks, Oh bogans.' She surveys the large crowd, with knots of men from different motorcycle clubs. 'But the thing is that in the end, it's going to be the bogans who are going to basically save us.'

Up on the stairs of the town hall, amongst the far-right speakers, a woman is brandishing a huge Israeli flag. Is this pissing off Blair, who wants a picture of Adolf Hitler in every classroom?

A beefy man takes the microphone. Lest you think he's not proud to be Australian, his top is emblazoned with 'Aussie Pride', the Australian flag, the coat of arms, and two Ned Kellys. His name is Ralph Cerminara. Because I'm a trainspotter of the far right, I know a little bit about him. He once led the Australian Defence League, an anti-Islam group that predates the UPF. Not long ago the cops arrested him for brawling outside a mosque in Lakemba, Sydney. One police officer ended up in hospital with a fractured shoulder.

'Before I go on,' Ralph shouts, 'I want to mention one thing. And that is the left-wing bigoted media.' The crowd hisses. 'You've got people like leftie John Safran – and I've seen him around here – he calls people Nazis. You're the fucken bigot, mate! You utterly disgust me.'

Turns out I'm not the only one with the internet. Dozens of 'patriots' turn to me and boo. I breathe in and try a smile.

Last rally, the small anti-Islam contingent had to be whisked away under police protection, to avoid being thumped by the large No Room for Racism crowd. Now that they've got the numbers, the anti-Islam folks scatter off from the town hall without a worry in the world and drink outside the pubs, draped in flag capes.

If Ralph were prime minister

My eyes can't make out the street numbers in the dark. I shine my phone on the bricks to check I have the right address. It was a twenty-minute train ride from Sydney's CBD to this block of flats in Marrickville, in the inner west. I push the buzzer.

'G'day,' I say, 'I wanted to speak to Ralph Cerminara.'

'Who is this?' a voice replies with suspicion.

'John Safran.'

'How'd you get my address?' he splutters, clearly bowled over by my detective work.

'I typed your name into White Pages.'

After several minutes of negotiation – he says I called the UPF Nazis, I counter I only called one of them an emo-Nazi – he buzzes me up.

Ralph is a man in his late thirties. His face is round and olive, with twitchy big brown eyes. We sit across from each other in his lounge room.

'So your surname is Italian?' I begin.

'Yeah.' He scratches his white singlet. 'Father is Italian, mother is Aboriginal.'

'Huh!' I say, thoroughly delighted by this development.

He addresses a favourite chant sung by anarchists and socialists at the rallies: Always was, always will be Aboriginal land. 'When you get the left wing chanting at us, "Oh, this isn't your land," and blah – hang on, my mother has won awards of parliament for community service with the Aboriginal community. She had all of this Aboriginal artwork that she'd done. Sold every single piece.'

Ralph says he was first drawn to anti-Islam after he asked for an

Angus burger with bacon at a McDonald's and was told there was no bacon. The store had turned halal, the girl behind the counter explained. He said, 'You've got to be fucken kidding me.'

That was 2010. He believes Sydney has become more Islamised each year and you now can't walk through certain suburbs.

'You do not go into Lakemba, simple and plain. I'd love to see you – as a Jewish person – walk down Haldon Street with a Jewish hat. You would be fucking bashed.'

'Oh really?' I say. 'What's the name of the street again?'

'Haldon.'

I write 'Haldon Street' on my hand.

It turns out Ralph was the guy who threw the Nazi off the UPF bus on the way to the Melbourne rally. He insists this proves that he, and the wider movement, are not Nazis. How can you be Nazis if you welcome Jews?

I ask about Blair's desire to hang a poster of Hitler in every class-room. 'I don't know anything about that,' he mumbles unconvincingly.

Ralph's interactions with Muslims all seem to be biffo-related. He once held an Australian Defence League meeting at a pub in Lakemba. He says a group of Muslims found out and burst in screaming, 'You Aussie dogs, you ADL fucking scum.'

'I'm not going to cop this shit,' Ralph tells me, 'so I turned around and said, "Well, Mohammed's a paedophile." Which he is. Under Australian law, Mohammed is a paedophile.'

'You would have known you were winding them up.'

'They said Aussie dogs,' Ralph retorts. 'Which, to me, is a racial slur. You're identifying my nationality. So it's the same as me going, "you Arab cunts".'

I'm trying to follow his train of thought. I ask him why he told them Mohammed was a paedophile, why he hadn't just called them Arab cunts.

'That's racist,' Ralph explains.

He grabs two beers from the fridge, then he pulls up a video on his computer. His buddy is filming as Ralph strides up a street in Lakemba, with 'Islam is Evil' printed in big black letters on his white T-shirt. He plants a BAN ISLAM. SHARIA LAW NOT WELCOME poster on a street pole.

'What are you fucking doing?' complains an elderly Muslim man approaching Ralph and spotting the poster. 'Who put this right here? Fucking piss off before I fucking kill you.'

'You got this, man?' Ralph asks his friend behind the camera. 'A straight-up threat.'

'A straight-up threat,' the cameraman smugly agrees.

Ralph presses 'pause' on the video and turns to me. 'He's being aggressive,' he says indignantly.

I'm confounded that Ralph thinks the footage paints the old Muslim guy, not him, as aggressive. What does 'ban Islam' even mean?

'If you were prime minister —'

'Every mosque demolished. Bulldozed. And put houses there for some homeless people.'

He's suspicious of Islamic schools too. 'They're building barbed-wire fences,' he says of a particular school, 'and it's monitored 24/7 by security guards. Why do they have it?'

'Maybe they think you're going to go there and attack them.'

Ralph doesn't see it this way. He believes that just as dangerous bikies conspire in clubhouses behind barbed wire, so too do the Muslims.

The burqa would be banned if he were prime minister, but the hijab is okay because it's really just like a hoodie. His liberal attitude to the hijab seems to be born of personal experience; he's ticked off about times he's been told he can't wear his hoodie.

The Qur'an, too, would be banned. Ralph takes me through his reasoning. There was a call for a ban of the blink-182 song 'I Miss You' after a girl quoted its lyrics in a suicide note, and 'there's nothing as bad as "kill non-Muslims, kill Jews and Christians" in the blink-182 song'.

I must have picked up a lucky penny today. I'm still perky from finding out that a leading 'white' nationalist is Aboriginal, when who should crawl into the room? Asian baby!

Ralph's wife is Vietnamese and, like Ralph's dad, an immigrant. I say that many people, looking at the UPF, see it as the type of group that would have been monstering Vietnamese immigrants a generation ago, and Italian immigrants two generations ago. But Ralph sees no hypocrisy. Just as he elucidated the difference between 'Arab cunts' (unacceptable) and 'Mohammed is a paedophile' (acceptable), he makes a distinction between ethnicity and religion.

And, as is the case with Blair, he might not like the Muslims, but he really hates the left. If it wasn't for the left pushing for multiculturalism and immigration, there wouldn't be a Muslim problem in Australia to begin with. Ralph enjoys beavering away on his Left Wing Bigots Exposed website. He digs up dirt on those who criticise the anti-Islam movement. He found photos of one next to a dead elephant in Africa.

'So you are going over there, you support killing elephants? And you call us bigots?'

I'm a little tipsy from the beer, so I can't figure out if shooting an elephant makes you a bigot. Or whether opposing Islamophobia but shooting an elephant makes you a hypocrite.

Because of his antipathy towards 'lefties', I laugh when he tells me, 'I take every test online, "Are you left-wing or right-wing?" It always tells me I'm left-wing! Fuck, man, I'm not a fucking left-wing bigot!'

Ralph asks if I smoke. I don't but I tell him I do. Don't really know why. To keep the conversation going? Out on his balcony, drizzle from the night sky hits our faces.

Maybe, he says, the online tests label him left-wing because he supports indigenous causes. He always clicks 'yes' on those questions. He's upset that the government is closing down remote Aboriginal communities. 'That's our land. That's Aboriginal land, and you're kicking these people off their own land because the government can't afford it?' Then he adds, 'Yet you're going to bring in Muslims from another country and spend millions a year?'

I cough from the smoke and Ralph pulls a weird face that I can't interpret. He reveals he had been writing a piece for Left Wing Bigots Exposed on me. He says he will kill the piece because it was nice I came over to chat.

He looks at my hand, where I've scribbled 'Haldon Street'.

'Don't do it,' he warns.

Parkour

Two days later, back in Melbourne, I pop into the Magistrates' Court. I'm curious about a case. Last month the police arrested a young man for goosestepping up and down streets in my suburb and shouting 'Heil Hitler' at anyone in a skullcap.

I watch on from the pews as his lawyer insists it was all a big misunderstanding.

'Is your honour familiar with parkour?' the lawyer asks. The magistrate shakes his head. The lawyer explains that this is a youth recreation, like skateboarding but without the skateboard, in which the practitioner leaps from place to place in the most efficient way possible. The lawyer contends that his client's parkour strides had been misinterpreted as Nazi-style goosesteps. He adds that at least one of the Nazi-like salutes was in fact his client flagging down a tram. The lawyer has no explanation for the shouts of 'Heil Hitler'.

The magistrate does not accept this version of events. He tells the young man, who is Fijian, that as he is from a minority community himself he should know better than to goosestep like a Nazi around our vibrant and multicultural city. He is let off with a warning.

Hey, it's not Kristallnacht, but there's been a constant drip of things like this in my suburb recently, sometimes with the assailant shouting words like 'Gaza!'

BOOK CLUB

Qur'an studies

By the end of this book Musa Cerantonio will be locked up in a jail cell, awaiting trial. The federal police will allege he was 'preparing to commit the Commonwealth offence of entering a foreign country with the intention of engaging in hostile activity' for an Islamic State-linked terrorist group.

But well before that all happens, the 29-year-old preacher shoots me a message on Twitter, signed off with a Japanese happy face emoticon: 'It may come as a surprise but I am a big fan of your shows and just recently re-watched Race Relations. ^-^'

Musa lives at his mum's in West Footscray, a traditionally working-class suburb in Melbourne. I tell him I want to find out more about the Qur'an, and soon I've driven over the West Gate Bridge, from my home to his, and am sitting on his couch. Musa's face is stuck in the fridge, in the kitchen area that runs off the lounge room. 'I actually . . . I got a drink yesterday, while I was at the super-market, and I didn't realise just how relevant it would be to give you.' He swings around. 'It's raspberry cordial!'

Raspberry Cordial was the name of my high school hip-hop group, something I covered in *Race Relations*.

'So,' I ask, 'is everyone in your family Muslim, or just you?'

'Certainly not – just me and a cousin of mine. He sometimes lives with us cos both of his parents passed away. I managed to get to him and he became a Muslim. But I've got three brothers. They're not Muslim and my parents aren't Muslim. Not yet, anyway.'

Musa converted when he was seventeen. By his mid-twenties he had become something of a big deal in the Muslim world as a TV presenter in Egypt. His show covered Islamic history. He chose kooky topics like the Islamic roots of the Dracula story. The station bigwigs had been impressed by his preaching at a conference in India a few years earlier. Why didn't the bigwigs just get an Egyptian to host?

'They have this fascination with white converts, and I've got blue eyes as well. They love blue eyes, you know? So they do love to prop you up. And I hate that – I absolutely hate the racism that's in the Middle East. Like, you find an African convert, "You should have him on the show," and they're just like, "No. He's black."'

Musa has recently married. 'She's really nice,' Musa says of his wife, sounding like he's preparing for a punch line. 'And she's also Eurasian, as you would describe her.'

That Eurasians are hot had been a recurring joke on *Race Relations*. Musa's wife is in the Philippines at the moment and isn't his first. He has two daughters from a previous marriage to a Lebanese Australian.

'You don't have as many Lebanese over here,' he says, comparing Melbourne to Sydney. 'Personally, I think that's not entirely a bad thing.' He chuckles darkly. 'They're always up to something.' With his white skin and Aussie accent, he could be an Alan Jones talkback caller.

I look around the lounge room. Owl figurines are perched on every shelf. Musa considers these to be graven images, but it's his mum's house so what's he going to do? She agreed to take down the Last Supper painting but was immovable on the owls.

Musa's brother Nick strolls in and makes his way to the fridge. He's wearing a black T-shirt featuring a pig's head. Why the non-halal T-shirt? Nick tells me it's a metal band. He loves metal and plays drums himself. He falls into giggles when Musa explains the confusion he causes his Muslim online followers when he references Monty Python.

'You don't become king just because some watery tart threw a bloody scimitar at you!' Musa squawks, riffing on *Monty Python and the Holy Grail*.

'Strange women giving us swords from ponds is no basis for a system of government,' Nick squawks back.

Musa and I duck out for lunch. He seems to know everyone in Footscray. He moseys down the street with his hand in his pocket, shooting '*Salaam alaikum*'s and small talk to the perfume salesmen in the mall.

We chew on flatbread in a Sudanese restaurant as he rants about a left-wing activist from his university days, when he was studying for an arts degree. On orientation day she had set up next to his Islamic Society stall. She came over and dropped pro-Palestine flyers on his table.

'So I said to her, "Please take them off. I don't want them here."' This is the first time I see fire in his eyes. This is a different Musa to the one at the house. 'She was giving me this confused look, like, Why not? I mean, it's for Palestine. I said, "Look, you're not a Muslim, you don't agree with Islam. As for us, that's what we want for Palestine. We want sharia law. You don't want that, so let's admit we don't want the same thing." She started to get a little bit offended. She's like, "Oh, but, you know, we have to work together," and I'm like, "No, we don't have to work together."'

Musa wipes yoghurt off his fingers, and is still fiery as he moves from Palestine to Syria. 'We believe that Jesus will return as the Messiah. We do agree with the Christians that it will be Jesus Christ, except when he comes back he's actually going to be fighting against them and show them that their religion has been corrupted. We believe that when he does return, he would return to Syria.'

'So,' I say, now that he's drilling down on scripture, 'I don't understand what happens under an Islamic state. Does that mean, like, all the rules of the Qur'an? Who decides what's literal?'

'Well, generally Muslims don't try to hide the reality. So yes, we know that there are punishments that do involve capital punishment.' Musa has had this conversation before – I haven't mentioned capital punishment. 'This is how it simply will be, and any Muslim who disagrees with that or rejects it isn't even a Muslim. The vast majority of Muslims are clear on 95 per cent of matters. You have to pray five times a day – nobody is saying it's six or four, we all agree. And the punishment for adultery for a married person is that they are stoned.'

I laugh reflexively, as if one of my sarcastic friends has said something transgressive for effect. But Musa isn't being sarcastic. I don't quite know what to say.

'So when did you . . .' I strain. 'When did you first, um, discover Monty Python?'

'Probably about year seven, I just watched *Life of Brian* and then got onto *Flying Circus*.'

That evening we're gobbling again, this time around the table in the lounge room. (The same lounge room ASIO officers will burst into after Musa is arrested.)

'Can you tell me something?' I ask the family as we tuck into the lasagne. 'Do you reckon Musa's voice – sometimes it goes up, like this?' I squeak and lisp. 'Like my voice?'

'He seems to have several voices, depending on who he's talking to,' Nick says. Musa's accent, according to Nick, goes a little Italian around Italians and a little Lebanese around Lebanese. While I'm trying to figure out if this chameleon voice means anything, the topic has triggered giggles around the table.

'Sometimes my mum loves . . .' Musa begins. 'She'll just grab the phone and say, "Come on, make a prank call!"'

'Oh God, he's good!' his mum says, passing a bowl of potatoes. 'Remember that time . . . I'm laughing already. He rang up about – was it army tanks or something?'

Musa had rung up Melbourne's CityLink private motorway to

ask how much the toll was to drive an army tank on the road.

'Do you want a sample?' he asks, dialling the CityLink number and putting the phone on speaker.

'What is your registration?' a CityLink woman asks.

'Okay, please,' says Musa, sounding a bit like Borat. 'Letter B, like for a broccoli. Yeah, A, like asparagus.' He makes a throaty 'ech' sound that's not quite any letter in the alphabet. 'Ech for echmen.'

'Is it H for hotel, the last letter?' asks the operator.

'No. Ech, like in echmen.'

'Sorry, is it S for sierra? Or H for hotel?'

This drags on for several excruciating minutes. The family and I squish our faces to muffle our laughter.

'Is it in the English alphabet?' the CityLink woman asks.

'No, of course not. I am from the Ukraine!'

'He's so clever!' his mum says as he hangs up the phone.

It spreads around the radical Muslim scene that I've caught up with Musa. A few days later, while I'm watering the cactus on my balcony, another stranger buzzes in my pocket. Hamza doesn't know Musa personally but is familiar with his preaching. He wants to know what Musa and I spoke about. I tell him Musa said adulterers should be stoned.

'They don't have to be stoned,' writes Hamza reassuringly. 'You could also chop off their heads.'

I still have those quotes from the Half-Jewess folded in my pocket. Hamza tells me he will be happy to clear up any questions I have about the Qur'an.

Pizza party

I roll through Doncaster, in eastern Melbourne, a suburb one up from my childhood home. I used to head here for its enormous shopping centre, with my mum, to buy jeans and hot chips. Now I'm back for Hamza.

He's a young man, draped in a thawb, which is a kind of Muslim muu-muu. We sit at the kitchen table in his unit. 'I'm a paladin dwarf,' he tells me, beginning to explain how it came to be that the government confiscated his passport. World of Warcraft is somehow involved. 'You get to choose your race, which is like as an elf or . . . What else is there? There is an orc, human, night elf, a few others.' He strokes his beard.

'What's a paladin?'

'You would call the dwarf the race and the paladin the class.'

ASIO turned up on Hamza's doorstep a year ago, after he and his mate, both in their mid-twenties, returned from Yemen. They weren't charged with anything but were placed on no-fly lists. Hamza is convinced ASIO is monitoring their phones and watching their homes. So, as a workaround, he, the paladin dwarf, and his mate, a gnome, skip through forests in World of Warcraft, chatting business over their headsets.

I ask him what he was doing in Yemen.

'Okay, now this . . . what you're getting to now, is a dangerous area.' He pauses. 'I was eating pizza.'

He asks for a selfie with me. He says the gnome will be stoked because they had to lie low at one point and were confined to a small apartment in Yemen. They passed the time watching *Breaking Bad* and *John Safran vs God*. Pretty chuffed by the inroads

I've made into the jihadi demographic.

I reach into my bag. 'I brought along my Qur'an,' I tell him, 'which no doubt will be the wrong one or something.'

'Soon find out.'

'I got it from, you know, just a regular bookshop.'

'Not the Penguin one?'

'Yeah, the Penguin one.'

'Get rid of it.'

Hamza returns with a Qur'an that carries a translation more pleasing to him.

A pug trots in behind him. It's his sister's, he tells me, patting its head. His sister, who isn't Muslim (Hamza is a convert from Catholicism), is staying here and —

Hang on. Muslims don't like dogs. They only like cats.

I tell Hamza about the Half-Jewess and her fiancé's sharia-motivated dog poisoning.

'That the dog is forbidden is absolutely wrong,' Hamza says firmly. 'This is more of a cultural thing.'

'What's the distinction between a dog and a cat?'

'Apart from the fact that one is a dog and one is a cat?'

I explain that the Half-Jewess's fiancé didn't have a problem with cats.

Hamza is seething, angry that this other Muslim has been spreading such bunkum (it's bunkum to Hamza at least). 'There's a saying of the Prophet, peace be upon Him: "If a dog licks one of your bowls you should wash it seven times."'

Hamza says some Muslims interpret this to mean a dog is dirty and therefore you should not own a dog. Hamza flaps his hands. 'If the Prophet wanted to say that the dog was dirty he would have said that it was dirty. But he didn't.'

Hamza might support beheading adulterers, but, to be fair, he's really liberal on the whole dog thing.

We open our Qur'ans to a surah, which is a chapter, called 'The Elephant'. Hamza says there's no need to start from the beginning because 'it's almost like you're watching *Pulp Fiction*. It's just all over the place; this is how the Qur'an was revealed.'

An army of elephants, mounted by pagans, invades the holy city of Mecca. Allah sends in birds, which pelt the elephants with clay pellets and the elephants explode. So this is a parable?

Hamza tells me this actually happened. Everything happened as written. 'If you were to use your own logic,' he says, 'you would think a bird cannot possibly take on an elephant.'

But can it also be a parable? 'If you're an ISIS fighter,' I ask, 'are you allowed to go, We are like the birds and America is like the elephants?'

'Absolutely.'

'Is it literally going to happen,' I ask, 'this war where Jews have to hide behind the trees and the stones? Literally?'

'Yeah, literally.'

'Then what happens if you're hiding behind the Gharqad tree?' I say of the tree that won't dob on the Jew.

'Then the tree won't say anything. I dare say the Muslims would probably know. "Gharqad tree, better check behind it."'

'I googled it,' I tell him. 'The trees don't seem to be available in Australian nurseries.'

'It's a small battle that's part of a larger war. It's nothing big.

Nonetheless, it is something that will happen.'

'I think it's considered a weed in a lot of places.'

'It's a strange little tree, I guess.'

I ask Hamza about the Jews Allah 'transformed into apes and swine', according to the Half-Jewess's notes. He emphasises that it was only some Jews who, after sinning, Allah (literally) turned into apes and pigs. Although on another occasion, Hamza tells me, Mohammed instructed his wife not to curse Jews as being the cousins of apes and pigs. So it's really swings and roundabouts with the whole Jews-are-apes-and-pigs situation.

Hamza's not rattled by present-day Islamophobia, he says, because it's foretold in the Qur'an. 'One of the recurring themes is persecution for your beliefs. The prophets before us were persecuted and they fought. You're going to find this recurring theme number one. Going through hardship, but then the ease that comes after this.'

'The ease that comes after it?'

'Yes. That's not just in this world, but more so in the hereafter – that everything you suffer with, ease will come.'

That's why he shrugs his shoulders when there's a Reclaim rally on the news. In fact, he clarifies, he's pleased in a way. It suggests the Messianic age is inching closer.

So whenever the UPF is marching through the streets, they are, unbeknownst to them, playing out characters in Hamza's Qur'an.

'You know when Muslims pray five times a day,' I ask, 'what actually are they saying?'

Hamza pushes his chair out and kneels beside the dining table. 'You always begin raising your hands, and you say, "*Allah Akbar.*"

God is the greatest. Always. After that you recite the first chapter of the Qur'an. After that you can recite anything you want.' Hamza bends forward, his forehead on the ground. 'If you want to say "O Allah, guide John Safran to Islam," you get to say that.'

I'm not the only one Hamza would like to upsell to Allah. As we wander to my car, we chat about Blair and Shermon from the UPF, with him deducing they don't know a lot about Islam.

'I mean, we'd love for them to learn more. We'd love them to be guided. And some of them do. We've had former neo-Nazis who embraced Islam.'

That's his reaction to watching UPF leaders blasting Muslims on the telly? The devout process the world in a different way to the godless shlubs.

A few days later I spot Muslim comedian Nazeem Hussain in a studio at Triple J, where we both work. I can see he's not on air and gingerly poke my head in.

'How's it going, brother?' he says.

I nod. 'Now listen, I hate to bring this up.'

'You hate to bring everything up,' he says, suddenly suspicious.

'What's your attitude to the Gharqad tree?' I ask.

He turns down the music. 'I have no idea what you're talking about. The gaga tree?'

'No, the Gharqad tree.' I tell him the story.

'I'm actually not familiar with the Jewish tree,' he says.

Is he doing that *taqiyya* thing – lying to a non-Muslim – that Pastor Daniel warned about? I lock my eyes on Nazeem's. Nope, I reckon he just doesn't know about the damn shrub.'

The Sufi in the garden

A young Sufi heard I'd been booed by the UPF at the rally and we began tweeting one and other. Now we're under the gaze of a Captain Arthur Phillip statue in Sydney's botanical gardens. In my imagination, Sufis are mystical and serene like kung-fu masters in the movies. *Grasshopper, jihad means inner struggle, not to kill. Now let's levitate.* I wanted to meet this Sufi – he's bearded and skull-capped – to get a counterpoint to Musa and Hamza.

'There's a longstanding suspicion amongst a lot of Muslims that there's a reason he didn't get arrested.' The Sufi is speaking of Hamza. Perhaps, he suggests, Hamza plea-bargained after returning from Yemen: no prosecution in exchange for feeding ASIO information. 'But I don't know,' he concludes.

While this meet-up was arranged to discuss the Qur'an, like all book clubs we're ignoring the book and just gossiping about people we know. We finally ease into the Qur'an when we find a point of entry that allows us to continue gossiping about Hamza.

Hamza, the Sufi tells me, follows a rigid version of Sunni Islam. 'They're literalist but . . . even more literalists than other literalists.' He says that Tasawwuf, the practice he follows, allows 'analogical reasoning'. For instance, he explains, 'Allah says that those who are blind in this life will be blind in the next,' and that would have to be an analogy, that can't mean literally blind. 'The Qur'an can't be just ones and zeros that you put into a computer,' he goes on. 'If the Qur'an's just a book of law, why is so little of it concerned with law? Why is so much of it concerned with tales?'

I keep floating into converts. A white Australian, the Sufi grew up in Maroubra. 'Have you ever heard of the Bra Boys?' he asks.

'That's Maroubra.' All sorts of threads led him from his non-religious upbringing to Islam: a chat with a Muslim girl in high school about Jesus; a book by a black American gangster who found redemption through The Nation of Islam. When the Cronulla riots erupted, just before his conversion, the Sufi's two worlds overlapped. Both sets of text messages shot into his phone: 'Let's fight the Lebs' and 'Let's fight the Aussies'.

Once a Muslim, he dressed the part. 'I wore a thawb. I wore a turban. And living in Maroubra, I got spat on, people threw bottles at me.'

His race shifted, too.

'Dudes drove past mistaking my race. Like, you know, "Arab dog," and "Go back to Baghdad!"'

We laugh so hard an old drunk man leaning against the statue turns and looks.

'Once I got off the train at Redfern and this guy, he's like, "Oh fuck me! It's an Abo in a dress!"'

The history of Islam, as he tells it, is intertwined with the history of resistance to colonisation. This is sounding familiar. 'You could have been an anarchist,' I say.

'I was an anarchist.'

Six months after converting to Islam, he met his wife while throwing fake blood over an army recruitment stall during a university protest. 'I got grabbed by security guards,' he giggles. 'I looked over and there's a woman in a hijab wearing an anarcho-feminist T-shirt and I was like, What the . . .? And then I ran into her afterwards, and everyone else had gone to the pub and obviously we don't go to the pubs, so I was like, you know, "*Salaam Alaikum.*"' This was nearly a decade ago.

It's hard to tell where the anarchist ends and the Muslim begins. He tells me he'd have no problem with a CEO 'who plunders the world's resources' being crucified, as that, he says, is the Islamic punishment for highway robbery.

I pull out the pages from the Half-Jewess and pass them across to him. I relay how she ended up in the United Patriots Front, upset by passages in the Qur'an. He only half looks at a page.

'Kill them wherever you find them, right?' he bristles, like I'm an arsehole for bringing this up. 'The entirety of that verse is missing. So where it talks about the attacks upon people? If people honour treaties, you honour them in return. I'm no Qur'anist scholar but even I know this verse has context, because it's thrown at us so often.' The Sufi folds up the pages and leaves them resting on the bench.

I push on. 'Do you think there's inflammatory stuff against Jews and non-Muslims in the scripture?'

He quickly steers the discussion away from scripture to 'the very good relationship' Jews and Muslims have enjoyed throughout history. 'Anti-Semitic conspiracy theories, they're not coming from Muslim history.' He mentions *The Protocols of the Elders of Zion*, an old European conspiracy theory about Jews controlling the world. 'It's that Muslims believe this stuff and then they look to the Qur'an and then they find it, they find a way to support it. These people were conspiracy theorists before they were religious Muslims.'

The Sufi happily concedes there are badly behaved Muslims and that these people should be admonished. Muslims can be flawed. Scripture? Absolutely not.

This talk of Islam, and whether it's open to criticism, rolls into the matter of the *Charlie Hebdo* doodlers. The Sufi says those critics of Islam had it coming. And their words and cartoons can't be seen as nonviolent. Not only were the cartoons part of a bigger story of France colonising Muslim lands and humiliating Muslims, but, like cartoons of hook-nosed Jews in Nazi Germany, they were inspiring further violence. 'Words and images can't be separated from context, right?'

'I guess so. I mean, yeah, but —'

'You want to say that the same thing is true about the Qur'an!'

The Sufi goes on to say that Islam would be fairer game for criticism if power dynamics were different. If Muslims made up the majority in Australia, he would have no problem with people criticising 'a think piece by a Muslim about how the Jews are cursed'. (I notice he's careful to make it a 'think piece' that is open to criticism, not the Qur'an, in his hypothetical.)

What about Bangladesh, I ask, a country with a 90 per cent Muslim majority, where Islamists keep killing bloggers critical of Islam: are the power dynamics in Bangladesh such that it's okay to criticise Islam?

He guides me through the twists and turns of Bangladesh's history to explain why the murdered bloggers are part of the power structure and the killers are part of the oppressed – and I'm an arsehole for bringing it up. This isn't turning out to be the conversation between the kung-fu master and Grasshopper that I was expecting.

The Sufi now pushes a case I've never heard pushed before. It's not just *Charlie Hebdo* who should shut up shop. Satire, the genre, should retire. The historical need for satire, he contends, was to weave around censorship, when you couldn't literally name names. There's little censorship in Australia, so goodnight satire. Even satire that aligns with his ideological views should hop in the bin.

A satirical piece might be sending up racism, for instance, but people can miss the irony.

'Satire runs away from you,' he warns.

'So there's more chance that satire will run out of control than religion will run out of control?'

'Well . . . yes.'

I'm thrown. 'Satire is more dangerous than religion?'

'Yes.'

I look down at my watch. 'We've spoken for two hours and nineteen minutes.'

'I haven't really spoken about Sufism at all, hey?'

Satire

I'm leafing through the Qur'an Hamza gave me. 'Do not treat the revelations of Allah as matters for jesting,' Allah instructs in one surah. The Sufi pointed to the history of colonisation and the demographics of Australia as reasons to not make fun of Islam. But he didn't bring up that Allah seems to command it in the book.

Catch the pants on fire

My head is overloaded and I just want time out from all this. But there's another buzz in my pocket: 'Hi, John. Were you aware that someone from Catch The Fire Ministries has written this about you on their website? "A prominent Melbourne journalist, writer and radio/TV presenter walked into a Catch The Fire Ministries meeting on Saturday night. At the end of the meeting, he was so touched that he talked with Pastor Daniel and then gave his heart to the Lord Jesus. Then Pastor Daniel laid hands and prayed for him.'"

First I think, What is this bare-faced lie? Then I listen to my audio recording of the night: I indeed did repeat after Pastor Daniel, 'Dear Lord Jesus, forgive me for any wrong I have done. Come into my heart and show me who you are.'

Jesus, I was just being social, like when I smoked with Ralph on the balcony. A strange feeling sets upon me that's hard to describe. Like I've been having a pleasant conversation with someone, then I look down later and realise they've nicked my watch.

Pastor Daniel has been on my mind quite apart from all this. I'm reading his self-published autobiography, *Worship Under the Sword*, which he uses to prosecute the case against Islam. Chapter one covers his early years in Sri Lanka: 'Sri Lanka was plunged into a southern terrorist uprising . . . the Church came under severe persecution and many churches were burnt down.'

Twenty pages in, I'm compelled to phone Pastor Daniel. 'I just wanted to make sure I was understanding something correctly,' I say. 'When you were in Sri Lanka, was the persecution by Buddhists or was the persecution by Muslims?'

'It was a Buddhist-oriented southern terrorist uprising,' he says. 'Not Muslims.'

That it's not Muslims is not entirely clear in the book. And Buddhists don't come up in his speeches about his persecution.

Later Pastor Daniel phones me back, to clarify that it's complicated. Rather than Buddhists versus Christians, it's more Sinhalese versus Tamils, the former being predominantly Buddhist, the latter predominantly Hindu. He's a Christian Tamil, though. Identity is exhausting.

45

Duelling swastikas

It's not just Catch The Fire Ministries that's trying to claim me.

I noticed at the Reclaim rally that both sides featured the swastika on their main banner. The right-wingers had I卐LAM: A CRIME AGAINST HUMANITY. The left-wingers had RACI卐TS.

Yes, they employ the swastika because it's universal shorthand for evil. But both sides invoke its anti-Semitic roots when I ask why they've stamped it on their banner. The right-wingers insist the Muslims are dangerous anti-Semites. (Look at the Qur'an, John!) The left-wingers insist the right-wingers are dangerous anti-Semites. (Look at Blair's Facebook feed, John!)

Ominous things lie ahead for the Jews, both sides warn. And both insist they're the ones at the forefront of stopping this menace. So both teams are pitching for my business.

The Jesuit

I'm meeting up with Hamza again, for another Qur'an lesson. But this time not at his home. In fact, my dad is responsible for tonight.

My dad loves public talks. He likes napping, too. He has slept through talks at museums and libraries all across Melbourne. He thought the topic of tonight's lecture at this Catholic church might appeal to me: Mary and Jesus in the Qur'an.

I knew this would interest Hamza, so I invited him. And he's brought along his World of Warcraft buddy. I suppose he has a beard and gnomes have beards, but unlike his video game avatar he's oversized, both tall and rotund. The gnome and I are nibbling on biscuits that have been laid out on a table in the church hall. Hamza has gone to the bathroom and the gnome is filling me in about the time Mohammed met a talking worm.

Hamza returns. He is wearing his thawb, like he did at home, but tonight a keffiyeh scarf is also wrapped on his head like a turban. I ask him if the worm tale is true.

'It's not authentic,' he answers, with a dark look at the gnome.

'Oh really?'

'Yeah. It's apocryphal, so to speak.'

'So as soon as you leave, he's leading me up the garden path,' I say. 'Literally a garden path, with worms.'

'Mmm, hope that ends well,' Hamza says.

The two dozen people here for the talk, most of them members of this church, are thrilled by the presence of a real-life Muslim in a robe and everything. They gather around Hamza like he's an exotic parrot.

The Jesuit priest, tonight's speaker, wears no such theatrical garb – just a jumper and trousers. Plastic chairs arc around him. He scratches his silver hair as everyone takes their seat. I'm squeezed between Hamza and my dad. We go around the room, introducing ourselves.

'I'm Hamza, I'm a friend of John's, I suppose,' he says a little reluctantly. Hamza tweeted recently that Muslims should not befriend the infidel. So I'm chuffed by his declaration. A bit like when a friend's cat hates everyone but you.

The Jesuit says he's a professor in Islamic studies. Hamza's face tenses up.

'I chose Mary and Jesus in the Qur'an,' the Jesuit begins, 'because this is a familiar story to Christians and to Muslims as well, so maybe we can find common points.'

Hamza's knee is bouncing under his thawb. The Jesuit senses his unease and adds, 'Maybe there are different . . . points also.'

The Jesuit shares a Bible passage that reveals Jesus could talk when he was born. Muslim scholars see it differently, the Jesuit informs us. They say Jesus could talk when he was three days old.

Hamza raises his hand. 'Which scholars?' The Jesuit lists the scholars. Hamza snorts. The Jesuit carries on.

Hamza and the gnome spool through the Qur'an on their phones. Hamza shoots his hand up again.

'The word used in Arabic, *sabiyy*, for a boy, usually means someone who is about three years of age – not three days.'

'So he received wisdom when he was three years old?' the Jesuit asks.

Hamza and his sidekick confer behind their hands. 'The word isn't really "wisdom",' Hamza says. '*Hukm* is more of an awareness of judgement.'

The audience is delighted. This is coming across as friendly interfaith dialogue. But I know Hamza well enough now. I can read the anger in his nostril puffs. I hope the Jesuit brings up Mohammed and the worm!

I elbow my dad, who's drifting off to sleep. Hamza keeps one eye on the Jesuit, the other on his Qur'an as the Jesuit continues.

'Christ said, "What God has put together let no man put asunder."'

'We don't say that he said that,' Hamza bristles. 'But no doubt that's one of the Christian traditions, yes.'

For half an hour they ping-pong over tiny things in the text. The crowd remains delighted. No more heat to this, they think, than a

Pole and a Russian quibbling over the best way to cook borscht.

My dad heads for the biscuits after the talk. For him, public talks aren't all about napping, they're also about the snacks. I ask Hamza, who's still flanked by the gnome, 'Could you convert my dad to Islam?'

'Could I convert your father . . .?'

My dad pats me on the shoulder. 'I think I'll have to, at this juncture, leave you three stooges to it.' He walks off nibbling his Monte Carlo.

A harsh wind is bending branches on trees outside the church.

'I didn't want to talk too much,' Hamza grouses. 'I would have told him to shut up quite a few times if I could have.'

'Yeah, I could see you were on your best behaviour.'

'I made sure to read up on him beforehand,' Hamza reveals. 'He is what I would call a cunning missionary. He says, "Oh, the Qur'an is beautiful, very beautiful," to sucker some Muslims in. Then he'll just put a few doubts in. And then start talking about themes of love and compassion, that Christianity has, which Islam is lacking.'

It's funny, I tell Hamza, how much clothes affect a situation. For all anyone knew, the gnome could have been the more educated Muslim. But he didn't come done up in his 'native dress', so they all flocked to Hamza.

'I thought, since I'm going to be going to a group of people who I'm vehemently ideologically opposed to, I just wanted to look as threatening as possible.'

I recall the delighted eyes in the room. It was as if a Japanese woman had turned up in a kimono.

'I think you're having bad flashbacks to your Catholic past,' I say.

'I sort of forgot just how strange some of them can be, the Catholics,' says the Doncaster paladin dwarf on a no-fly list.

'Why does Islam make sense if Catholicism doesn't?' I ask.

The gnome climbs into his car while Hamza braves the wind to answer. He insists the Qur'an's logic is watertight while the New Testament is riddled with inconsistencies. 'One verse says he hanged himself,' Hamza says of the death of Judas. 'The other one says he fell over and his stomach exploded. Which one is true? I've asked questions. They can't answer it.'

I have to stop myself from blurting, Who cares? 'I don't know,' I try. 'There could be a parallel universe. There could be anything, because it's God. Why can't he have died two ways?'

'Because of the fact that you can't die in two ways.'

'God can do anything.'

'We would say that, yes, God is all-powerful, but it's absurd to suggest that God would lie. If you come across a science book or a mathematical book and it contains basic errors, you have to question the integrity of the author.'

Is this why the Sufi, Hamza and other Muslims are so touchy about people criticising the Qur'an? They think everything falls apart if there's an 'error'?

Pastor Daniel would be proud. (Maybe Jesus entered me after all!) I propose it's good that Judas dies two ways in the New Testament. 'It puts out there that we're humans and we're never going to know the absolute truth, only God is going to know that.'

'God does not speak in incomprehensible riddles,' Hamza tells me.

From across the street we watch the Jesuit priest turn the keys and lock the church door.

'A very cunning and evil man,' Hamza says.

Duelling swastikas II

Australian Jewish organisations are very careful with words. The general line of thought is: Muslims and Jews are part of the same Abrahamic family. We live in a successful multicultural country, and any grievances we hold relate to the Middle East, not here. And even over there it's about Palestinian, Egyptian or Iranian leadership. Not Muslims or their faith.

But recently, darker conversations have crept into the letters page of the local Jewish newspaper. Maybe local Muslims aren't so good for local Jews after all. Week by week, two cantankerous Jews fight it out:

'. . . You have to hand it to Henry for finding problems where there aren't any. He acknowledges that Pauline Hanson has no problem with Jews, but says the Jewish community should make an enemy out of her just in case she changes her mind! We have more than enough enemies already. Henry, redirect your energy and enthusiasm on attacking the anti-Zionist Greens, socialists and Labor left.'

'. . . But she is against halal. What next, will it be kosher food?'

The white rooster

A synagogue where Jews dress like they're in 1930s Poland sits across the road from my home. An old schoolfriend, Michael Roth, leans against the bookshelf that runs along the back wall. I'm about the only Jew here lacking a black hat and beard. Jews like me, who don't turn up for much, still turn up today for Yom Kippur. God decides on this holiest of holidays whether He'll write you in the Book of Life for one more year. Michael mentions the rooster. I'd forgotten about the rooster!

'You slaughtered the white rooster this morning?' I ask.

'I didn't slaughter it myself but I swung it around my head.'

For an orthodox Jew, the sins fly out of the man and into the rooster.

'I left it to someone else to slaughter,' Michael says. He asks me where I was.

'I was too busy.'

'Sleeping?'

'I was concentrating on how this Thursday the Muslims sacrifice an animal for Eid.' Musa had invited me along to a sacrifice in a park, but called yesterday and told me that the man in charge doesn't want me there. 'I was too busy thinking about how I could hustle my way into a Muslim goat sacrifice. I forgot that right in front of my eyes – literally across the road – the Jews were slaughtering roosters.'

'Next year,' Michael says.

I had thought the Muslim sacrifice would be grisly. 'The Christians are right,' I tell Michael, remembering that Jesus parable. 'Before you look at the splinter in someone else's eye, take a log out of your own.'

Slouching in the pews with another schoolfriend, George Weinberg, I tell him what I've been snooping into. And we remember the Torah stories we learnt in high school.

The Torah is filled with horror. Don't worry about goats and roosters – following God's instructions, Abraham binds his own son to an altar for sacrifice. He only stops bringing down the knife at the last moment because God tells him to.

The catchy explanation for those who want to slam the Qur'an but not the Torah is that bloodthirsty Torah tales are 'descriptive, not prescriptive': the Abraham story doesn't tell you to tie your own son to an altar. But not all darkness in the Torah is descriptive and not prescriptive. George advises me to ask his mother about one such matter.

Back home I burrow through old computer files, searching for a satirical column I wrote for the *Australian Jewish News* years ago. I find the line I was looking for: 'The Australian Jewish community is facing one of its most difficult tasks – how to make the Muslims look cuckoo for wearing funny hats when we wear funny hats too.'

The gett

I pluck a herring from the plate on the kitchen table. George Weinberg has invited me over to Saturday lunch with his mum. I knew that when George was tiny his dad had bailed on the family, but I had no idea his mother is a 'chained woman'. These are the women forbidden under Jewish law from remarrying because their husbands have refused to hand over a religious divorce certificate – a gett.

'What led up to you marrying what's-his-face?' I ask Mrs Weinberg.

'Maurice,' George interjects.

'I fell in love with him,' Mrs Weinberg says. 'And I was a very shy person and he was full of life.'

They married in 1970, she tells me, and she left him seven years later, convinced he was cheating. She asked for a gett. 'He just said to me, "I don't want you to get married again."'

Mrs Weinberg looked for support. 'I asked one of the synagogue secretaries to help me – a big synagogue here in Melbourne. The guy said to me, "If you give me five thousand dollars I'll try to get you a gett."'

'What do you reckon he meant by that?' I ask. 'Like, threaten Maurice or something?'

This isn't as mad as it sounds. A renegade rabbi is on trial in the United States, accused of plotting to abduct and torture Jewish men who refused to grant their wives a gett.

Mrs Weinberg doesn't think it was this. She suspects at least part of the five thousand dollars would have gone to paying off Maurice. A single mother with two children to support, she didn't have the money.

Would she have remarried if Maurice had granted a gett?

'Maybe,' Mrs Weinberg says. 'I wasn't like today, I was young. I was in my early thirties, I was tall, I was nice, I had hair, I had teeth.'

After she separated from Maurice, she refused to date again. 'I knew I didn't have the gett, and I wasn't a person to just play around, you know? If I would have gone with someone, it would have been to get serious, and get married, and I couldn't.'

'Wow, so he really . . .'

'Ruined my life? Yeah.'

Mrs Weinberg is now in her mid-seventies.

George, at the kitchen sink, pipes up, 'What would happen if tomorrow you went to the supermarket and across the prune aisle you saw a man who you connected eyes with, and then you fell in love, whirlwind?'

'Well, I would maybe try again to get a gett,' Mrs Weinberg says. 'Maurice might have mellowed a bit with age, and maybe he would give it.'

George scribbles down his father's address for me, and I trek to the central coast of New South Wales and turn up on his doorstep.

Bald, thick glasses, he's thrown by my unannounced visit, but invites me in for tea and biscuits. He's an artist, and drawings of Michael Jackson and *Diff'rent Strokes* actor Gary Coleman line his walls.

'When I got divorced, she had done the wrong thing on me,' he complains in his British accent from his little kitchen table.

I tell him that even after thirty-seven years, Mrs Weinberg pines for a gett. For closure.

'She wants a gett?' Maurice says. 'Let her phone me up.'

'Oh, really? What happens if she phones you up and asks you for the gett?'

'I won't give her one.'

'What do you care if you sign a gett or not?'

'What's she want a gett for? Who's going to marry her?' he says meanly.

I tell him it sounds like he's withholding the gett to maintain power.

'It doesn't give me no power.'

'It must be giving you something, that you want to —'

'No,' he butts in. 'It's because what she done to me.'

'That's like revenge,' I say.

'Why should I make her feel better than me?'

'Isn't that revenge?'

'You can put it what you like.'

I shlep back to Melbourne and visit a man called Rabbi Jacks. He holds the office of associate judge at the rabbinical court that oversees getts. Sitting at his dining table, in between soup slurps I pitch a rational explanation for the gett law: it's an obstacle to make couples think hard before deciding to split.

Rabbi Jacks shakes his head. We need not seek a rational reason. 'If my three-year-old wants to play with a shiny knife,' he explains, 'when I take the knife away from her, she thinks I'm a monster. Basically I have to tell her, "Look, you're only three years old. Your maturity and understanding is far inferior to my adult understanding." We look at God's rules in the same way.'

God spake this law unto Moses three thousand years ago. It's in the Torah: a man takes a wife and possesses her. She fails to please him because he finds something obnoxious about her, and he writes her a bill of divorcement, hands it to her, and sends her away from his house.

'This is the most tragic thing,' Rabbi Jacks goes on solemnly. 'If a woman without a gett has a child with another man, that child is a mamzer.'

'Is that a bastard or something?'

'Yeah,' Rabbi Jacks concedes. A mamzer is prohibited from marrying anyone, except another mamzer. 'It's a stigma that's passed on forever.' He adds, 'Some rabbinical authorities say a mamzer could also marry a convert to Judaism.'

I think of Australian suicide bomber Jake Bilardi. He said Jewish scripture proved Jews thought they were 'superior to all other races'. Was this one of the things he read? That bastards are only able to marry other bastards – or those who were once non-Jews?

Not long ago hundreds of women stared down at Rabbi Jacks in a school hall. The National Council of Jewish Women had called a meeting to discuss 'chained women'. Why wouldn't rabbis change the law? 'You have the absolute responsibility to answer our question now!' one woman screamed as an excited 'Oooh' rolled through the crowd.

'We can't change the religion. That's not an option,' the rabbi tells me, shaking his spoon, exasperated. 'They are asking us to go to God and to tell God that He made a mistake!'

My son the Grand Wizard

Hamza told me something the Sufi had brought up too. Television host Waleed Aly gets grief from coreligionists for 'selling out' and pandering to the non-Muslim 'system'.

Strange to learn this. I guess I assumed Muslims would celebrate his success. Maybe I'm projecting. Because celebrating is what Jews would do in such a situation. If the Grand Wizard of a Ku Klux Klan chapter is revealed to be a secret self-hating Jew, his mother is telling all the other Jewish mothers: 'You know, Grand Wizard is the top position. You can't get higher than that in the organisation.'

THE CASTE SYSTEM

The putrid and the pure

Shermon clucks his tongue. (I'm watching him on my laptop.) A curtain, perhaps a shower curtain, is draped behind him.

'Just as the rally was ending, right?' he is telling his Facebook fans. 'And I'm there talking to police and stuff. Next thing, I just hear this annoying, screechy voice go, "You're nothing but bogans!" And I look up and here's this leftie, right? With a sign REFUGEES ARE WELCOME, right?'

The UPF leaders hold blue-collar jobs. Shermon has been a garbo. So I'm assuming he is about to attack the left for being latte-sipping, inner-city condescending shits. But I'm wrong. Shermon continues: 'This leftie has one of the greatest mullets I've ever seen.

He's wearing this T-shirt where there's, like, holes missing out the side of it. Looked like one of the T-shirts that some bloke wears, on the piss, out at the farm. He jumps fifty barbed-wire fences and snags himself, and rips half it open. Anyway, so he's there, giant mullet, holes through his T-shirt, this weird spiky fringe, and he's calling me a bogan? Oh fuck, it was funny.'

I also would have thought left-wing folks would be shy about tossing around the word 'bogan'. Isn't it loaded with class snobbery? Aren't the left against that? Again I'm wrong. One of the big anti-UPF sites is called The Anti-Bogan. In fact, the online psychological warfare between the left and right essentially consists of everyone calling everyone else a bogan. Or a wanker.

'These lefties are fucking retarded,' Shermon goes on. 'No wonder they're starting to lose the battle and the right wing's rising. They've fucking spastic, fucking drug-fucked hippie degenerate scum in their rallies. Dickheads.'

Blair has also hit 'record' on his webcam. He has an announcement to make. A man in Arizona is organising a global day against Islam. 'He's called upon all nations of the world to participate, to rally on the same date, later this month. Germany, Sweden, Britain, France, and other European nations. The United Patriots Front will make its contribution to this worldwide rally in Bendigo. Our next big public demonstration of community pride and strength. Make sure you get there. Keep watching the page for more details.'

I notice the view count on this video. It's tipped over a hundred thousand.

The Brahmin

Shermon's video makes me think it's time I caught up with the other side.

'Shermon just blabs on and swears every two seconds,' declares Aish, a No Room for Racism organiser. 'Whereas Blair is a bit more – he's trying to reach a more sophisticated . . . Like, "I'm intelligent, I know what I'm talking about, so you should listen to me."'

We're drinking at this bar in Collingwood, inner-city Melbourne, discussing UPF videos like we're David and Margaret on *At the Movies*.

The far right aren't the only ones with an online strategy. 'You're going to run into some pictures of penises and breasts,' Aish warns, pushing her phone across the table towards me. A socialist, she explains, has been posing as a fascist online. 'A man pretending to be a woman, a very blond and attractive woman.' The fake fascist has lured right-wing Aussies into sending dick pics. Now he/she is revealing them to the world.

Aish tells me she was born into the top caste in India but dumped Hinduism for socialism long ago. When Reclaim calls a rally, her group, the Socialist Party, pulls together a counter-rally, branding itself as No Room for Racism, with a cartoon panda logo.

Three months before my first Reclaim rally, the actual first Reclaim rally was held at Melbourne's Federation Square. The socialists rocked up early, Aish remembers. Being the debut rally, they didn't know who'd show. Pauline Hanson's 'mums and dads' flapping Aussie flags? Or out-and-out neo-Nazis? Both types arrived, then a third. Indian men in turbans.

'Like, this is really embarrassing!' Aish recalls. The socialists, largely consisting of white people, felt their moment of disorienta-tion. White Australians blocking brown people – in turbans! – from having their say? Is that on? Furthermore, can you thump a brown Reclaim supporter like you can thump a white one?

What confuses her comrades makes sense to Aish. She knows from growing up in India that it's common for Hindus and Sikhs to attack Islam.

'You have, for one, the RSS. They're Hindu nationalists, or basi-cally Hindu fascists, in a way.'

In Aish's view, the career of a certain man reveals much. He was complicit, she says, in a riot where thousands of Muslims were killed. That didn't stop Indians electing that man prime minister in 2014.

I remember one of my posts from the day of my first rally. 'Listen,' I'd typed under a photo of a tattooed skinhead, 'I don't want to jump to conclusions. He might have chosen the swastika not for its Nazi connotation, but in its capacity as the Buddhist and Hindu peace symbol.'

Aish tells me her left-wing friends say similar things: '"Oh my God, the Nazis have taken the swastika and appropriated Hindu culture. They've turned this really peaceful religion into something that's the exact opposite."' She leans forward, pressing her hands on the table, more impassioned than when discussing the UPF. 'And I'm trying to explain to these idiots there's a reason why the Nazis picked it!'

Before Shermon posted his first video, before Pauline Hanson made her maiden speech, Hindu gods divided people into the pol-luted and the pure. That's what attracted the Nazis to Hinduism, Aish insists. 'Caste and Hinduism are intrinsically linked. You can see it written throughout the holy texts. They have the Vedas, Shruti, and all these texts, they talk about how different castes behave, what is expected from you, what is your role.'

I sip my beer and it strikes me: Aish talks about Hindu scripture the way Reclaim talks about the Qur'an.

I once met a Buddhist, I tell her, who was suffering through multiple sclerosis. The Buddhist said she must have acted badly in a previous life to earn the disease. Aish's face travels from fury to sadness as I talk.

'I don't know why people get so excited,' she says of the hippie fascination with Eastern mysticism. 'I think it's the LSD and the dope that they've been consuming that's helped shape their views.'

Aish's comrade, Stephen, slides in next to her. He has the answer for a question that's been bugging me: why aren't Muslims really drawn to these rallies? If there's an anti-Israel rally, for instance, there're keffiyehs and hijabs everywhere.

Stephen says the Islamic Council of Victoria supports No Room for Racism but has told Muslims to steer clear. 'The danger is Muslim people will bash the crap out of these fucking neo-Nazis, and the headline in the *Herald Sun* the next day will be, JIHAD COMES TO MELBOURNE, because these guys . . . It's like, you know, when I go out to the mosques to speak, you feel like you're in a fucking gym. Like, they're seriously big guys.'

He believes Labor MPs in Muslim areas have also warned Muslims off, as the rallies are run by the competition – the Socialist Party.

Then Stephen cautions me: these far-right guys might look goofy in Facebook videos, he says, but particularly as I'm Jewish,

I shouldn't drop my guard. 'There are a hardcore minority who are neo-Nazis,' Stephen says. 'No question about it. Like Neil Erikson.'

Neil Erikson rounds off the trio of UPF leaders. It's him, Blair and Shermon. Neil has just finished serving a one-year supervised community correction order. The prosecutor wanted him behind bars. Neil pled guilty to stalking a Melbourne rabbi. Among other things, he repeatedly called the rabbi's synagogue and hissed, 'Give me the money, Jew, or else I will get you.'

Stephen had to call the cops himself not long ago. A 'patriot' – soon to face court – made a late-night phone call.

'He was drunk,' Stephen recalls. 'Not only did he say he wanted to kill me, but – it slipped off his tongue – he said he wanted to rape my face.' Stephen made sure the media found out about that. 'I knew that most of his homophobic friends, they would be like, "Mate, it's okay killing the commos, but don't rape 'em . . . you fucking poofter."'

Back home, at two-thirty in the morning, I fall down an internet rabbit hole reading white nationalist message boards, in the dark, in my bed. My name comes up.

'One face I did recognise at the front of the UPF rally was John Safran. He's a Jew, so I take it his presence at this thing is for intel gathering. Or does he fancy himself as some kind of storm chaser of the far right, relishing the thrill of being a Jew among it all?'

Someone else who spotted me at a UPF rally expresses surprise that 'no one has bitch slapped' me 'back to Israel' yet. After Stephen's warning, I take this loose talk of violence a little more seriously. Despite Ralph's and the Half-Jewess's assurances, it's hard not to feel that this movement is kind of a bit Nazi-ish.

Divine intervention

Okay, I've woken up and I can't find the audio memory card that I used to tape Aish. It was in a red box, I just cannot find this red plastic box. I start thinking, Oh, this is like Hindu karma. You know, spirits trying to take this card away from me because it holds the audio where we were challenging the gods.

I tell you this story because some people think I'm on Team Richard Dawkins. But my head is in the same space as the Sufi and Pastor Daniel and the rabbis with the big furry hats walking up and down my street. I'm one of the lunatics in the asylum.

(The red box had fallen down the back of my bed.)

Zion

Pastor Daniel's name starts flashing on my phone. As if he knew I'd settled into thinking the movement is anti-Semitic, he tells me that Catch The Fire Ministries is hosting a special Jewish event this Sunday morning. He invites me along. I'm assuming that by 'Jewish event' he doesn't mean anti-Jewish event. But he does endorse the UPF. Of course I have to go.

The church is forty minutes up a highway I'm never on, in a direction I never go.

The *Age* awarded Hallam the distinction of 'Melbourne's least liveable suburb of 2011'. The colour palette in this semi-industrial zone stretches from cement-grey to asphalt-grey. Inside Catch The Fire Ministries, however, vivid colours fly everywhere. Congregants rush up and down the aisles with flags, some emblazoned with crowns. It's incredibly multicul— multiethnic! White families are mixed in here too. Behind the band, on the stage, hangs the Australian flag. Well, a version of it. Prayer hands are printed on the flag along with the Union Jack and Southern Cross.

(Later, a friend argues that the addition of prayer hands is, technically speaking, flag desecration. Indeed, Pastor Daniel's efforts to be Australia's most patriotic citizen sometimes produce 'un-Australian' quirks. At rallies he holds his hand on his heart during the national anthem, something his Anglo companions there don't do, and nor would the governor-general. It isn't the Australian custom.)

One more flag is worth noting. The Israeli one hangs over a lectern on the stage. Just as Pastor Daniel is more Australian than the Australians, he's more Zionistic than the Jews. I've never seen an Israeli flag in a synagogue.

'We all actually keep all of the Jewish feasts,' a regular whispers in my ear. 'It reminds us where we come from.'

The cultural mash-ups are only just beginning. This week also sees a Jewish festival in which Jews eat under a sukkah, a structure roofed in palm leaves. The entire point of the sukkah is that it's assembled outdoors so you can look through the leaves to the stars. Catch The Fire has built theirs indoors, so you can only look through to the fluorescent lights. I hope I don't sound like a jerk. I love a cultural mash-up. Buy a bagel and fill it with ham today.

'I'll ask my brother from Uganda to come and pray,' Pastor Daniel announces from the Israeli-flag-draped lectern.

'Hallelujah!' the Ugandan man, who's sporting a goatie but no hair, rasps at the rainbow coalition of congregants. Several hundred folks have turned up this Sunday morning.

'We pray for the salvation of Israel!' the Ugandan man cries. The organ moans in the background. 'It all started with God promising Abraham the covenant. From chapter seventeen of Genesis: "I assign the land you sojourn in. To you and your offspring to come. All the land!"'

The Ugandan is shaking and weeping. I'm worried he's peaked too early.

'Lord, You make a covenant,' he wails. 'A bigger covenant was made when Christ died for that land. No one can break that! Not the UN!'

'No!' shouts the congregation, a drum now beating over the organ.

'Not Obama! Not Pope Francis! Not the demons, nor the Devil himself!'

The Ugandan man drops to his knees. (I was wrong to fear he'd peaked too early.) 'I will thank You, Lord, for the IDF! The Israel Defense Forces!'

This is way more entertaining than synagogue.

'Hallelujah!' wails the congregation.

His prayer over, the sweaty Ugandan is led off like he's James Brown.

I think about Pastor Daniel's dictum: immigrants must assimilate to the Australian way. Sure, Pastor. Because there's nothing more 'strayan than dropping to your knees and weeping to Christ for the IDF. I imagine Dennis Lillee is doing this right now.

'Look!' A Chinese woman has now taken the stage and thrusts a giant bible at us. 'This is the land title. This is the formal title for the land of Israel! Nobody can dispute that.'

I'm reminded of Hamza and his Qur'an – if it's in the book, that's that.

'Lord, we thank You,' the Chinese woman goes on. 'This Yom Kippur, the Palestinian young boy who doesn't know God, and the love of God, wanted to bomb Israel and the bomb detonated in his hands!'

The congregation 'Hallelujah!'s this news of the blown-up Palestinian.

Now Pastor Daniel walks back to the lectern and calls up a very special guest. A man blessed with an impressive walrus moustache, and a Jewish skullcap, struts to the stage.

'My name is Jonathan. I am from America. I'm a living miracle. I ought to be dead many times over.'

That was Pastor Daniel's opener back in Mildura – that he ought to be dead.

Jonathan, born Jewish, walks us through his downfall. As a young man he screwed up his big break in a Disney World a cappella group by forgetting his words. He fell into a funk, overdosed on cocaine and found Jesus. Now, he tells us, he is a Messianic Jew.

That group's logic: the Torah mentions a Messiah, so why can't that be Jesus? And therefore, why can't you believe in Jesus and still remain a Jew? This is heretical to most Jews, who see Jesus as a false Messiah. Religious Jews from my school would throw rocks through the window of the local Messianic Jewish synagogue. They were the ultimate traitors in in my schoolmates' eyes.

'Hava nagila . . . Hava nagila,' Jonathan croons as he swaggers across the stage with a lounge-singer arrangement of the Jewish classic.

A Chinese man in the congregation springs to his feet, whipping out a shofar, a ram's horn. In a synagogue, a rabbi solemnly blows the shofar on holy occasions, producing a few mournful bleats. This Chinese man is somehow blasting out 'Hava Nagila' like he's Charlie Parker.

Is this why Pastor Daniel invited me? To show I could accept Jesus and still be a Jew?

Next, the Jewish lounge singer who believes in Jesus belts out the rabbinical classic 'Moshiah! Moshiah! Moshiah!' while Filipinos, Maoris, Nigerians, and Anglos too, leap to the front and dance in circles like Chassidic Jews.

Just as I'm thinking this is peak cultural mash-up, Blair Cottrell strides into the church. The UPF leader and Hitler enthusiast has walked into this multiethnic celebration of all things Jewish. I can't believe my luck.

Blair is accompanied by a blond woman with handguns printed on her yoga pants. He's trying to find a seat, but the Ugandan is pulling his sleeve, trying to coax him into Jewish dancing.

Blair blushes, and with a smile politely pulls away. He and Handgun Yoga Pants sit next to Pastor Daniel. Blair nods a hello to me. I don't know why he's here. He's mentioned he's not a Christian in one of his Facebook videos.

Jonathan has taken a break from crooning, but the band pounds on. One young dancing woman, overcome with the spirit, has collapsed. A blanket is thrown over her body – for 'modesty', I'm told. Other blankets are stored along the wall, so collapsing congregants must happen a bit here.

Ten minutes later, the Chassidic dancing winds down but the

organ keeps burbling through the speakers.

Jonathan is back at the lectern. 'The spirit of anti-Semitism is alive today in the Church,' he cries. 'You guys don't need it. It will keep you from knowing Jesus and who he really is. I would just recommend that you take this opportunity right now – today – to come up here and to ask God to forgive that spirit and get rid of it!'

The churchgoers rise and file up the aisles. Jonathan lays his hands on them, one by one, and prays to drive the spirit of anti-Semitism out of them. I find it difficult to believe that all these Maori and Chinese people are possessed by such hatred.

Meanwhile, the one guy who might need such an exorcism – the guy who wanted a picture of Hitler in every classroom – sits and fidgets with his car keys.

Pastor Daniel drops to his knees, squeezes his eyes shut and mumbles to God. Did he invite Blair along for this? To try to drive the demon of anti-Semitism out of his soul?

More congregants collapse, more blankets are thrown. I fall into a conversation with the Chinese shofar virtuoso. When I turn my head back I see two empty chairs. Pastor Daniel and Blair have disappeared! Where to? Handgun Yoga Pants is still here. I scan the room and spot Pastor Daniel and Blair ascending a staircase at the back of the church. The staircase leads to the pastor's office.

What are they up to? I'm antsy as hell. I want to run up that staircase and burst into the office more than anything. More than fourteen-year-old me wanted to break into that Freemasons' hall to find out all their secrets.

I loiter near the sukkah. A middle-aged woman tells me I have to see the Australian World War I epic *The Lighthorsemen*. 'It was

God's plan,' she says of the battle the film is based on. 'He used Australians to set Beersheba free, to put up the British flag after – eight hundred years, was it? I don't know. It was a long time that the Turks had Ottoman rule.'

I've never heard Australian history told through the filter of religious miracles.

Blair and Pastor Daniel return but will reveal nothing about their absence. 'Come,' Blair says to Handgun Yoga Pants, and the two are soon out the door.

Pastor Daniel senses I've been thrown by Blair's drop-in. He leans over to me and claims that when he met the UPF boys they were filled with hatred, but he's been steering them in the right direction.

I ask him if he's heard of Blair's plan to place a photo of Hitler in every classroom. He says, unconvincingly, he doesn't know anything about that.

Outside, turning the keys in my car, I remember a Triple J Hottest 100 broadcast, one Australia Day. We the DJs pressed the buttons and spun the tunes from a stage in a park. In our dreams – and those of Triple J management, too – we would be looking out at multicultural Australia. That's who we wanted our audience to be, but most of the thousands of faces staring up at us were white.

Every Melbourne institution, from the Melbourne Theatre Company to the Melbourne Writers Festival, would kill for Pastor Daniel's ethnically diverse crowd. They hold meetings (I've been to some of them) where they brainstorm how to draw a 'less white' demographic.

Hey guys, ring Pastor Daniel for tips! Only catch is, they don't like the Muslims. I zoom back down the freeway sniggering like Muttley.

By the time I'm home, the Case of the Disappearing Hitler Enthusiast up the Staircase is solved. Blair has uploaded a new video. He stands next to Pastor Daniel in his Catch The Fire Ministries office. The office features an ornamental crucifix so large you could perform an actual crucifixion on it.

'In light of Australia's second terror attack,' Blair begins, referring to the fatal shooting two days ago of a police worker in Sydney, 'it's more important than ever that we stand up for our way of life. Next weekend, the UPF will be holding its biggest rally to date.'

So this is an ad for that global rally against Islam.

'Yes,' Pastor Daniel pipes in, 'I want to encourage everyone who's watching this – walk with me for the next generation. This is not a rally that is racist, no. Look at me. Look at Blair. We are . . . we are our nation. If you have a problem with that, go back to where you came from.'

He and Blair give a thumbs-up to the camera. Travelling through the walls of Pastor Daniel's office I can hear the faint crooning of the Messianic Jew.

Shermon's sermon

A big blue sky hangs over the backyard. Shermon paces back and forth in front of a tree. A punching bag dangles from a branch.

'One of the greatest things I hear these days from the Christians, facing this Islamic problem,' he begins, 'is "God will sort it out." Or the other one I hear is "It's in God's hands. There's nothing we can do."'

Shermon's hands flap in exasperation. 'This is the very rea-son Christians are having their arses kicked in France, England and Sweden!' He rolls through a litany of violence that has befallen Christians across the globe.

'Don't you think God gives you the strength to do things for yourself?' he pleads. 'Let's look at this. Imagine you're out some-where and there's a man, say a group of two or three men. They're attacking a woman. They tackle her to the ground and they start tearing her clothes off, and a man sits there and he starts praying: "God, please stop them." Afterwards, that man praying looks up and says to God, "God, why the hell didn't you do anything?" Don't you think God would look down and go, "How come *you* didn't do any-thing? You were there!"'

I remember a rabbi delivering pretty much this exact sermon in high school, although he had a Torah behind him, not a dangling punching bag.

'We have many faiths in this movement: Christian, Pagan, Buddhist, Hindu.' Shermon's eyes are alive. 'Wake up!' he demands. 'The time for relying on your deity to do everything for you is over!'

One of the gods must be displeased with this decree. Shermon breaks into a sneezing fit.

'Must be some halal food cooking somewhere. Fucking allergic to that shit. But anyway, I'm the Great Aussie Patriot. Catch you later.'

This video has earned him thirty thousand more views than his previous.

BENDIGO

Global anti-Islam day

Twenty police officers sit on the grass in the shadow of a giant tree. Fifty 'patriots' have already gathered across the road from them, an hour before the advertised start time.

'You?!' a UPF man squeaks in disbelief. The squeak doesn't match the bulk of him. He's the shorn-headed guy who blocked my camera at the last rally. He reveals his grievance: I had posted a photo of the man with the swastika on his neck. Bad for the 'family values' brand the UPF are trying to cultivate. He tells me not to publish lies. I tell him it wasn't a lie. There was a man with a swastika tattoo at their rally.

'No lies!' Squeaky demands again. 'We know what you look like, we'll hunt you down, mate. We'll all fucking hunt you down.' He fans his hand across the crowd. 'Look at how many people who will hunt you down, mate.'

One of the fifty who'll apparently hunt me down is holding a sign: PUT UP A STRIP CLUB NOT A MOSQUE.

I fall into a conversation with a scruffy patriot leaning against the mailbox of one of the houses in the street.

'I heard that a train left Melbourne with lefties, 94 percent full,' the man tells me. That's a precise number. The UPF statistician must have been on board the train. 'They're here now, I don't know what they're up to.'

Squeaky has followed me over. 'Danny Nalliah, I think, is bringing his whole church,' he adds. 'Like two buses, wasn't it?'

'It's all right if I get killed today,' the scruffy patriot says. 'Danny can bring me back to life!'

We all laugh.

'You seem to like talking to Neil, mate,' Squeaky says. 'Do you have a bit of a homosexual fantasy about him?'

Neil? Oh! I connect the dots. This scruffy patriot is Neil Erikson, the man who did a one-year supervised community correction order for stalking a rabbi. The 'give me the money, Jew, or else I will get you' guy. Should have clicked earlier. I've been watching his vids online.

Neil knows who I am. 'Well, Iran's getting the nuke, mate,' he says. 'They've got it set on Jerusalem.'

I can't figure out if he's happy about this or whether this is his pitch to me to join the brotherhood of anti-Islam.

'Is it true,' he asks, 'that Melbourne is the second-largest Jewish population after Tel Aviv?'

'We're only 0.5 per cent of Australia, so it can't be that much. I guess that's one in two hundred. Too many for my liking,' I jest.

'You're harsh,' Neil says. 'Self-hating Jew, I love it!'

Blair and Shermon have arrived. Women flock around them for selfies. They are the One Direction of anti-Islam.

On foot, I thread through laneways and backstreets. The patriots will soon be marching to the park for their family day. Police aren't just stationed on the streets, but on balconies in private houses, and I get that *Where's Wally?* thrill every time I spot one.

The sun throws a golden glow over the gazebo in the park. This must be where No Room for Racism will be assembling. A professionally printed banner is draped from the gazebo. In the style of a child's drawing, kids of different races hold hands. YES TO PEACE IN BENDIGO FROM THE PEOPLE OF BENDIGO is stretched across the banner.

I'm wrong. This isn't where No Room for Racism will be assembling. My eyes catch another slogan on the banner, beneath the kids of different races holding hands: WE STAND TOGETHER AGAINST ISLAM.

This is a UPF banner. There's also a swastika on it with a red line struck through it. It's unclear whether this is signalling that the UPF don't want neo-Nazis at their rally or that they think Muslims are like Nazis.

Blair's mob has pilfered other slogans of the left: NO RACISM and NO VIOLENCE AGAINST WOMEN.

Several men who look like bikies start patrolling the gazebo, murbling into walkie-talkies. Laminated passes hang from their necks: 'Event Management'.

Jesus! Two rallies ago, Blair and Shermon were winging it on the back of a ute before their tiny band of supporters. Now they have Event Management.

'What's your role here?' one asks.

'I'm in charge of sarcasm,' I tell him.

Big men, without laminated passes, are now rolling up. Their muscular shoulders stretch out the slogans on the backs of their T-shirts: I'M THE INFIDEL ALLAH WARNED YOU ABOUT and VAN DIEMEN'S LAND CONVICT.

I'm not the only interloper. A student is scribbling notes for his PhD on crowds and police. 'It's a great banner,' he says of the huge canvas number with the rainbow coalition of children united against the Muslims. He means it's great propaganda.

I look around the crowd of rough blokes in sunnies. 'I think an issue, at the moment, is these people don't look like the people in the banner.'

The official UPF march must be approaching and it must be big; Mr PhD and I can hear the booming chant: 'Islam loves well-hung gays! Islam loves well-hung gays!'

We try to unpick the tangles. These guys don't care about gay rights unless . . . but ISIS is killing homosexuals . . . but it's a poofter joke . . . but the left pretends . . .

We give up and hold our bellies and laugh as the roar draws closer and closer. Soon, over a thousand people are stretched out around the gazebo. And the real world is looking more like the banner.

An Aboriginal teenager wants me to take a photo of him and his mate, who is white.

'We look gay,' he says, looking at the photo in the viewfinder.

'Do another one.'

No matter how many snaps I snap, I can't make them not look like a gay couple, so we give up.

A patriot, who doesn't trust we'll understand his metaphors, holds a sign: NO MATTER HOW MUCH LIPSTICK YOU SMEAR ON A PIG (ISLAM) IN THE END IT IS STILL A PIG (ISLAM). Near him a man leans against a tree, with what I assume is some sort of nationalist symbol tattooed on his arm. I walk closer – it's the *Transformers'* Decepticons logo.

'Khe Sanh' bursts out of the gazebo speakers and hundreds of fists pump into the air. Jimmy Barnes announced last week that he doesn't want Cold Chisel's music played at events like this. Blair smirks from the gazebo, his finger on the mixing desk. He looks blown away by the massive crowd.

Event Management is stopping a woman from climbing the gazebo steps. She's stretching her arms out to try to reach Shermon. I overhear a girl tell a friend, 'Neil's my favourite one.' Mr PhD informs me, 'You know, there is a Niall in One Direction.'

Rosalie Crestani, from Catch The Fire Ministries, steps to the microphone. She's the woman who jumped on the back of the ute and thanked the traditional owners at my debut Reclaim rally.

'If you are racist this is not the rally for you, so you should go home now.' This earns her a polite golf clap. 'However, if you are an Australian patriot, who cares about protecting Australia against jihadist Islamic terrorist attacks, then, yes, you're at the right place and you are a part of history-making!' This earns a roar.

Then Blair takes the microphone. 'I think,' he shouts, 'this is probably more important than sitting around in pubs drinking wine and eating cheese while our country rots from the inside!'

The local business group has cancelled a wine festival, which would have drawn thousands of visitors today. It felt it would be bad for the Bendigo brand if a race riot broke out while so many tourists were in town.

Blair skates lightly over Islam, merely stating that it 'could pose no threat' if it wasn't for another treasonous force. But who or what is this treasonous force? 'Have you ever heard of a concept called subversion?' he rasps. 'Subversion is the steady takeover of a nation from within. Subversion is when your institutions, your television networks, even Hollywood, everything, serves a single agenda.'

It must be just Jewish paranoia that makes me suspect he's referring to the Jews. After all, the banner clearly states this isn't a Nazi rally.

Online, the socialists and anarchists have started picking up that Blair doesn't rant against Muslims that much. Usually a person can get away with not being an Islamophobe, but when you head up Australia's pre-eminent anti-Muslim group, it's the kind of thing that sticks out. Like me, the socialists and anarchists suspect his real target is the Jews.

'The only way to stop us now is to kill us, and good luck!' is Blair's strong closer.

Pastor Daniel leads a chant: 'No sharia law! No sharia law!' A surfie dude next to me leans in and larks that when sharia law is introduced he's going to take two wives: Pauline Hanson and Jacqui Lambie.

The next orator holds his notes to his nose and discusses the role of the Queen in all of this. I can't figure out if, to him, the Queen is good or the Queen is bad. Just as Blair won't spell out who the 'treacherous force' is, and Pastor Daniel doesn't bring up Jesus today, here's another man with a cloudy second agenda.

Then there's Mr Normal. 'I'm a former soldier,' says the handsome man on the gazebo. 'My name is Scott Moerland.' He looks down at a pack of bikies. 'Some pretty staunch dudes here that I don't want to run into in a dark alley, I'll tell you what.' Everyone laughs. 'I've done two tours of duty, one in Iraq and one in East Timor, and I can tell you now I'm more nervous standing in front of them lot than I ever was overseas.' A relaxed family man, chock-full of dad jokes, Scott could appear on *My Kitchen Rules*. Or host it. 'So guys, I've got a little baby boy now. In twenty years' time, my biggest fear is whether the left get their way and Islam has, you know, got a foothold in this country and terrorism has gone through the roof; I don't want him looking at me saying, "Dad, you didn't do something about this because you were afraid some fuckwit was going to call you a racist."'

The Aboriginal teenager and his white friend are spraying water on each other, laughing. Couples are shimmying to 'Run to Paradise' on their picnic rugs. Pastor Daniel's rainbow coalition threads through the crowd. The counter-protesters are sealed off, half a kilometre away across a lake, so no negative feedback is feeding through. A rainbow glimmers on a giant bubble as a girl circles the grass with her giant bubble wand.

Hands rested on the balustrade, a delighted Blair looks out from his golden gazebo. The UPF family day – he's nailed it. A young patriot shuffles by with a sign: WE SHALL OVERCOME. I pull out my phone and google. I'm right. That was the chant from the Martin Luther King Jr marches.

The organisers have their tricky little agendas where one thing means another, but the folks with the homemade signs are less complicated. The white Martin Luther King insists that the local council have overthrown the will of the people by accepting the mosque proposal. A woman brandishing YOU KEEP YOUR BURQA, I'LL KEEP MY CLITORIS argues her case with sincerity. Another woman strolls by with ISLAM. THE MOST RACIST RELIGION ON EARTH. That's been a popular placard today.

Blair has pulled off something bigger than a family day. Unbeknownst to No Room for Racism, the folks on this side think they're at the anti-racist rally.

The crowd is thinning out. The police haven't been able to block off the counter-protesters entirely. Little fights are breaking out between No Room for Racism and UPF supporters. On the border of the park an Arab dude is shouting at a white guy.

'I know what the prayers are about,' he shouts. 'I'm Arab!'

I could detail the argument back and forth, but the thing you need to know is that the Arab, a Christian, is the UPF supporter.

'I think that hate can be overcome with love,' says the white guy.

The afterparty

I've slipped into this pub because I saw the flags and such and I'm thinking maybe this is where the UPF guys are hanging out. Guys like Ralph and Blair and Shermon. But now I see these people are all in T-shirts saying 'NA'. and I realise that means Nationalist Alternative. They're like the UPF except they don't sugarcoat their views on Jews.

They recognise me. 'Oh, that's John Safran.' There's a whole gang of them and I just get the worst vibe, and so I decide to leave. I skol my beer.

Sunscreen is burning my eyes and that beer's the only liquid I've downed all day. Are they following me? Is the NA following me? I won't stop to tie my shoelace and I hasten my stride. What's that boy in the yoghurt shop waving at me for? It's six o'clock in the evening and the shop is closed. He unlocks the door, lets me in and locks it again. He runs the place, he says, and saw me from the window and wants to offer me a yoghurt. I think, This is the part of my Hobbit adventure where I pause at the inn in the woods for replenishments. Or maybe it's like World War II where a local hides me from the Nazis.

A silhouette travels past the window. It's Squeaky from the UPF! I've picked up the trail again. I lick my spoon, bid farewell to the innkeeper, and escape out the yoghurt shop door.

'Serve this man a beer!' slurs a shaven-haired man in his twenties. We're crammed against the wall outside a different pub. So many folks are squeezed up here and squawking, I can't hear the nearby traffic tearing by. The United Patriots Front and the Nationalist Alternative are not the only groups of their type. This guy is part of the Patriots Defence League Australia. He pushes a schooner into my hand.

'I wanna watch your back,' he whispers in my ear, rubbing his very red eyes. 'I wanna keep an eye on you.'

'There's not much chance I'm gonna get clobbered here, is there?'

'That's why I'm fucking watching your back.'

I take this to mean he's got my back, but maybe I'm being an optimist.

Squeaky spots me. 'What are you doing here?' he whines. 'You fucken . . . you could smell Erikson, couldn't ya?'

There is supposedly tension between the UPF and the Patriots Defence League of Australia. But it can't be that tense or they wouldn't drink at the same pub.

Squeaky sighs in resignation. 'We're gonna have some shots, man – our shout.'

I skol my beer again and Squeaky pulls me by the arm inside the pub. 'Have a shot with us and I'll never have a go at you again at a future rally.'

The barman spreads a round of tequilas across the bar.

'We're gonna put it on the UPF page, yeah?' Squeaky says.

'No!' I laugh.

Neil Erikson, two other UPFers and I slam down the tequilas. Uncanny X-Men blasts through the room.

Squeaky's phone is hovering about. 'I've gotta get a photo of you together,' he says. 'I won't post it on Facebook, it's more for my personal entertainment.'

I shut my eyes, I open my eyes. Neil's opposite me in a booth. He asks if I'm still in trouble with my high school, Yeshivah College, for breaking into the grounds and cutting Footloose.

I tell him that since I filmed that stunt, a couple of staff members have been thrown in jail for molesting students. 'So now it's like there's no way I'm the worst thing, I'm good publicity for the school.'

Neil laughs. We throw down our second tequilas. 'Have you spoken to Gutnick?' he asks.

Rabbi Dovid Gutnick was the rabbi he threatened. 'No, not yet, nooo,' I manage, my head stinging.

'Hey, tell him from me I apologise.'

'Oh, you're apologising?'

'I'm apologising.'

There are several Rabbi Gutnicks. I don't know his one, but I tell Neil I'll hunt him down. Bad choice of words, considering.

He asks if I'm 'mates' with an anti-Islam group called the Q Society. I've heard of those folks. From what I can tell, the Q Society is for the white-collared and middle-aged. Which sets them apart from other anti-Islam groups, like the ones in this pub. And they must have money behind them because they tour international guests. Ones so extreme they're on hate watchlists. The Q Society is very secretive. I haven't been able to rap my knuckles on their door because their address is a PO box.

'They're Zionist Jews,' Neil declares.

This momentarily pulls me out of my tequila daze. For Jewish organisations across the board – Zionist, non-Zionist, left-wing and right – the position is uniform: we live in a wonderful multicultural country and Australian Muslims are part of our Abrahamic family.

Neil says most of the Q Society members come from Melbourne's Jewish suburbs.

'Oh really? Where'd you hear that from?'

He tells me everyone in the anti-Islam scene knows. 'It's mainly about Israel.'

I fancy myself as Australia's pre-eminent Jew detective. If what

Neil says is true, how has this group been operating under my nose, in my own goddamn suburb, without me knowing?

I throw down another tequila.

'You and me again!?' Squeaky slurs. I've stumbled outside for air. 'I tell you what, man, let me just shut you down right now. I am not going to be your new boyfriend. You stick with Neil.'

'I'll stick with Neil,' I slur back. 'The social pages of the Jewish news, when it's got the picture of me and Neil under an interfaith wedding and . . .' I'm too smashed to finish whatever the joke was when the sentence started.

Scott Moerland, the UPF's Mr Normal, lumbers over and he's slurring too. 'Mohammed, he came up six hundred and fifty years after bloody Jesus got crucified! And he said that Jesus was not really crucified. It was a trick, God played a trick on everybody!'

What the hell is Mr Normal on about?

'I reckon we're living in the end of times,' he continues. 'There's five thousand revelations to come true in the Bible. Two thousand have already come true, to the letter. There's more prophecies in the Bible about the times that we're living in now than there was when Jesus actually walked the earth.'

So Mr Normal is not really Mr Normal after all. Like Blair, Pastor Daniel and the Queen man, there's something else going on. He's some sort of doomsday Christian.

'Most people when they hear your speeches,' I say, 'they would take you as being this Aussie ex-soldier who's pissed off, on some secular level, with Islam. They wouldn't, like – as soon as you started bringing Jesus' prophecies into it they'd get confused.'

'I leave that out of it because, bloody, that exact reason. Because, bloody, ah, I am, I pride myself on being the epitome of an Aussie bloke, right? Not many people actually know that I am a full-on Christian.'

A familiar man threads through the crowd. It's Ralph Cerminara.

He slaps my shoulder. 'Got a hundred and eighty back!' He explains that he was paying for a silent number. The fact that I was able to find his details on whitepages.com.au meant the telephone company reimbursed him a hundred and eighty dollars. 'I appreciate it!' he says.

I feel I've inadvertently played into his far-right preconception that the Jews are good with money.

'The left-wing dickheads counter us,' Mr (Not) Normal slurs. 'And I believe this has got something to do with God as well, because they say everything works for good. Even evil. Dickheads bloody counter us, gets the attention, gets us the opportunity to put our message out there.'

Just as the UPF are playing out characters in Hamza's Qur'an, the left are playing out characters in Scott Moerland's Bible.

Neil jumps onto a table. He shushes everyone. He has a joke, he has a joke, he assures us. Amazingly, the scores of drunks all shut up and turn.

'The reason [redacted] wants a mosque in Bendigo,' Neil begins, 'is because the imam of the mosque promised to cure his gay son's AIDS!'

'Haaaa haaaaa haaaa,' everyone cracks up.

Good one, Neil, you fuckwit.

A young man leaps onto the table, pushing Neil along. 'This isn't a piss-on!' he slurs. 'This isn't a piss-on! This is about us! Stop drinking! Listen! Listen! This isn't about drinking . . . about friends or anything like that . . . this is about us uniting as a front —'

'Shut up!' yells a woman.

'We need to stop!' he goes on. 'We need to stop. This is not about alcohol! We need to stop!'

'Shut up!'

'Aussie, Aussie, Aussie! Oi! Oi! Oi!' the young man chants, falling off the table.

I snap a photo of the pub.

'Saw that!' It's the guy from earlier who said he'd watch my back. He's changed his tune. 'You get the fuck out of here, all right?'

My eyes are three-layers stinging – sunscreen, tequila, and taxi high beams. I trip into a Bendigo house. It's flimsy. I fear my elbow will go through a wall if I lean against it. I turn into the lounge room, although there isn't any furniture. This is the UPF Global Rally Against Islam afterparty.

'Beers are in the fridge,' says one guy.

'Shit, I haven't got many ciggies left,' complains another.

They discuss rolling a joint, and whether they should mix it with tobacco because the dope is so strong.

Someone flicks a switch and the harsh fluorescents overhead light up everyone's yellow teeth. 'Turn it off!' growls a woman and the lights go out.

'Thanks for having us, man,' says Ralph.

'No worries, bro,' says the host, a gangly guy with sores on his face.

'You realise you have some big leaders in your fucking house, man,' Ralph tells the host. 'Give it half an hour, ASIO will be here.' He looks around. 'Neil here?'

'No, no,' I say. 'I think he had to go home to his wife or partner.'

'Oh really?'

'I think she was screaming at him on the phone or something.' That's my memory of the taxi ride.

A UPFer is staring at me. 'You look like Andrew Denton. Are you related?'

I shake my head.

It's only when I see Ralph return that I realise he must have ducked off for some reason. 'You want a joint?' he asks.

'Yeah yeah,' I say. You know, to be social.

'Go for it, mate.' He passes the joint. 'F''king get into it.'

'Take it easy,' says a man.

'Suck it in,' instructs a woman.

'What do you think of that?' Ralph asks.

'What do you mean, what do I think of that?'

'What do you think of this one?' He hands me a plastic bag of grass.

'I don't know. I don't know anything about this stuff.'

'That . . . that's the good stuff,' Ralph assures me.

'Yeah, looks good,' I say.

'You've been on TV, haven't you?' someone asks. 'You're ABC. John Safran.'

'Yeah yeah.'

'Don't worry. What you do stays here.'

My phone buzzes in my pocket and I topple to the bathroom. A stranger – a woman with an Indian name – has Facebook-messaged me. 'Hi John, have you come across any stories that spirits can live inside technology devices which have data storage? Video consoles, newer model TVs, smartphones? My friend's kid said he saw demons come out of a TV while playing violent video games. Many thanks!'

I topple back to the lounge room.

'You know he's Muslim, don't ya?' the host of the party tells me. He points to a short guy – Indonesian maybe? – leaning against the wall, hands tucked behind his back. I'm well past the novelty of brown people at white nationalist meet-ups.

'What?' Ralph snaps, overhearing.

'Yeah, he doesn't like it – being Muslim. He hates it,' explains the host.

'But you're a Muslim?' Ralph asks the maybe Indonesian.

'Yeah.' He's either shy or scared or his English isn't that good. His friend tells me he's immigrated to Australia recently and he's married to a UPFer.

'But a Muslim by demographic?' Ralph asks.

'Yeah,' says the maybe Indonesian.

'Yeah, demographic is different – I understand.' Ralph moves back to glugging his beer and I slip outside. I don't understand what 'Muslim by demographic' means.

Outside, ten minutes later, I blurt into my dictaphone: 'Hello? Okay? I got a taxi back to my car at the pub, but now I'm going to go back to the goddamn party where the United Patriots Front are.

Cos they're all sitting there – I hope my dictaphone battery didn't run out when this happened – they're sitting there with this Muslim dude, this Muslim immigrant . . .'

· 'Welcome back, bro,' says the host as I stagger into the house, to the dope-smoke-filled kitchen where the party has shifted.

'Oh beauty,' says another. 'D'you want a beer?'

'No, no, no, cos I'm trying to un-beer,' I slobber.

I turn to the room. 'I don't understand!' I announce to the whole kitchen. 'The entire day was spent about "Oh listen, we've got to worry about Muslims and Muslim immigrants." But then, we end up here at the end of the night, partying with a Muslim immigrant! I mean, like —'

A female UPFer stomps past the grubby fridge, waving her finger. 'Yeah, no, hang on. You can speak to me, right?'

'Oooooh!' Ralph rolls.

'Just stand there and listen to me,' she demands woozily.

'Don't you understand why I'm asking the question?' I whine.

'My husband, Sito, is Muslim by birth. He's from southwest Java.'

'Cool.'

'Okay? Now, he doesn't practise, because he believes that the Islamic family he was born into comes from your heart. So, you don't have to go to a mosque, fucken every day. You don't have to eat halal food. It is what is in your heart or you believe in, right?'

I glance around. I can't spot the Javanese in question.

'You got me there so far? Now, he's come to Australia as a legal immigrant, right? That cost a lot of money and a lot of time. Four years, the immigration part. So, he's come here now and he's Muslim. But, loves his pork roast, has a beer. He doesn't have to go and put his arse up in the air, five times every bloody day.'

'So he's not a Muslim?' Ralph asks.

'Well . . . he is, because he says he is, cos he's born into a Muslim family.'

'It's what you do, right?' Ralph concludes. 'It's what you do that defines you, right?'

'Eggsakly!' the woman says.

'Fair point,' I add.

This is like stoned *Q&A*. And I'm Stony Jones.

Ralph, not happy with this closure, winds things up again. 'The fact that you're defining him as a Muslim is insulting.'

'But that's the way it is!' the woman insists. 'According to his Indonesian citizenship.'

'No, no, no. No, no, no,' Ralph counters. 'No country – and especially Australia – defines individuals by their religion. Every country defines the individual by their ethnicity, all right?'

'But on his papers that we had to have for him to come here, we had to declare that he was a Muslim.'

'Oh, no way,' Ralph says. 'Well, he's a piece of shit.'

'No, he's not, man!' pleads the host. 'We know Sito, man. He's a good bloke. I've met him before in the past.'

'Do you worship a paedophile fucken prophet or not?' Ralph shouts at the woman.

'No, I don't and he doesn't!'

The host is trying to calm Ralph down. 'That cunt's smoked fucken big-arse joints with us, mate. He is cool, I've known him in the past. He's come to all the fucken rallies.' The host motions for Ralph to leave the kitchen with him.

Minutes later, Ralph re-enters. 'Oh look, I apologise,' he says to Sito's wife. 'I guess I'm very apprehensive naturally, because they come to my house and try to kill me.'

'Well, not my husband.'

'I stand corrected. And I do apologise.'

'But, I've stated my case and . . .'

'You're a lovely woman and you stood your ground – especially against someone like myself. And I can be very, very savvy.'

For the second time tonight I flop out the front door, to a not quite full moon.

'I'm Islam but I'm anti-Islam too,' Sito assures me, hands tucked behind his back, leaning against the garage door.

'He's an Australian assimilator,' a woman adds.

'He's a good bloke,' confirms another.

How has this happened? What's wrong with everyone? Some madness has settled over the party where the UPFers – the guys who just threw the All-day Anti-Islam Gazebo Jamboree – are standing up for the Muslim against intolerant Safran.

'He's not an extremist.'

'Yeah, but —' I protest.

'He's an Aussie.'

'But that's what lefties say! They say you've got to understand, just because a person is born Muslim and because they're an immigrant . . . No one seems to understand what I'm getting at!'

'Oh, Sito is just a good bloke. He eats bacon. It's his favourite breakfast.'

The morning after

My phone's convulsing under my pillow, a succession of strangers.

'What the fuck is going on?'

'Big fan of yours for a long time, tell me, what's the deal with . . .'

'Have you joined the UPF?'

I click through to the UPF page. There I am, slamming down the tequila, with Neil and co stumbling out of frame. Beneath, Squeaky has typed: 'John Safran has shots with UPF. He's seen the error of his ways and joined with us.'

I spend the morning putting out spot fires, telling folks I haven't joined the UPF. The Melbourne Anarchist Club – those guys turn up to the rallies with their faces wrapped in bandanas – seem particularly miffed: 'We hope there's a good explanation for why John Safran went out for drinks with the United Patriots Front last night. Fairly sure there's no solid journalist or satirical explanation for having shots with neo-Nazis. We are excited to hear John's response. We hope it's funny and not just depressing.'

'So you've taken shots with them?' It's a man called Jay on the phone. He does security for No Room for Racism/the Socialist Party.

'Yes, I guess. Needless to say, it's a slight misrepresentation.'

I've been trying to catch up with Jay for weeks; suddenly he's all cheery and wants to meet. By evening I'm pulling up a chair in a bar in the city. Jay's here, and a woman is sitting at the table too. I recognise her from online. It's Mel Gregson, the No Room for Racism matriarch. The all-seeing eye on the top of the pyramid. When I spoke to other socialists they told me I should really talk to her.

Jay heads to the bar, leaving us alone. I realise this is like the Mafia movies, where a henchman takes you in to meet the Godfather.

Enormous mirrors with ornate gold frames hang everywhere, so Mel's striking red hair hits me from all directions. I tell her that I think the No Room for Racism branding is great, with the cartoon panda. Because most folks wouldn't want to turn up to a Socialist Party event.

Mel frowns. This small talk has come out all wrong. I meant to compliment the panda but it's come out like . . . I try again. I tell her Neil told me Zionist Jews are behind the Q Society. The logic running through my head and which I hope is running through hers: this validates breaking bread with the UPF, right? New information. Also, even-handedness. Not just digging for dirt on the Muslims, digging for dirt on the Jews.

'Why does it matter?' she asks, exasperated.

The panda isn't the only No Room for Racism marketing device, there's that killer photo: a skinhead with a swastika inked on his noggin and a cool-as-fuck black dude staring each other down. That image keeps the message simple. Those against Islam are white supremacist skinheads. Meanwhile here's a-hole me scuttling around town: 'Hey look, Pastor Danny is black!' 'What's this Israeli flag doing here?' 'Ralph's mum won an Aboriginal art prize!'

Mel says the UPF are paranoid about the media, cut off, marginalised. And that's very helpful from her perspective.

'I don't want you becoming friends with those boys,' Mel says, fingering her unlit cigarette.

Coming down

There's that stereotype of the radical who's not really one. Follow the shabbily dressed socialist with the Che Guevara tattoo back to his home, you'll arrive at a two-storey house in a swish suburb where he lives with his mum and dad. And it's a removable tattoo.

The UPF leaders are the reverse of this. Strange people with radical thoughts – from national socialism to apocalyptic Christianity – hitting the streets and playing dress-ups as regular Australians. But the UPF have to do this if they want to succeed. Because, just my observation, mainstream Australia doesn't do radical. Act too strange and you're cut off.

I've been following the far right out the corner of my eye since high school. People as extreme as Blair form groups that usually draw six people, to a pub or a lounge room. Not the thousand-plus who made the pilgrimage to the UPF gazebo.

The day before the UPF triumph, a different group against Islam, Party for Freedom, called a rally outside a Parramatta mosque. Fifteen people turned up to that. Party for Freedom doesn't have larrikins like Shermon Burgess and Scott Moerland who distract from Blair's weirdness and telegraph to a mainstream crowd: This is as normal as turning up to the cricket or Splendour in the Grass.

REDFERN

Community outreach

Six months before my first Reclaim rally, something curious happened:

A poster has started popping up on walls in an Aboriginal area in Redfern, Sydney. In the middle of the poster, a Chinese dragon is chomping into the Aboriginal flag. STAND UP FOR YOUR MOB. BLACK HOUSES ON BLACK LAND – LET'S STAND WITH OUR COUSINS AND FIGHT. NO ASIANS IN REDFERN.

The poster is tapping into a tense local matter. Mick Mundine, an Aboriginal businessman, oversees a stretch of land known as the Block. Once, it provided low-cost housing for Aboriginal people. But Mick decided that drugs and crime had destroyed the area, so he tore down the houses and moved the Aboriginal people elsewhere. Now he plans to build apartments on the Block for Asian international students.

A few days after finding out about the poster (a buzz in my pocket from a random, as usual; I like how my phone is the hotline for race awkwardness), I head to Sydney. Who is pasting these things up?

The taxi driver taking me to Redfern, a Muslim immigrant, tells me he doesn't like to come down this way. He points to the perspex window that separates him from his passenger. 'When I open this to take the ten dollar, he punch my face, ha ha! And he pick up my coin bag. And run away, ha ha! After that, when I see the Aborigines, I don't like to pick them up.'

Protesters against Mick's development have set up an Aboriginal tent embassy on the Block. Big white slabs of wood on the grass spell out SOVEREIGNTY NEVER CEDED. A small group of people are shielding themselves from the harsh sun under a canopy.

'G'day,' I say from outside the perimeter of the grass. 'Am I allowed to come on here?' I'd been advised to ask this. Not to treat the Block like a public space.

'Well done,' says a Maori woman. 'Good on you, darling, for asking.'

'Hey, um . . .' I begin.

'Hey, um,' the Maori woman mocks. 'You English? Of English descent?' she asks pointedly.

I tell her I'm not.

'Irish?' snaps an Aboriginal guy.

I tell them I'm Jewish and they become more welcoming, now knowing I'm not 'classic white'.

'So good on you then,' the Maori woman says, 'for not using their bastardly language correctly and throwing that "um" in there.'

I ask about the poster.

'We don't know who it is – person or persons unknown,' says an Aboriginal woman. 'We don't want to get into a battle about vilifying Asians. We cop that every day ourselves. So we don't want to put that boot into anyone else.'

The Maori woman thinks the poster is a dirty tricks campaign by Mick's company. To make the embassy cause look racist.

'An interesting place to hang out,' the Maori woman advises, 'and perhaps stretch your ears, is Pride of Redfern.' This cafe, she says, is where Mick's employees take coffee breaks. She feels that a Tongan family, in particular, is having an unhealthy influence on matters. Mick needs these Tongans because he can't get Aboriginal support for the development, she says.

'Just sit and listen,' she continues. 'And come back and tell us what they talk about!' Everyone laughs. 'Will you? They're not easy to miss. A Tongan family. The father is a short man. Walks with a bit of a laboured left leg. Ugly. So if you found a good-looking one, you've got the wrong one.' Cackles break out again.

She spots a white guy crossing the Block with his shopping and lifts herself from her chair and bolts towards him. 'You didn't actually ask,' she snaps. 'You just crossed without asking.' She points at the PRIVATE PROPERTY sign. He argues back but eventually gives in and edges off the grass.

'I've always been on their team,' he says, sounding hurt, as the Maori woman marches off.

I find the Tongan man with the laboured leg at a nearby gym

and boxing centre. His name is Alex and he manages the place.

'I've lived in the community here for twenty-five years now,' he says. 'I've got eight kids and they were all born and raised here.' He says it's a bit rich of the embassy to label the Tongans as outsiders. Many of the protesters are new arrivals. 'She's only just come in with the tent embassy,' he says of the Maori woman.

Alex says he doesn't know anything about the poster but to ask his wife, Lani. She's the general manager of Mick's company.

I wander for five minutes up a hill. A two-storey-high photo of Alfred Cameron Jr, a 'Black Anzac' who served at Gallipoli, is pasted on the company building. In the boardroom Lani opens a coffee table book with the redevelopment plans. The illustrations look chic, a bit futuristic.

'It looks modern,' I say. 'Was there any pressure to try to make it more identifiable, so straight away you're going, This is like an Aboriginal place?'

'What? Have a boomerang or something?' she says sharply. 'We're an urban community.'

Lani turns the page in the big book to photos of the project's multicultural team. One woman is Sudanese, another South African and Maori. Lani thinks the redevelopment is a multicultural vision in itself, literally knocking down a wall that hides the Block from greater Redfern.

She's no help with the poster. She says she has no idea who stuck it up.

I poke around town. A local bar owner not only hasn't heard of the poster, he hasn't heard about the embassy just down the hill, a minute from his business. Asian international students don't know what I'm talking about either. They just look at me like I'm asking them for two bucks for the train.

Finally! A white guy at the pub claims he knows who's behind the poster. And it's not the tent embassy protesters or Mick's people. He says it's Party for Freedom. He's seen those blokes pitching their wares around here, trying to bring Aboriginal people into their fold.

Over the phone, Party for Freedom's chairman, a guy called Nicholas Folkes, denies he's behind the poster, but says he has recruited Aboriginal members. 'They're seeing increasingly large numbers of Asians coming in. They feel that they're being squeezed out economically. They're competing for jobs, housing, the kids are competing on a school level.'

He says his party is picketing auctions with Chinese buyers. 'Let them know they're not welcome.' But he's not a racist, he assures me. 'I'm married to an Asian. An immigrant. But I don't support further Asian immigration.'

While I try to tease out the loophole that lets the head of an anti-Asian immigration party have an Asian immigrant wife, down the phone line I can hear a ruckus. Nicholas is in the car with some mates.

'We're on our way to Canberra. Hopefully, it'll be on the news this afternoon! One of us is wearing a burqa, one's wearing the Ku Klux Klan outfit, and one's wearing a motorbike helmet. We're trying to get into Parliament House today.'

He predicts the 'Klansman' and 'motorcyclist' will be denied entry while the 'Muslim woman' will be allowed in – the stunt exposing what Nick sees as the hypocrisy of multicultural Australia.

'Which one are you wearing?' I ask.

'I'm wearing the burqa, mate.'

Back at the tent embassy an Aboriginal dude also thinks a far-right group is behind the poster, although he thinks it's another group, called Australia First Party. 'They self-admittedly got a guerrilla group that's specifically designed to do this kind of stuff and cause division. They're just manipulating shit.'

So off I go. The shopfront headquarters for the Australia First Party sits on a busy road opposite a Japanese car parts factory, a few suburbs up from Redfern. The roller door covering the headquarters has been kicked in, presumably by the anarchists who have pasted their posters all around. The Australia First Party likes to describe itself as 'European nationalist'. Its enemies go with the blunter 'white supremacist'.

I knock on the side door, down a laneway. The party chairman, an old man with a grey moustache called Jim Saleam, is initially friendly. But he shoos me away when I mention I've written for *The Age*. 'Smear-mongering, lying, criminal arseholes,' he mutters.

I sit at the bus stop across the road, impotent, unable to confirm my suspicion that his group is the one 'manipulating this shit'. I suspect his group because its website covers in great detail the little-known story of the poster. Jim gloats over the bind he thinks the left are in. Will they support Asian immigration or Aboriginal sovereignty? Ultimately, he feels, the left will back immigration and 'Aboriginal people will see in return how false the friendship of this gang really was.'

Back at the embassy tents, the Aboriginal dude who dobbed in Jim is throwing wood on a fire. He says a few Aboriginal people with 'colonised minds' fraternise with the far right, but not many. He says there's a bond between blackfellas and Asian people, rolling back to before white invasion. Similarly, he says, there's a special bond between blackfellas and Muslims. 'Muslim people support our people and our fight, because they've understood dispossession. I've been to Bankstown. For the first time, I walked around without feeling like I'm being stared at. Cabbies have pulled over to give me lifts.'

I don't tell him that the Muslim taxi driver who dropped me off was unambiguous: 'When I see the Aborigines, I don't like to pick them up.'

A black guy, born in Bermuda, has stopped by. Here on a holiday, he saw the Aboriginal flag flapping from the Redfern train station and wanted to know what was going on. A white girl, a British tourist, is also under the tent canopy, her eyes moistening. 'It was my country that did this, not just here,' she tells the Maori woman. 'They've done this all over the world. It's absolutely disgusting.'

I think of the local bar owner a minute away who has no idea this embassy protest is going on. Yet these tourists somehow found their way here.

The Maori woman spots a young white couple strolling across the grass. 'How are you?' she shouts. 'Come and have a chat. Have you got five minutes? Come on, guys, you're trespassing!'

'Trespassing?' the young Aussie man says.

'Look to your left. There's a sign. Private property.'

'Gee!' says the young man.

'Sorry!' shouts the young Aussie woman.

'Sorry I stole your country,' the Maori woman mutters. 'Sorry, sorry.'

The young couple don't stop for a chat.

Almost a year later I'm back in Redfern. I've fallen into a conversation with a young Aboriginal Muslim man, Youssef, at the foot of an elevator. He knows of Ralph Cerminara.

'They've been pumping the Aboriginal connection, these guys,' he says of the far right. He's sceptical of their commitment to Aboriginal issues. 'Where were they thirty years ago? Where were they two years ago?'

I hold my phone up to him. A 'patriot' group has included this disclaimer in an advertisement for an upcoming rally against Muslims and refugees: 'We would like to make it clear that we are not rallying against our Aboriginal brothers and sisters and support them as the first Australians.'

Youssef shakes his head and we head off for a bite.

'I was married to a pious Muslim girl, you know?' he tells me at a nearby cafe. 'That was about a year and a half ago. But she wanted a divorce because I stopped praying one day. I look back and say, How beautiful is she to ask for a divorce because I stopped praying.'

Youssef converted to Islam ten years ago. 'Blackfellas come through Islam really in one way – through jail. You'll meet a couple of Leb boys and you've got the environment where you can discipline yourself and focus on it.'

In fact, that's not the only way a blackfella can come to Islam. Youssef fell in with a couple of Omanis at university whose family own a Gulf airline. They once took him out to a dinner where the bill at the end of the night was eleven thousand dollars. (Good Lord!) He admired their humility, despite their wealth, so looked into Islam further.

Initially his Muslim brothers weren't satisfied with his commitment. 'I got told to choose between sharia law and my communist side,' he says. 'It took me a while to let go of Fidel Castro.'

Youssef is fond of Libyan revolutionary Muammar Gaddafi, and he shook the hand of Sinn Féin leader Gerry Adams when he toured Australia. 'Doesn't mean I respect the IRA, their method is wrong, but their ideology was correct in the sense that it resists the imperialism of Britain. King Henry wants to chop every wife's head off – why? Because he wants a son. "By the way, I'll just switch churches and remove parts of the Bible." That's what I like about Islam – it doesn't progress.'

'What's wrong with progress?'

Youssef motions out the windows of the cafe. For hipsters, McDonald's and Starbucks ruin an area. For Youssef it's the hipsters and their cafes that are the problem. 'It breaks my heart. I haven't been in the area. I come back and there's like nine coffee shops.' Youssef fondly remembers the instant coffee at the one Greek takeaway in his youth. 'Now they've got restaurants, a culture of people, but they did it on account of removing the Aboriginals.'

I tell him I've been down at the Block and his face droops.

'I went down there,' Youssef says. 'One of the elders got up and is going, "You don't know what you are, Youssef!" I go, "I've just come down to see how you're going." And she goes, "You're not welcome here!" And I go, "What?" She goes, "You know what for."'

'Because you've become Muslim?'

Youssef nods. 'I was really hurt by it, ay,' he says.

(Later, I tell people this story and they're surprised. But why? They wouldn't be surprised by news of a rabbi rejecting a Jew who leaves his faith.)

This wasn't the only time things didn't fit neatly. 'I went through a full black nationalism stage – in the sense of empowering the indigenous people – but the Arabs were the ones that sorted me out, the Omanis. They said, "Man, go easy on your black power."' Youssef says Malcolm X travelled the same road, concluding that too intense a focus on blackness doesn't square with Muslim teachings.

So why didn't Youssef dig into Aboriginality for his spiritual fix?

'Alcohol has destroyed those roots,' he says.

A few years back, up in the Northern Territory, his family wanted him to go through law, which Youssef explains as a coming-of-age ceremony, deep in the bush with secret rituals. He didn't want to go through with it. 'I hid in the police station,' he says. 'I know it sounds like I've sold out. I can't ever go back to my people's ways.'

But he can't leave his Aboriginality behind. 'I have my battles with my Muslims. I'm always fighting my heart. My biggest thing right now is scholars have said, "Can you pray on stolen land?" Some say Allah won't accept your prayers if you do.' Youssef is frustrated that clerics aren't joining the dots. He told one: 'Hey Sheikh, this land's been stolen. Maybe we should seek permission off the indigenous people.'

Youssef tells me that last time he was down in Melbourne a white guy racially abused him, but not for being Aboriginal. He thought he was Indian. We cackle like Heckle and Jeckle.

Youssef notices that I'm scribbling my notes with a pencil.

'Are you a hipster?' He winces.

'I don't know.'

'Hope not, brother.'

He puts up with the far right, but you have to draw the line somewhere.

JEWISH AUSTRALIAN PRINCESS?

Neil's rabbi

I keep my promise to Neil that I'd hunt down and apologise to the rabbi he stalked. Rabbi Gutnick's synagogue is a white building squeezed between two brown ones in Melbourne's CBD. Just around the corner from Parliament House, the site of my first Reclaim rally.

When I arrive, the rabbi is pacing in his office, shouting into his phone. 'He just said, "The syrup's no good but the pill will be fine! But he was wrong!"' The rabbi adjusts his skullcap. 'Okay, I will. All right, no problem. Goodbye!'

The rabbi turns to me and says, 'They had chametz in my antibiotics!'

We are in the middle of the festival of Pesach (Passover), when it's forbidden to eat wheat, known as chametz. The rabbi tells me he's just discovered that his pills contain wheat starch.

We stomp up the stairs to a loft – the choir used to sing from here when there was a choir – that overlooks the synagogue interior. The rabbi has pushed bookshelves and a table into the tiny space.

'Once you're into this business, there's no limit to the amount of rules and regulations you can create for yourself to be serving Judaism in its most optimum way. It does reach a point where it gets very ridiculous.'

'Don't tell me,' I say, 'it's the people who are just a little bit more religious than you? They're the nutbags, are they?'

For the Jews, anyone a touch more religious than you is a nut-case, anyone a touch less religious barely a Jew.

'It's not even about religion any more,' the rabbi sighs. 'It's become some form of OCD.'

The rabbi says religious Jews try to out-pious their neighbours. Not only can't you eat chametz at this time of year, you must cover your dinner table because it has touched chametz during the year. 'They say, "Oh, I would put two cloths on my table on Pesach." And you say, "I actually shave a layer off my table on Pesach and then put two cloths." I've met people that do that, actually.'

'Wow, they shave a layer off the table?'

'Yeah,' the rabbi confirms. 'They sand with an electric sander. That's simply because chametz has touched, possibly, maybe. The table's growing thinner and thinner; one day it's going to be gone.'

'I met Neil Erikson,' I tell the rabbi. 'He said to me – cos he thinks all Jews know all Jews – "Can you apologise to Rabbi Gutnick for me?"'

'Apologise?' Surprised, he scratches his beard.

'So I pass on his apology.'

'Has he rehabilitated in any way?'

'Well, he's moved on from abusing Jews to abusing Muslims.'

'So he still wouldn't be good for keynote speaker at our annual lunch?' the rabbi says. 'That guy, Erikson, he wasn't the worst I've ever had, I've got to tell you. A guy called my phone. He talked about how he's going to come after me, and what he's going to do. He's going to attack my daughter. He talked about cutting and things. This was my first introduction to people that stalk rabbis. It's a whole genre of society that stalk rabbis in their spare time.'

The rabbi reported the caller to the police. 'They reverse-traced his calls. He was a seventeen- or eighteen-year-old guy, sitting at home in his parents' house. Apparently he also called priests and bothered them. He was quite non-discriminatory.'

'Cross-cultural,' I say.

'Interfaith,' the rabbi adds.

'He was anti-racist. He would do it to everyone.' Oh no, I'm caught in a sarcasm loop. 'Someone we should look to, to . . .'

'To emulate!' the rabbi concludes, winning the sarcasm battle rap. He says the policewoman who handled the case chided him because he kept chatting to the guy on the phone.

'I said to her, "In my tradition, most times when people meet me, even if they've been sceptical or hesitant, after we get to know each other, often we become quite good friends. After a while you can break down almost anyone, I've found." Then it turns out you can't. She explained to me that there are just crazy people in the world.'

After Neil's threats the rabbi took up Israeli martial arts. 'I did six weeks of Krav Maga training. Now I can catch bullets and throw them back at people.' He feels that the fear Neil struck in him was 'the Lord's reminder that I'm supposed to be different. I've got a mission in the world. Erikson was just a messenger from the Lord to remind me that I've got a unique role to play and stop trying to pretend I don't. Anyway, who knows?'

Like Hamza and Scott Moerland, Rabbi Gutnick sees his foe as part of God's big story. This soothes them all.

Over Pesach, Jews read from a book called the Haggadah, which tells a story that is also told in the Torah: Moses leading the Jews out of slavery in Egypt towards the Holy Land, Israel. (The Jews had to flee Egypt one morning and there wasn't time for the bread they were baking to rise. So during Pesach we only eat unleavened bread. That's why the rabbi can't take his antibiotic pills.) I pull my Haggadah from my bag. I didn't just come here to pass on Neil's regards.

'In my Haggadah they've got a beheaded person.'

My copy of the Haggadah was illustrated by a Polish Jew, Arthur Szyk, in the years leading up to the Holocaust. A full page shows Moses killing an Egyptian who had been beating up a Jew. Another shows David strutting with the head he severed off Goliath. Neither of these tales are traditionally part of the Haggadah, but Szyk threw them in anyway. He was a Zionist and wanted to tell Jews to get militaristic and not go like lambs to the slaughter in Europe.

'People aren't comfortable with killing in the Torah,' the rabbi says, looking down at David clutching the head. 'They get stuck at David beheading Goliath and then say, "That looks like —"'

'ISIS?'

'Yeah. Then the argument is, "Well, that was two thousand years ago." The problem with ISIS is they're still doing it now.'

Nonetheless, the rabbi doesn't think you can reverse-park the Torah into political correctness. For beheadings to feature in Jewish scripture means the practice had to be 'ethical, and true, and proper, regardless of its historical context. They had to do it to create a victory and dispirit the enemy. It's fine. It's got my endorsement as a military tactic. The grim reality is, you bag the Qur'an for stuff, you have to look in the Torah as well.'

I learnt in high school that when the Jewish Messiah arrives, the Jews will travel to Israel on clouds with wings of eagles, and a court will convene where capital punishment can be dished out to homosexuals, adulterers, witches and Sabbath-breakers. Sounds to me like the Jewish version of the Islamic State. The safety clause is 'when the Jewish Messiah arrives'. The court can't convene until after the supernatural event. This theological detail is important to atheists who want to argue that Islam is more dangerous than other faiths, including Judaism.

I ask the rabbi if he's read the Qur'an.

'I don't know enough about Jewish scripture to start reading Muslim scripture,' he says. 'I only know what gets repeated. Things about rocks and trees and people hiding behind them. It sounds like a game of hide-and-seek, capture the flag. It sounds like we could do a camp. I don't fully fathom. I mean, you've got all types of weird stuff written in religious things.'

'Yeah, but Jews know the power of words. Doesn't the power of words in scripture mean something?'

'Bottom line is how it translates in action,' he says. 'If that translates into pogroms, that's the problem. In Australia, my thirty-six years I've been here, I haven't had a pogrom yet.'

'Do you reckon the Haggadah is dangerous?' I ask. 'That it can easily be superimposed on a modern setting? The Haggadah warns: "In every generation enemies rise up to destroy us." So if you're there at the Pesach table you can think, like, Oh, the Palestinians are the enemy for this generation. I can kill a Palestinian.'

The rabbi insists the Haggadah can't be taken this way, because the punishments – from raining frogs to the death of firstborns – are doled out by God, not by Jews. Still, Arthur Szyk took the leap and sprinkled the Haggadah with Jews taking vengeance. (But he was inspiring the Jews to fight the Nazis. So that's good, right?)

At the very least, the Haggadah – with its cry of 'Next year in Jerusalem' – transformed the world. Its yearly reading, around the dinner table, inspired Theodor Herzl, the father of modern Zionism. He was ethnically Jewish, but reportedly did not believe in God. Scripture bleeds everywhere, not just over the devout.

'Is it weird,' I continue, 'that we're telling kids there will be a court, and witches and adulterers and homosexuals could be killed? Is that unhealthy?' An orthodox Jew had recently wandered around a gay pride rally in Israel and knifed people.

'I have no doubt his relatives need to take responsibility for the way he was brought up or trained,' the rabbi says. 'That's the thing about any of these laws. You need to be able to contextualise it. That can't be: your kid walks in at six years old to prayer, and the first thing he learns is stoning, strangulation, hot lead down the throat.'

Something's been bugging me for a few weeks and I think

I've worked out what. 'We're always being told, socially, no micro-aggressions,' I say. 'Be careful, if you meet a transgender person, to use the right pronoun, because you don't want to upset them. The spirit of our age is to not offend. Then, on the other hand, we have the Qur'an and the Torah —'

'It's just a dance. It's just a balance.' The rabbi concedes that the Torah gets sold at Dymocks, yet if I wrote a book saying homo-sexuals should be stoned, it probably wouldn't get stocked.

'There is certainly more latitude given to religions, because of their historical role. Frankly, I give my religion more latitude because I believe it's the stuff that God said. We're looking at it through an angle of Western secular society. Some of the stuff is very, very hard to swallow. I've met transgender people and gay people. Very hard for them to read through that portion —'

'Leviticus 20:13.'

'How do you even know that?' the rabbi squeaks.

'Because I like to drive Father Bob crazy by bringing it up,' I say of my Catholic priest radio co-host.

Leviticus 20:13 states: 'If a man lies with a male as one lies with a woman, the two of them have done an abhorrent thing; they shall be put to death – their bloodguilt is upon them.'

'What does Father Bob say about Leviticus 20:13?'

'Well, Christians get off the hook,' I tell him, because of the New Testament. 'Because Jesus died, things got reset or something.'

'It changed.'

'Yeah. Something happened. It's like a Spider-Man reboot.'

The rabbi tells me that I should be more like Waleed Aly. Waleed fudges Islam to make the religion look good, the rabbi claims, and I should do the same for Judaism. 'You don't have to be purely objective about your own people.'

That night I type into Facebook Messenger: 'I forgot to ask you. Do you forgive Neil?'

'I would be keen to forgive him,' the rabbi types back. 'Hatred ultimately consumes the hater more than it does the hated. We could do a great coming together for your book. An embrace in the synagogue on Rosh Hashanah. Although I think he's not allowed to come within 50 metres of me. I told you he saved me 600 bucks right?'

'No. Do tell.'

The rabbi's wife was pulled over for yakking on her phone while driving. The policeman checked the registration and saw that the car was owned by a Dovid Gutnick. The cop asked if this was Dovid Gutnick the rabbi, who'd been recently harassed by a neo-Nazi.

'My wife said yes,' the rabbi tells me. 'He said he did the case and felt bad for me so he's waiving the ticket. It would have been over 600 bucks! So the neo-Nazi who accused Jews of being money hungry saved this Jew 600 bucks.'

'I better not tell Neil. It might tip him back from the Muslims to the Jews.'

'Seriously, I think the threatening calls were worth it for that savings,' the rabbi says. 'That's not feeding the stereotype, is it?'

The Q Society

I trot up the staircase of the Israeli martial arts gym in Caulfield, a suburb one up from my flat. This is where Rabbi Gutnick trained when he was frightened Neil might come and clobber him.

'Did you bring the flag or what?' shouts a buff young man, Avi Yemini, as I walk inside. Punching bags shaped like people are dangling here and there. Avi owns the place and is a trainer himself. 'My mum's against the idea,' he goes on. 'She's against burning the flag.'

I'd told Avi I'd like to pop by to chat, and he offered to burn a Palestinian flag as 'colour' for my book.

'I thought you were joking,' I say.

'Why would I joke?'

'I don't know,' I concede. 'I guess you wouldn't – you're not an Ashkenazi Jew.' Those are us white Jews. 'It's only Ashkenazi Jews who are sarcastic.'

'No. I'm black. I'm a black Jew.'

Avi's family fled Yemen for Israel in 1948, so as well as being Jewish they're Arab. Avi's not some oddity, as rare as a four-leaf clover. Jews from Arab and Muslims countries, and their descendants, make up the majority of Israel's six million Jews.

This muddies the simple story where the Palestinians are like the Aboriginal Australians and the Jews are like Captain Cook and the First Fleet. So certain folks leave this bit of the story on the cutting-room floor.

'You're an Arab,' I say to Avi.

'What can I do?' he says ruefully.

A man in a tracksuit stands with Avi, listening in.

'Are you Jewish?' I ask.

'No,' he says. 'I would like to be, though.'

'You're a JINO. Jew in nose only.'

'Okay,' he says.

Avi is a former Israel Defense Forces soldier and his business is called IDF Training. (He's got his story ready if lawyers come after him: his 'IDF' stands for 'Individual Diet and Fitness', and it's not his fault if people confuse his acronym with that of the Israel Defense Forces.) His marketing prowess doesn't end with the business name. Avi is super-talented at tapping into neuroses in the community. A week after the Lindt Café siege he ran a workshop: 'Learn the correct way to respond to a terrorist attack!' He also held themed workshops after two Arabs bashed a local Jew, after a carjacking and after a murder in a park. The 'ripped from the headlines' themes draw in the newspapers and current affairs shows.

Rabbi Gutnick may have trained here, but I didn't drop by to talk about that. I'm chasing a lead. A local Jewish opera singer, who I bumped into outside the chemist, told me that Avi knows about the Q Society, the group Neil spoke of while slamming down tequilas.

I need to know if it's true. Is there a secretive anti-Islam group run by Jews operating under my very nose?

'They had a meeting with me once,' Avi says.

'Huh!'

Someone phoned him out of the blue. A stranger. 'And they go, "Hey Avi, I've got a meeting for you that I think you should really come to."' Avi turned up to a house not far from the gym, not knowing what it was all about. He sat around a dinner table with other people, none of whom he knew. Some were Q Society members and some, like him, guests. The guests were asked to offer up ideas on how they could help 'combat the rise of Islam'.

'I was just sitting back and listening,' Avi says. 'Then they turned to me and they go, "And what do you think about organising some training?' We've got groups of guys that are ready to go, that need the training, that are ready to fight when we need.'"

'Training guys for what, though?' I ask. 'For some future race war or something?'

'I think that's where they were going. They wanted me to train up some little militias.'

The Q Society people told Avi that they feared attacks by political opponents. 'But they're a bunch of fucking headcases,' he says. They hectored him with what sounded like conspiracy theories, about the halal industry funding terrorism. There was something cultlike about it all. They wanted him to come to another meeting. 'I just walked out. I go, "No, look, I've had a think about it, it's not for me."'

'But were they Jewish?'

Avi shrugs.

Two dozen people in tracksuits are jumping around on the mats next to us, thrusting rubber knives and pointing rubber guns at each other. Avi once ran an Israeli Army-style course with real guns. Waleed Aly attacked it on his television show: 'If I rocked up with my mates Mustafa and Hamoudi do you reckon they'd let us train?' Waleed said if Muslims were out training with real guns, there'd be hysteria. Avi saw this as another chance to promote his business, and now runs Waleed's editorial on a loop on a big-screen television in the gym.

Unsurprisingly, considering his business's name, Avi has attracted the attention of those against Zionism.

'We're a hot target for Israel haters because we're so vocal and we're ready to fight.' He says people online threaten to come down and thump him, but so far it hasn't happened. 'Sometimes I think I'm going to egg my own place or throw a firebomb in the middle of the night. You know how much media I'll get?'

We stroll next door to the kosher restaurant for falafel. Avi might think Q Society are cuckoo, but not that cuckoo. 'Look at Europe, it's just exploding and Jews are the first ones to cop it,' he says. Avi thinks the most difficult thing for Melbourne Muslims who want to attack Jews is the travel.

'Traffic. From Coburg to here is just annoying.' (There's a big Muslim community in Coburg.) 'The layout of Melbourne protects the Jewish community. How long will that last. Who knows?'

Avi says that now and then he still thinks about his meeting with the Q Society. 'When I walked away from them that night and I just analysed it, I'm like, That was some of the weirdest shit that's ever happened to me. But when I was thinking about it later, I'm like, Are they just geniuses that are seeing the future?'

I find another man who has been invited to a Q Society meeting, a non-Jew who self-identifies (or at least used to) as a fascist.

'Are you still a transcendental fascist, or whatever the hell it's called?' I ask Richard on the phone.

'I don't know.'

Seems to me you should know if you're still a fascist or not. I haven't spoken to Richard for forever. Since I met him in the late 1990s he has made films, run film festivals, and managed a bondage club. There were often swastikas on the promotional posters for all these – mulched-up art, sincerity and irony.

He once phoned me, upset. He'd programmed a video in his film festival, a talk by Holocaust revisionist David Irving. He'd been excited by the thought of university activists protesting outside the cinema. Like with Avi, it was all fun and games. He was shaken when elderly Jews who had survived the Holocaust turned up to protest.

Richard says he attended a Q Society meeting a few years ago. He reckons many there were Jewish.

'Were they wearing skullcaps?'

He says they weren't. So how did he know they were Jewish?

'It just seemed there was a presence there.'

Both he and Neil Erikson have a swastika-tainted past. Don't these types of people think Jews are lurking in the shadows everywhere?

Richard tells me it's not the fascists I should be worried about anymore, pointing to a new novel by Michel Houellebecq. Set in the near future, it's about 'what happens when Muslim immigration essentially takes over a Western country. Basically, a lot of Jews in France have to leave for Israel because they're under threat. Fascinating book. You'll love it.'

'Yeah. It's just that I'd be too embarrassed to go into the bookshop, because I don't know how to pronounce the guy's name.'

'Michel like Michelle, and Wellbeck.'

I grab the Michel Houellebecq from a bookshop in the city and duck into a bar and start drinking and reading.

Burnt cars on the streets of Paris. A Muslim party has clawed to power. French women just know to dress modestly now. The far-right Front National pushes back.

I order another drink. I had planned to see a film but I think, No, I've got to keep reading this.

The French Jews just know to leave. The main character, a non-Jew, is envious his Jewish girlfriend can escape. 'I don't have an Israel,' he says, kissing her goodbye.

Facebook Messenger buzzes. It's a random. 'I'm a fan of your show. Do you believe in Jewish deicide?'

'What do you mean?'

'The belief that Jews collectively are responsible for the death of Christ.'

'Is that what you believe?'

'A little, but it's the reason why so many people hate your kind.'

Jesus! Thanks, buddy. I really have the most wonderful fucking fans.

I tuck my phone back in my pocket and keep drinking and reading the Houellebecq, but my mind is drifting, from the Front National to the United Patriots Front, from the French Muslim Brotherhood to Hamza and Musa.

I shut the book and, with three whiskeys in me, wander out of the bar and through the city, and end up passing an army disposals shop. I glance in the window and there are knives laid out. I think, Oh.

There are some that make sense. Leatherman, workmen knives, and Swiss Army ones. But there are others that look like . . . I'm not sure what you'd use them for if not to protect yourself, although I'm just as sure there is some other reason. I think to myself, Maybe I need a knife. Maybe I should carry one in my pocket.

I drift on into the store and I feel embarrassed, like I've wandered into an adult bookshop. I say to the man, 'Ah, you know. Just browsing.'

He says, 'Ah yes. Well, this is the shop to browse.'

There are nice items with wooden handles. Little ones you can fold up. There are knives with rubber handles that have a spider on the blade.

'My niece, she's turning eighteen,' I tell the man. I feel compelled to give a cover story. 'She's always camping. And I just walked by the window and thought, For her birthday, why not get her a knife?'

The Q Society pop up again, but this time they're not in the shadows. They're quite public. A federal election is on the horizon and the Q Society reveal they're forming a party, Australian Liberty Alliance. For the launch, to be held in Perth a few weeks from now, they're flying in far-right Dutch politician Geert Wilders. I click on ALA's brand-new website and skim their frequently asked questions page.

Q: 'Did it occur to you that ALA can be pronounced so it sounds like Allah?'

A: 'Yes, and this is of no concern. Members and voters care much more about our values and policies – plus we have a very cool logo.'

I spool through 'Values & Policies'. The only foreign country presented in a positive light is Israel.

I phone the number on the website and get through to ALA president Debbie Robinson. She says no worries, we'll be able to catch up for a chat. Some secret society, Richard and Neil! The question 'Are you Jewish?' is on the tip of my tongue, but I decide to hold back until our face-to-face.

The day before the Australian Liberty Alliance launch, an email shoots through. 'Dear John, Regret to inform you that we are unable to accredit you for the Perth media conference. Thank you for your kind interest in the Australian Liberty Alliance.'

I call around. A journo friend from the ABC and another from Al Jazeera were accredited. This is a me thing. Goddamn. I bet they thought I was going to start trouble.

ALA president Debbie Robinson is a Jew. A wily Jew. I can tell now. She's out-wily-Jewed me by leading me on – 'Yes, yes, yes, we can catch up for an interview' – and then at the last moment denied me even media accreditation, something she's doled out to every shmuck in town. If Debbie had knocked me back when I rang I could've prepared a plan B.

Of course I don't know for sure she's Jewish. I call her but the phone bumps to voicemail. Jesus. Why didn't I ask her if she was Jewish when I had the chance?

I recall the comment of Mel from No Room for Racism: 'Why does it even matter?'

Well, it matters to me because I'm the Jew Detective and I still can't believe a (possibly) Jewish secret society has been operating in my home town. But it's more than that.

Blair and Pastor Daniel both dress up their agendas – white nationalism and evangelical Christianity – as 'everyday Australians' being concerned about Islam. Are Australian Liberty Alliance 'everyday Australians', or have they also got a precise agenda –

Zionism? Are all those claiming to be average in fact more extreme than they're letting on?

I pack my bag for Perth.

Debbie's husband, also an ALA director, practises out of a medical clinic in a quiet Perth suburb. The building just looks like a big house from the street. I park around the corner. I only have a half-formed plan. I'll book an appointment. He's an orthopaedic surgeon specialising in knees and shoulders. My knee used to play up at the gym. I'll have to fake *ouch*es when he touches me. I'll go in with a skullcap. As the appointment is wrapping up and I'm buttoning my shirt I'll be like, 'Hey, you're Debbie Robinson's husband, right? Is she Jewish?' and it'll seem normal because I'm wearing the skullcap. I doubt he's Jewish. 'Robinson' is as WASP as it comes. But that's not her original name. Her maiden name's probably Bagelsteinberg or something.

Hang on. I can't give a fake name for the appointment, can I? I'll have to show a Medicare card. 'John Safran' will set off alarm bells. I need to think this through more. I drive off to the cactuses.

The socialists want to protest the ALA members-only launch starring Geert Wilders. But, like the journos, they don't know where it's being held. (The media conference will run afterwards, at a yet to be revealed location. The journos have to wait for a text from the ALA.) So the socialists have taken to a stage in a popular outdoor mall, next to a cactus sculpture. A sign on the stage says The Wiggles will be appearing here next week. For now, a Pakistani-Australian woman in a hijab preaches against Geert while shoppers stroll by, seemingly oblivious to her. An old white guy brandishing an anarchist flag takes over. Apart from the woman in the hijab, the socialist gang is an all-white affair, so they perk up when two brown dudes stop at the foot of the stage to listen, the first members of the public to do so. They perk up further when the two dudes offer to help hand out pamphlets.

One of the dudes mumbles as he passes a pamphlet to a woman pushing a stroller, 'Oh, I can go mean-ass on these fellows, these Muslims.'

Huh?

'What's this protest about?' I ask the dude.

'Muslims, is that it?'

'Yeah,' I say. 'Is it for them or against them, though?'

'Against them. It's against the Islamic! We're Pacific Islanders. We're peaceful folks, you know? We don't like terrorists.'

I don't have the heart to report this back to the socialists.

Every journo's phone in Perth (besides mine) buzzes. The ALA text message has arrived, and a journo here by the cactuses tips me off. The press conference will be held on the lawn of the state parliament.

I pull up early to survey the lie of the land. Six suited security men with ALA passes dangling from their necks are hovering on the grass. One snaps that I need a sheet of paper with media accreditation to walk further.

'Mark Safran?' bellows a smart-looking bloke as tall and sturdy as the security men. It's Andrew Horwood, another ALA director. I recognise him from a YouTube video where he asks supporters to film Muslims at their mosques, shops and homes on the last day of Ramadan. He doesn't explain why he wants them filmed. And I'm not sure why he's calling me Mark. He insists I'm not allowed to be here.

I rush around trying to find the entrance to Parliament House, but no matter which side of the building I go there doesn't appear to be one. In the distance I hear the bustle of journos arriving on the lawn for the press conference. I lean against a tree and call the front desk of Parliament House. I'm handballed from staffer to staffer until I end up at the ear of the Executive Manager of Parliamentary Services. He's furious that the ALA are holding a press conference (the ALA hadn't alerted him to this) and that they're blocking me from the lawn (it's a public space). He tells me that of course I'm allowed to be there. And to call on a parliament security guard if the ALA gives me trouble.

I dart to the lawn in time to see the back of Geert's and Debbie's heads as the two climb into a four-wheel drive. I've missed it. I stroll over to Andrew Horwood and tell him I was allowed to be here. He shrugs.

Out-wily-Jewed again. I mope off to my Airbnb and fall asleep reading Houellebecq.

The Australian Liberty Alliance is always banging on about *taqiyya*, the Islamic law that supposedly permits Muslims to lie to outsiders. The Australian Liberty Alliance has been *taqiyya*ing me every which way it can. (By the way, Muslims say that *taqiyya* doesn't mean you can lie to outsiders. Conveniently, the anti-Muslims can dismiss this explanation as yet more *taqiyya*.)

The next morning, I'm once again parked around the corner from Debbie's husband's medical clinic. I'm slurping a thickshake. I haven't worked out my plan but figure I might as well brainstorm here until something pops into my head. By the time I've finished the thickshake, a police car has pulled up in front of me.

'What are you up to, mate?' one of the cops ask as I stumble out of my car.

'I was hoping to . . . I'm a journalist and I was hoping —'

'Boom!' the cop says to his partner.

His partner tells me he guessed I was a journalist.

'Go on, tell me Mr Journal why you're here? Two days in a row.'

So I've been noticed.

'To be honest —'

'We like honesty.'

'Yes. To be honest, as a writer, you're sort of thinking of approaching people,' I say, 'but yesterday I just decided, I just decided to not approach them.'

'You're making absolutely no sense whatsoever,' the cop advises. 'You're talking in conundrums, you really are. Question is, why are you parked here now?'

I tell them that the orthopaedic surgeon in that medical clinic heads up an anti-Islam party and I'm trying to find out if his wife is Jewish.

'Write them an email or a letter or something,' the cop recommends. 'Rather than parking around here and wasting two of your days and being a bit creepy.'

The Warsaw Ghetto Uprising

I've finished Houellebecq. Scary book. Fiction, but could it be foretelling the truth? The West makes incremental changes to accommodate Islam and next thing you know, polygamy seems normal and banning blasphemy seems reasonable, as does dressing more modestly.

I have moved on to a new book. This one is about Jewish resistance fighters during World War II. It's a true story.

Leon Rodal waits with his fellow fighters in a pockmarked building. They're waiting for nearby Nazis to wander into their range of fire. Frustrated that it's taking too long, Leon pulls on a stolen Nazi uniform. He marches out of the building and, posing as an officer, instructs the Nazis to follow him. He leads them to where he needs them, tells them to stay there, enters the building and throws a hand grenade from the window. Later in the war, he orchestrates a fake funeral procession to escape a town. Jews posing as corpses in caskets are carried by Jews posing as mourners. Leon leads the procession.

I've been feeling miserable about my failed Perth mission, but this book is pumping me up. Leon, a master of disguise, was a wily Jew in situations far more high-stakes than anything I've been thrown into.

I stare into my bathroom mirror, preparing to shave. Debbie is hosting an Australian Liberty Alliance event in Sydney in a month. I return the shaver to the rim of the sink. No, I think I'll grow a beard.

LAKEMBA

Blair compromised

Compromising photos of Blair Cottrell have fallen into the hands of an anarchist group. They've passed them on to *Daily Mail Australia*, which has published them. The headline reads: LEADER OF FAR-RIGHT PATRIOT GROUP IS PICTURED AT THE COUNTER OF A HALAL KEBAB SHOP. The article goes on to say: 'An infamous far-right, anti-Islam campaigner who helped lead a boycott against halal certification has been caught out ordering from a kebab store which locals claim is halal certified.'

The photos show Blair chatting to the kebab shop woman serving behind the counter. According to the source, Blair 'had indeed ordered a kebab mixed with hummus, garlic yoghurt and barbeque sauce' and was waiting for his order at the time of the photos. 'We also understand that it was ordered as part of a combo with fries and an orange juice.'

The United Patriots Front have gone into damage control and released a statement claiming Blair 'only ordered an orange juice from an Aussie'.

To hammer this home, Neil Erikson has annotated a photo. A red arrow points to the orange juice, which is labelled 'Not a kebab'. A second arrow points at the kebab shop woman, who's labelled 'Aussie chick'. Neil has added 'Paparazzi Fail'.

By the end of the day a screenshot is doing the rounds on the internet. It's Blair and a UPF member exchanging texts just before the photo leak. Turns out the man who leaked the photos of Blair is a UPF member himself.

Blair: 'I'm going to caution you against what you're about to do.'

UPF member: 'Sorry, I'm being an actual Australian and eradicating poor behavior from so called leaders.'

Blair: 'There will be consequences.'

UPF member: 'Probably.'

Blair: 'No I am telling you there will be. Call it a hunch.'

UPF member: 'If that's a threat I'll take you down too.'

Lakemba, simple and plain

I never did follow up on Ralph Cerminara's dramatic claim. But I'm in this part of town, so I might as well do it now.

'You do not go into Lakemba, simple and plain,' Ralph told me in his flat. 'I'd love to see you – as a Jewish person – walk down

Haldon Street with a Jewish hat. You would be fucking bashed.'

Okay, so now I'm pulling up in Lakemba wearing a yarmulke, the Jewish skullcap. I'm also wearing my tzitzit – they're those strings that dangle out the bottom of your shirt. I've gone the full *Fiddler on the Roof*.

Walking from the car. I'm also carrying a copy of *Australian Jewish News*.

Lord, it's hot.

Walking past these kids near the train line. I brace for them to say something, but they just continue bouncing their tennis ball.

I'm now up on the main street, Haldon Street, passing by the shops. People are everywhere – Africans and Arabs – in thawbs and hats as well. They're not attacking me, Ralph.

People aren't even looking. Everyone seems to be just minding their own business, Ralph. A bus speeds by.

'Hi, how are you?'

'Good. How are you?'

Ralph, I just had my first verbal exchange. A man on a box outside a grocery shop. You know that I would love, for the sake of this book, to be mildly beaten up but it's just not happening. I walk on.

I'm fanning myself in the scorching heat with my *Australian Jewish News*.

Over to my left is the Lakemba Uniting Church. So if the Muslims can put up with them maybe they can put up with me. Oh! There's a Greek Orthodox church as well.

There's no one noticing me. Not one person. Here comes a woman in a full niqab. I'm not being noticed.

I'm feeling the sweat soak through my socks and the sweat run down my back. I've stepped in bubble gum. That's how much drama hasn't happened: I'm making a note that I've stepped in bubble gum. Ralph, the readers thank you for this thrilling addition to the book. This swashbuckling adventure.

'Just that, thank you.'

'Sixty cents, please.'

Bought a Chupa Chups, Ralph. From a Muslim. Ralph, you are an idiot. Care factor about the man in the Jewish hat wandering around Lakemba: zero.

Car's pulling up near me. Hopefully, if I'm lucky, some guys will jump out and beat me up.

No.

Okay, I'm now walking past a dumped mattress on the side of the street. That's the most dynamic thing that's happening, Ralph.

There's a sheikh-looking guy! He's rolling towards me in an electric wheelchair. Maybe the sheikh will run me down.

Nope.

My god! I'm back in the car. Turn on the air conditioner. Jesus!

My nose is sunburnt. Thanks, Ralph.

I cool down and head off to lunch, with my Warsaw Ghetto Uprising book in tow. It's an electrifying story, but depressing. Why didn't more Jews fight back against the Nazis? I think about what I would have done, as kebab juice drips onto the pages.

I'm in this part of town because Lakemba Mosque invited me to its open day. The email promised 'Q&A with religious elders to break down misconceptions about Islam', as well as a jumping castle and face-painting. I in turn invited the Half-Jewess; she certainly had questions she wanted answered when we were discussing inflammatory passages in the Qur'an. And – good Lord! – she's brought along a friend, a UPF leader called Farma John. So named because he's a farmer.

Fifty or so people are fanned out on the carpet in front of an imam. Labor leader Bill Shorten is looking down ruefully at his socks. They're red-and-white striped and I've got the impression he would have gone with a low-key black had he remembered you have to remove your shoes when entering a mosque.

Farma John stands up. He looks to be about thirty. A plastic tag, like you'd find on a suitcase, is threaded through the band of his akubra hat. Printed on the tag is a map of Australia and 'Fuck off we're full'.

'My name is Farma John,' he begins.

Why does he put his job in his name? Is Bob the Builder here too, waiting to ask if it's haram to build on Ramadan?

'People have always heard, myself and others are known as infidels. Why do you guys segregate us as separate? If I called an Aboriginal a coon, that would be offensive to a black person. If you call me an infidel I find that quite offensive. It would be like me turning to Mr Safran and saying, You're a tight-arse Jew.'

Hey, don't drag me into this! I'm skittish about being seen with a UPF member. I don't want to be dragged before Mel the matriarch again.

'Thank you for your question,' says the imam. He explains that 'the Qur'an refers to Christians and Jews as "People of the Book". Very respectful and very reverent. It teaches us to respect one another.'

Before I can work out if that answers the question or dodges it,

Farma John has a follow-up question: 'Have you ever tried bacon?'

'No,' smiles the imam. 'I'm actually guilty as charged. I haven't had bacon. Never in my life. I've smelt it a lot.'

I pull out the loose-leaf sheets of paper with the Qur'an quotes that so upset the Half-Jewess. I noodge her to ask the imam about them, but she's gone all shy.

'What are your thoughts about the drought at the moment?' Farma John continues.

'That's a very interesting question,' the imam says. He explains there's a specific prayer to ask Allah to alleviate a drought. The Prophet encouraged not only men, women and children, but also livestock to go into an empty field for this prayer. 'Can we come visit your farm?' asks the imam. Farma John says yes. 'We would love that,' says the imam.

A young man in a yellow T-shirt, Mohammed, approaches Farma John after the Q&A session. 'You have no religion?'

'I worship,' Farma John says. 'I worship a woman's beautiful body. That's honest to god.'

'You can't just let him get away with that!' I squeak at Mohammed, thrilled that a Muslim appears to be about to try to convert a member of the UPF. 'He clearly needs God.'

'He's worshipping his vice,' Mohammed tells me. 'His situation is mentioned in the Qur'an.'

Mohammed turns back to Farma John. 'God talks about people like you. Desires will lead to your destruction in the end. Are you chasing girls?'

'I don't chase,' Farma John says smugly. 'Trust me.'

Mohammed tells Farma John he was once like him. 'It killed my heart, chasing women. It will lead to mental problems.'

'I like fine things,' Farma John says. 'I like a fine luxury vehicle. I like a beautiful woman.' Not sure why he's suddenly talking like a 1960s car ad.

'The Qur'an says you're allowed to have sex but you need to ask for her father's permission and marry her.'

'That's fair enough,' agrees Farma John.

'Do not go behind the door or jump in the window,' instructs Mohammed. 'You go to the door and say, Listen I want to marry your daughter.'

'I did that already!' Farma John bemoans. 'I was engaged for five years. I asked her father. Did everything right. Then she screwed me over.'

Mohammed passes him a Qur'an. 'There's a lot you don't understand about Islam. Once you read that, it explains everything.'

Farma John leans against the wall of the mosque and begins to read his Qur'an. I tell Mohammed that the Half-Jewess has more questions. Prayer time is starting, so Mohammed ushers us out of the mosque to the building's underground carpark. We sit around a plastic table next to a couple of wheelie bins. Another Muslim has joined us, a man from Bangladesh.

Mohammed runs his finger along the Half-Jewess's scriptural quotes: '"In truth, the disbelievers are an open enemy to you . . . Take not the Jews and Christians as friends."

'It doesn't mean we're enemies,' Mohammed explains. 'But it means we're not best friends, because I'd be lying to you. How can we be best friends if I have to pray five times a day and you're sitting there watching me? How does that make us best friends?

You're going to say, Get out of here, man, I want to go to the pub. It doesn't work. Do you get it?'

The Half-Jewess nods her head.

'It doesn't mean you're racist. It doesn't mean I'm racist,' Mohammed says. 'It just means reality. I love Big Macs, you love cheeseburgers.'

'I love big tits,' Farma John adds for some reason. Everyone pretends they didn't hear him.

'Next question, please.' Mohammed slaps his palms on the table.

The Half-Jewess still won't speak.

'I wanted to know,' I say, pointing at the relevant verse, 'about the stones and trees that will say, "there is a Jew behind me; come kill him".'

'Zionists,' Mohammed clarifies. He says Zionists are the ones who'll be dobbed in by the talking trees because 'They are the ones who design all the problems in the world.'

The Half-Jewess softly groans.

I tell him that while Zionists are responsible for some things, seeing there are only fourteen million Jews on this planet I don't buy that they're responsible for 'all the problems in the world'.

Mohammed leans in and asks rhetorically, 'You reckon bin Laden dropped two buildings down?'

'It's the Israelis who did 9/11?'

The Bangladeshi man interrupts and looks sternly at Mohammed. 'Brother, don't talk all this.'

'It's a hundred per cent sure,' Mohammed goes on. 'You know the Rothschilds, in Britain, and the monarch? It's all pushed by the Zionists. And America is linked. All the senators in America are all . . . They're linked to the Illuminatis and —'

'At the end of the day,' the Bangladeshi man interrupts again, 'definitely I want to be your friend. You want to be my friend?'

'Yes,' I say, 'absolutely.'

He tells me to come back to the mosque whenever I like. The Half-Jewess offers an annoyed fake smile and heads off to her car.

Walking through the front garden of the mosque I notice that a section of the jumping castle is droopy. The attendant tells me it has a puncture.

I picture a scene in my head: Mohammed wandering by and blaming the Jews for bringing down the jumping castle. I tee-hee-hee and walk out the front gate.

Farma John invites me for a drink, so I hop into his car, which I notice isn't 'a fine luxury vehicle' but rather a shitbox. 'You were in the army?' I ask as we turn onto the main road.

'I joined and then I pulled out. I said, I'm not going to war for something I don't believe in.' The war he's talking about is the invasion of Afghanistan after 9/11. He had an Afghan friend who showed him pictures of his homeland. Farma John says he asked himself, 'Why are we going to war? These people aren't asking to be attacked. Only some radical stupid people went and blew up a building.'

So when it came to attacking Muslims in the most violent way, the UPF leader declined. He's from a military family, and relatives disowned him for his decision.

'They just said, "Mate, you let us down. Your grandfather would be turning in his grave."'

'You pulled out of the army, and now joining the UPF is making up for it in some way?'

135

'No, that's a misconception.' Joining the UPF, he says, can be traced to a 2009 bushfire, when he was a volunteer with the Country Fire Authority. 'I do this because after Black Saturday . . . Yeah, I went through that and I won't really go into details, but people died and I couldn't help them.'

The CFA wouldn't let him back on a fire truck because he was suffering post-traumatic stress disorder. (A humiliation, because his father was a well-regarded CFA captain. 'When he died, there was 400-plus people at his funeral.') So Farma John sought out another 'volunteer community group'.

He says the UPF is like Lions Clubs or Rotary. 'We go to small towns and you feel that people go, *Wow*. You give them hope, a sense of pride in community, getting people together as one.'

Is that really what's rolling through his head when they march through Bendigo? While others see Nazis goosestepping into town?

'Yep, we sing "Aussie, Aussie, Aussie" – yeah, it's a bit bogany. It's not just about that. It's saying we need to work together to bring back what we had. We're losing ourselves, we're losing our way as a nation.'

Farma John is a third-generation cattle farmer but sold all the cattle when his dad died. 'You want to know how Islam affects an Aussie farmer?' He turns left into a roundabout. 'When you've got people that come to this country not knowing any better – dodgy people take advantage of them, pay them less than an Australian worker.' This drives down wages, he says. 'I really feel that that's something we need to educate people on. Educating the refugees when they come here to not settle for less, work together in unity with the Australian people and say, We deserve better. We shouldn't work as slaves.'

He was a conscientious objector to the war in Afghanistan and he thinks refugees are exploited. I tell him he sounds like he should be on the other side of the police line at the rallies, with the left-wing folks. What's his problem with Muslims anyway?

'At the shopping centre they scowl at you. They talk in Arabic and they grease you off. And they have a go at you or your partner or your children because of what they're wearing. It's a bit frustrating, because you don't feel welcome. They call you . . . You hear the term "infidel" a lot.'

We sink into armchairs at a bar attached to a theatre. He tells me Reclaim Australia have something big up their sleeve, they are organising a nationwide day of rallies. He's concerned about the Melbourne one because the UPF have wrested control of it from the other groups involved in Reclaim Australia. But he's a member of UPF. Why's he worried?

He says motorcycle clubs and other outlier groups are attaching themselves to the UPF. 'There's people holding stockpiles of weapons in Australia that are ready to rise up against the Muslims. I have people coming up to me saying, "Can you get me guns?"'

I want to know more, but that's all he'll say on the matter.

But not all these outlier groups are fans of the UPF. To promote the last rally, the UPF dressed up as Muslims and beheaded a dummy in front of a Bendigo council building. Farma John says a local motorcycle club was furious.

'I had a death threat. They actually wanted to shoot us. They felt very disrespected that the UPF had come into their town without asking their permission.' Farma John had a connection to the leader of the club. 'The only reason the UPF boys have not got a bullet in the back is from me and another mate saying, "I'm sorry you felt disrespected. It was not meant like that."'

He says the UPF is also stepping on toes in Sydney, with its talk of a pilgrimage to commemorate the tenth anniversary of the Cronulla riots. A lot has changed over the decade. Now, according to Farma John, 'Lebanese' and 'Aussie' crime gangs are in alliances. They don't want these morons from Melbourne making waves. 'When someone rings you up and says, "You're dabbling your foot in the pool of death," well . . .'

Farma John sips on his red wine. 'I'm tired of this, man. It's not going to end well. It can only end in bad things happening. I don't want bad things happening, John.'

PARIS

UPF

'Just waking up to the bad news,' Neil reports from his doorstep. 'France is in lockdown. There are multiple shootings, bombings, and even a hostage situation happening simultaneously.'

Terrorists have killed scores of people at a rock concert. The next day, Blair is holding a bouquet of roses – red, white and blue.

'We're here at the French consulate in Melbourne,' he announces. Neil and a few others stand beside him. 'We're here for France, because we are France. We all come from Europe in one way or another, which makes Europe our mother, and when you hurt our mother, you hurt us too. We all feel it, because we are all linked in spirit. We are Europe. The son of France, the son of Europa.'

They lay the flowers and drive off in a ute, an Australian flag and a French flag propped up in the flatbed and blowing in the wind.

The French consulate posts a photo of Blair and his mates offering the flowers. An hour later, the photo has disappeared.

Charlie Hebdo, published weekly, can quickly respond. The cover of the new edition shows a man drinking champagne and the champagne spraying out of bullet holes in his body. 'They have weapons,' the caption reads. 'Fuck them. We have champagne.'

Seems defiant and cheeky and good-natured to me. But another narrative is developing. A local dude on my Twitter feed thinks the cover is sinister. The *Charlie Hebdo* guys are covering up the fact that the French do respond with weapons. The French are part of the coalition dropping bombs in the Middle East, after all.

This dude wants something else known: the shooters were reacting to a bigger picture of empire and colonisation. It strikes me he's done a lot of heavy lifting to make cartoonists, not the murderers, the villains in all this.

Hamza

'Since I last saw you quite a bit has happened, to say the least,' Hamza tells me as we stroll up his street in Doncaster, the shopping centre on the skyline.

He thinks the terrorists struck Paris to try to draw France into fighting Islamic State. 'ISIS wants to clearly put people in two camps: the camps of the Muslims and the non-Muslims.' Hamza says terrorist attacks 'force all the Muslims sitting on the fence to take sides'.

He's evasive about what he thinks about all those dead people (a hundred and thirty in total). And I'm evasive about asking him. This is a strange relationship.

Hamza points towards a park. 'This is actually where I grew up. There were two trees at the end that we would use as football goals,' he says, remembering his pre-Muslim life.

'Will there be more stuff like what happened in Paris, do you reckon?'

'I don't know the future,' Hamza says. 'Let's just say this: John, have you known the Islamic State to lie?'

'No.' (I guess I haven't.)

'When the Islamic State says, "Expect more," you're going to have to take their word.'

I tell Hamza what Farma John told me. That Reclaim Australia is planning a nationwide day of rallies, and that he's worried about the UPF getting out of hand at the Melbourne one.

'Well, it'll be interesting to see with the . . . the UF? The UFP?'

'UPF.'

'UPF,' Hamza says. 'I think that shows how little I care about them. By the end of your book, they're just going to be a little disparate group of ninnies who probably can't even get their shit together. The Islamic State remains and expands.'

'It *will* be interesting what happens at the next Melbourne rally,' I tell Hamza. 'I'm predicting not big numbers.' I don't know why I'm predicting that.

'Paris,' Hamza says happily. 'People don't mess with us anymore because they're literally afraid they're going to get their heads chopped off. We're not the oppressed Muslims anymore. We're not,

"Oh, that poor little guy." Things are changing.'

Back home I message a couple of friends. 'This is a faux pas I think we can all relate to. I was at ISIS supporter Hamza's house today and I forgot I'd changed my iPhone screen saver to the cover of the *Charlie Hebdo* Paris massacre edition and he saw it.'

'That is such a niche faux pas,' my friend types back. 'Lol!'

This isn't the first time the Paris theatre, where the main massacre took place, has been targeted. In 2011, police captured Muslims planning an attack on it. The Muslims said they'd chosen the theatre because the owners were Jewish. The fear that Jewish-connected events are being targeted ripples across the world. SECURITY RISKS PROMPT CANCELLATION OF MELBOURNE JEWISH EVENT, announces the local Jewish newspaper. A religious Jewish organisation, Chabad, pulls the plug on its annual Chanukah in the Park (which had been scheduled for three weeks from now), where thousands turn up for kosher fairy floss, ferris wheels and fireworks.

Avi from IDF Training texts me. He reckons Chabad are gutless wonders. The show should go on, he says, with Krav Maga-trained Jews spread over the park. I'm three-quarters of the way through my Warsaw Ghetto Uprising book, and the world and the book are blending together. I keep looking at Jews in my neighbourhood and wondering what they would have done in the Warsaw Ghetto. Pretty sure Avi would have organised a posse to scalp some Nazis.

'My Aryan'

That night I fall down another internet rabbithole. Laptop on belly in bed, I can't stop watching these UPF videos. The UPF is expanding, opening a West Australian branch. A new leader, Dennis, has emerged as its man in Perth. In his debut Facebook video for the group, he's cuddling his two daughters in a park. They run off ahead. 'See you at the pool, Dad!' yells one.

Like an infomercial host, Dennis turns to the camera. 'Those are my girls. Aren't they beautiful?' He takes a moment to reflect. 'I love their whiteness.'

Huh! The UPF haven't quite gone here before. Publicly, that is.

'Their blond hair. One of them's got green eyes. I love that about them! I love their racial features.'

It must be said that his daughters' hair is so dark blond it's arguable whether it can be called blond. I don't care, but he's making a big hoo-ha about it, so I feel compelled to pass that on.

'When I talk like that, does it trouble you?' he continues. 'If an Aboriginal dad looked at his daughters and said, "I love you, my indigenous princess," there'd be honour in that. The left would get behind it. If a Chinese father said, "I love you, my oriental princess. . ."'

I wince so hard I nearly fall off my bed.

'. . . again, that would be promoted and celebrated. But if I feel that way about my kids, that apparently makes me a neo-Nazi, or a white supremacist. I don't want supremacy, I just want equality.'

The video cuts to his daughters. A caption fades up beneath them: 'My Aryan'. (Don't know why he's chosen the singular.)

All this white pride is reminding me of something else. I pull up an *Age* article from earlier in the week. The headline reads WHITE FLIGHT: RACE SEGREGATION IN MELBOURNE STATE SCHOOLS. 'In the Greens-voting socially liberal enclaves of the inner north,' the article begins, white middle-class families are deserting schools populated by large numbers of Somali and Muslim students.

I recall a podcast featuring American white nationalist Jared Taylor. He claims that for every important decision in their lives – where to live, whom to marry, where to send their children to school – 'liberals are no different from members of the Ku Klux Klan'.

And, if you believe the *Age* article, in the only federal electorate held by the Greens, families are making their schooling decisions as if they're in the UPF.

LEFT-WING PINKOES AND RIGHT-WING DEATH BEASTS

It was never meant to be anything bad

Farma John is not the only one worried about the Melbourne rally. I've been invited to a secret rendezvous: Mel, the No Room for Racism matriarch, will be meeting her counterpart from the other side of the police line, Barbara, a founder of Reclaim Australia.

Mel's foot soldier, Jay, told me my name somehow came up when negotiations for the meeting were being bashed out. Barbara wanted me there. I don't understand why, anymore than you. I'm not withholding any information. Maybe she saw me at a rally? I've never met her.

So I walk down a stairwell in the city to a bar and slide into a booth. Mel, Jay and Barbara are sipping mojitos.

Barbara explains that Reclaim Australia has gotten out of hand. That when it began it was meant 'to provide a space where people could air their concerns' about all sorts of issues, like ice in the community, and public housing waiting lists. 'It was never meant to be anything bad,' she claims.

Mel looks sceptical. She's previously told me she 'grew up bogan', so doesn't buy that class backs you into a corner where you have no choice but to lash out at Muslims.

Barbara says that after the Lindt Café siege some people in the group started talking about Islam. That's when the blokes from the UPF latched onto Reclaim Australia. She says she tried to keep them out but, as she found out later, a certain Reclaim attendee was a mole. That attendee was Pastor Daniel.

'We would have meetings and nut things out, organisational-wise, and he would send that straight over to the UPF.'

Barbara says the UPF are becoming more reckless each rally. According to her, it is now cosying up with a motorcycle club called 19CC. The CC stands for Citizen Crusaders, referencing the Crusaders who fought the Muslims in the Middle Ages.

'If we were to propose to you,' Mel says, 'that we could do something on that day that was positive, rather than an anti-Muslim rally and then us doing a counter-rally and everyone fighting and hating each other – that instead we found points of agreement and rallied together, would you be interested?'

'I would,' says Barbara.

The 'points of agreement' would be things like addressing the ice scourge and the public housing crisis.

'You could do media in the lead-up to it, saying, "I'm the founder of Reclaim Australia but I object to the racism of it. I reject that they're focusing all their attention on Muslims. That's not what we're supposed to be about. I'm leaving Reclaim in order to say that this is the way forward."'

'Mm-hmm,' Barbara says and sips her mojito.

A Clockwork Orange

The UPF pulls up to the Melbourne Anarchist Club. (They're the ones who were furious because I slammed down tequila shots with the UPF.) And Blair and co just walk on in and start clomping around. The one anarchist inside yelps, 'What? Get out of here!' Blair and co flick through Marxist books on the shelves and the anarchist runs out the front door. (The UPF filmed all this and uploaded it to their page.)

Then they're hitting the nearby community radio station. They scramble through the corridors, fearless. They hate the anarchist show – I think they think the host will be there, but he isn't and they roll on out.

The UPF have invested so much time, with their family days and gazebo, trying to prove they're not thugs. Why have they done this?

Shermon wasn't at the Anarchist Club that day. And today he's freaking out on his bedroom webcam, his sweaty face leaning in. 'So an Islamic psychopath by the name of [redacted] wants to murder Blair Cottrell. According to his Facebook, he reckons he's going to find Blair and then he's going to come after all the other "patriot dogs".'

No one knows yet what violence lies ahead. The cat is out of the bag about Blair's past, though. The anarchists have dug up an educational video, shot in a prison in 2013, and are passing it around. The face is blurred and the prisoner is identified as 'Bruce', but there's no doubt who it really is. I learn that Blair, then twenty-two, has convictions for trafficking testosterone and for violent assaults, including torching the garage of his ex-girlfriend's new boyfriend.

'I had this little tomahawk,' Blair says, 'that I put inside my jacket, and in the middle of the night, at one and two o'clock in the morning, I would go out the front of his house and hover around. As soon as the door would open, my heart would skip and I would stand up and be holding a knife because I'd be ready to kill him.'

I feel around in my pocket, realising that I now carry a blade too.

Rapper's delight

Two weeks before the rally, the 19CC Motorcycle Club pulls up next to the park in Bendigo. The patch sewn on their jackets features a red crucifix and the words 'No FGM', as in 'No female genital mutilation'. UPF folks are milling around a barbeque. This is supposed to be a private function for 'patriots', but Farma John has let me tag along. I brought a beer, thinking it would help me fit in, but most of the 'patriots' are either not drinking or drinking bottles of water.

Blair and two blokes are chatting under a canopy. I wish I could hear what they're saying.

Blair's striding over!

'You are everywhere, aren't you?' he tells me. This guy who I've watched for months on the internet. It's disorienting. Like if Donald Trump came up to me at the tram stop and started chatting.

'It's weird,' I tell Blair. 'When you watch all the Facebook videos you think you've got some sort of relationship, that's not actually there.'

'I was talking to Neil last night,' Blair says of Neil Erikson. 'And he had this idea. He said we should do a podcast but we should get Safran to host it. Would you do that?'

I evade answering by pitching a TV idea that's been stewing in my head. A book club with members of the UPF and members of the radical Muslim group Hizb-ut-Tahrir. 'But instead of sitting around and discussing *Twilight* or *Hunger Games* you could sit around discussing the Qur'an.'

'I actually don't know a lot about the Qur'an,' Blair pushes back. He says his podcast idea is stronger than my book club idea.

I can't believe that John the Jew is finally meeting Blair the Hitler enthusiast and our conflict is over 'creative differences'.

'It's not something people would expect of us – "the Nazis" and a Jewish character hosting,' Blair says. 'They'd be all like, What's going on? But we try to keep things unpredictable.'

When he says 'the Nazis', Blair uses finger quotes. Online, he has mastered his weasel-speak. The Nazis, he argues, are, factually speaking, confined to a time and place – World War II Europe. It's no longer 1935–45 and Blair lives in the outer-Melbourne suburb of Frankston. So he can continue to admire Hitler and propagate his theories, but he's no Nazi.

I ask him about the last Bendigo rally and the huge crowd. 'Do you reckon it's just going to reach a peak?' I say of the movement.

'It will die off just as fast as it started,' Blair says, happy to be frank. 'The idea is to see it through and try to do your best to transcend everybody else and remain the only group.'

Blair says the UPF might have to move on from Islam. 'In my opinion the anti-Islamists will become more mainstream gradually. You'll get the popular official parties capitalising on it and it will quickly become boring.'

If the UPF are moving on from Islam, it begs the question: 'remain the only group' for what?

'I think it's important to always plant the seed of something a little bit more controversial,' Blair explains. He points to the recent video from the UPF's man in Perth. 'At the end he says "my Aryan",' Blair laughs. 'Can you believe he said that? I saw that in the video and I was like, What is this guy doing? But I thought, Fuck it, we'll leave it and see what people will think in an hour or so. The views kept going up, not really any negative feedback.'

'What is the master plan?' I ask. 'Like the big endgame?'

'Just power and influence. I mean, that is the only reason anyone does anything in politics. It's easy to become infatuated with the issue of the moment, but you just have to keep your focus on the fact that you're trying to get influence over the majority of your own people, national influence, and that is essentially power.'

His 'own people', he says, are first and foremost white Australians.

'Fewer policies you have, the more value you get. The more policies you give out, the more reason you're giving for people to disagree with you.'

He says he looks to Judaism and Islam for this blueprint because they all have a single and uncompromising philosophy. 'In Judaism you've got the chosen people and the gentiles. Islam – the Muslims and the infidels. No compromise. For symbolism, simple as all hell, everything is simple and just repeated, and then bang, suddenly this powerful force.'

Blair started his political journey on the other side of the aisle.

'When you're seventeen years old you pretty much just hate everything. I remember I saw a Marxist poster – the idea is to challenge the system, and I'm thinking, Yeah, that's what I want to do. I would go into weird bookshops and buy Occupy-type books, like occupy this street and that street. Eventually I kind of just started reading the opposite-type stuff and nationalistic-type authors and learned a different idea of history. Then I kind of realised, Okay, equality is bullshit, and it all went from there.'

One reason 'equality is bullshit', according to Blair, is because 'the physical differences in people are important'.

I try to understand what 'nationalism' means to him. For him 'nationality', 'whiteness' and 'culture' are all mixed together.

'Culture is actually an expression of the inner being of a specific people. If you lose your specific identity – your nationality – then gradually the surrounding culture morphs and changes and actually regresses as well.'

I glance around the park. The guy flipping the sausages has a slight slant to his eyes.

'What happens if it's too late and you've become mixed already?'

'We are not who we were,' he admits. 'And we are never going to be that again. We've lost it. There is a natural regeneration process that will take place, I believe, if we just bring ourselves together and remember who we were. We've got a lot of good stuff remaining.'

Blair asks me if I've read *The Protocols of the Elders of Zion*. I tell him I haven't. 'I don't know if it's real or not,' he says of this so-called transcript of a secret meeting of the Jews (according to conspiracy theorists). He says he likes one of the concepts within. That there are 'highborn' Jews with better genes and 'lowborn' Jews with worse genes, and the highborn must lead and rule the lowborn. He looks around at this bogan- and bikie-filled park. 'Similar situation here.' He explains he's the highborn who must lead these lowborns.

'I always enjoy talking to Jews,' he says. 'They are always more appetising than regular people.' He tells me to have another think about his podcast idea.

Farma John is showing around a photo of a car belonging to a 'patriot' that's been destroyed by fire. Farma John says a socialist or anarchist is responsible, but doesn't offer up any proof.

'We're moving it to Melton?' Farma John whispers to a bloke. The bloke nods. 'Good, done,' Farma John goes on. 'We're not going to tell the lefties until the last minute.'

Farma John sees that I've overheard. He says they're changing the location of the upcoming rally from the Melbourne CBD to Melton, a suburb an hour's drive from the CBD. The reasoning? Their rallies outside of Melbourne always run smoother because fewer socialists and anarchists turn up to counter-protest. He says this is because 'lefties are dong-beaters who can't afford a car or a licence and they ride pushbikes and they can't travel far from Melbourne'.

Farma John locks his eyes on mine. 'Don't you tell your leftie mates.'

lair, would you say my book is better
worse than *Mein Kampf?* (UPF leader
lair Cottrell)

UPF supporter (right). Such a fine line between looking like a menacing fascist and looking like you're just back from the Royal Melbourne Show where you bought the *Ghoulies* show bag. On that theme: no, he didn't bring along a kewpie doll from the show, that's UPF leader Shermon Burgess (left).

or those wanting to know what Ralph Cerminara
oks like . . .

Trust me, it would have come up in the book if Pastor Daniel Nalliah (left) was a dwarf. That's the kind of detail I would have loved. He's just kneeling. (Catch The Fire Ministries)

Non-Jews, the first time a Jew tells you about 'blowing the shofar', feel free to do a gag about 'blowing the chauffeur', but know it's well-trod territory. Here's the player at the Catch The Fire Ministries.

Labor leader Bill Shorten getting cold feet, partly because he's suddenly realised he's in a conversation with a UPF leader (Farma John) and partly because it's a mosque, so he had to remove his shoes.

TOP: Policing these rallies has cost taxpayers millions of dollars. But I'm sure you'd agree that's a small price to pay for shtick for my book.

ABOVE: UPF, stop being bad for the Bendigo brand. Take your race war to Wodonga or somewhere.

LEFT: You know you're wasted when a convicted neo-Nazi (Neil Erikson) carting a slab is looking at you like you've taken things a bit too far.

Cronulla Riots 10th Anniversary. LEFT: Lamest sequel ever. Organiser Nicholas Folkes (right) promised a race war but this was the only butchering that went down on the day. BELOW: You're going to think I'm telling you not to eat the pig because I'm a Jew, but I swear it's not cooked through.

Hey, I'm looking for the pro-Australians at this rally. Are you guys pro-Australian? (Melton, Victoria)

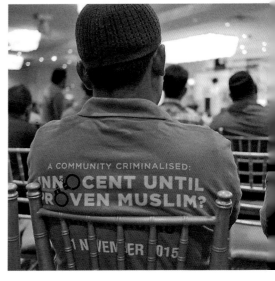

The whole day at the Hizb-ut-Tahrir conference in Sydney I couldn't get out of my head: 'I love Hizb-ut and I cannot lie, you other brothers can't deny.'

AUSTRALIA WELCOMES ALL RACES & RELIGIONS EXCEPT BARBARIC, EVIL ISLAM

bet this photo really annoys you. That's why I made it so big. I'm always negging my audience.

Jay the henchman from No Room for Racism. You may have spotted he's black but I didn't mention he's black in the book. That's because I don't notice race.

Boring! Hippies are not interesting. Nazis are interesting. Get out of my book, buddy.

Aish, the socialists won't be there for you when life gets serious. Return to Hinduism. Co-signed, your mother and Vishnu.

Are you trying to seduce me into anti-Islam, Mrs Robinson? (Debbie Robinson [centre] at the Australian Liberty Alliance launch in Perth.)

No lie, Geert Wilders; I was hanging with punters from a distance, and no one was talking about whether they liked you or didn't like you, they were just talking about your hair.

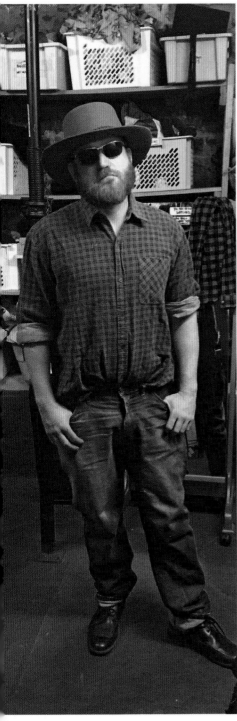

My Farmer John disguise.

Can someone smuggle this book to Musa Cerantonio in a cake or something?

The Jews have burqa'd the Christmas tree! Chanukah in the Park at the racetrack.

Avi goddam Yemini! Stop plugging your gym in my book. Out!

Interfaith relations between me and the JINO (Jew In Nose Only).

'Hey Johnny Boy.'

It's Neil on the phone. I've only been home from the park for a few hours.

'I've got Blair here.'

Blair has moved on from his podcast idea and has another project to pitch. 'You know that song "Fuck tha Police" by N.W.A?'

I tell him I'm familiar with the Niggaz Wit Attitudes hit.

'I was thinking we could make a Jewish version of it, yes? Instead of Ice Cube you could be Ice Berg. You can do this, man. This would be funny.'

I still prefer my book club idea.

Blair could be the N.W.A guy, he continues excitedly, who demands to hear the truth, the whole truth and nothing but the truth, but he'd change 'black ass' to 'Jewish ass'. 'Then you launch into it, "Fuck the Nazis," and we do a whole song. What do you think?'

'I'll have to think it over.'

'In other words, not a chance,' he says, disappointed. 'I thought it was funny.'

Maybe he and Musa should do a comedy show together. Musa with his prank phone calls, Blair 'Weird Al' Cottrell with his songs.

Later that night randoms start lighting up my phone. A sinking feeling hits my gut. Over at the UPF page, a doctored CD cover has been posted. There I am, photoshopped with Blair and Neil, the three of us wearing baseball caps. The CD is titled *J.W.A. Straight out of Elsternwick*. Beneath Neil Erikson is the name 'EZ-ERIK'; beneath Blair, 'DR. FASH'; beneath me, 'ICE-BERG'.

'Me and Blair were just on the phone to the one and only John Safran,' Neil announces. 'We need all our supporters out there to inbox John Safran's Facebook page and tell him to join our group. This is going to be bigger than One Direction.'

I head to bed, but not before watching another video. A man sporting a T-shirt and a cap, both bearing the Australian flag, stands before an Australian flag. 'G'day, my fellow Australians, my name is Shermon Burgess, AKA the Great Aussie Patriot . . .'

Except it's not Shermon Burgess, it's someone taking the piss. And it's not a left-winger taking the piss, but a fellow patriot, although not one I've come across before.

'. . . filming live from my mum's basement. You might know me from such hits as "Stalking Miss Daisy" and "I Bash Kittens and Puppies". There's a lot of so-called patriots out there hanging shit on me . . . Hang on, hang on, guys . . .'

The man leans out of frame and pulls on another cap, which features a larger Aussie flag.

'Teasing me and mocking me and I don't know why . . . Hang on, guys . . .'

He pulls on a cap with an even larger Aussie flag.

'It's not fair and I don't like it. I'm an Australian. I have feelings! I have feelings! . . . Hang on . . . hang on . . .'

He pulls on a final cap with the largest flag of all.

'I wish you'd all stop, and if you don't I'm telling my mum. I've already told her once and I'll tell her again.'

A few hours later the real Shermon Burgess is reporting from in front of a tree.

'Hello patriots,' he begins. 'I'm just letting you know that the Cronulla tenth-anniversary rally will be my last. Now, I don't mind putting up with death threats from Muslims. I don't mind the dogs in the left-wing media. But when your own fucking people start turning against you and having a laugh, after all the sacrifices you made for them, that's where I draw the fucking line. And I'm done. I'm fucking done.'

Shermon scratches the side of his Aussie flag cap.

As I start drifting off to sleep, a stranger buzzes on my bedside table. I reach in the dark and the bright phone screen stings my eyes.

'You Talmudic son of a bitch,' the stranger's Facebook message begins. The neo-Nazis love dropping the expression 'Talmudic', I've noticed. Although this isn't a neo-Nazi; the man tells me he's a Muslim. 'Zionist ho. You make a mockery of God. Don't forget it was He that made you jews a "super race". Y do you think you jews are so 'smart'. U imbecile. Did it come from circumcising each other? I've watched your stupid shows making fun of religion. The day will come when you Zionists will feel his wrath. It's soon. Rott in hell with ur master.'

It's two in the morning and this line of talk feels a bit chilling.

'Who's my master?' I type.

'Satan.'

Golden Dawn

That Muslim man isn't my only non-fan. A story I wrote over a year ago – well before the UPF or Reclaim formed – is about to come back and haunt me. So I'll give you a little outline.

I'd rocked up to a street in Brisbane. Fascists were rallying in support of the Greek fascist party, Golden Dawn. The left had organised a counter-rally. I wrote:

The police line is weak and the fascists and the left have met up at points. But only a subset of the left, the trade unionists. The hippies and others are standing well back. A dozen big men surround one skinny fascist in a leather jacket.

'Why's he shaking, mate?' an old grey-haired man from the CFMEU sarcastically asks a colleague.

'Because he's shit-scared,' a handsome young guy with a red beard replies.

'Is he?' singsongs Mr Sarcastic.

'He's petrified,' says Red Beard.

'You mean he's scared of us spilling some of his claret on this cement?' continues Mr Sarcastic. He turns to his army. 'None of youse would spill any of his claret on the cement now, would ya?'

'Nah!' scream the workers.

'Fucken oath!' announces one.

An Islander goes nose to nose with the petrified fascist. 'Welcome to the future,' snaps the Islander.

The fascist ducks between the men.

'Weak!' one man shouts after him.

'NAZI SCUM OFF OUR STREETS!' roar the rest.

Another fascist, a pasty guy with a ponytail and acne, is drifting through the crowd, waving a large Eureka flag. A workman stabs his finger in the air. 'Don't fucking use our union flag, you heap of shit,' he says. 'Forty-five nationalities at Eureka, you fucking clown. Docile fuck. Go read a bit of history, genius, hey?'

Four unionists pounce on the pasty kid. Next thing he stumbles out of the pack with his flagpole stripped. Soon I see a young trade unionist walk out from the crowds wearing it as a cape.

A young fascist leader in a shiny suit comes to try to calm things down.

'Love your op-shop fucking suit!' screams someone. The crowd of university anarchists and greenies and workers laugh at his cheap suit.

'Look at you – you little anorexic fuck,' spits the Eureka historian. 'You fucking dog, you're the hard man in the crew, are ya?'

Laughter rolls through the crowd again.

'You were the cunts that got picked on in school!'

After the rally, my story revealed, trade-unionists stormed a pub and bashed a mob of fascists. Five men were injured; three were taken to hospital, including a Greek Australian man in his late sixties. Seemed a fair enough story to me. After all, that's what had happened. But then . . .

Mrs Sneer and Mr Snort

There are more hot anarchists than I expected here. Don't get me wrong, there are also flabby radicals who wouldn't be able to throw a Molotov cocktail without breaking into a wheeze, but still. The Melbourne Anarchist Club, a converted shopfront along a busy road, has thrown open its doors, inviting the community to show solidarity with them. It's a response to the UPF recently rolling up to the club and thugging around.

'So I hear you're starting up a rap group?' a woman snaps as I walk in. It's the day after Neil announced his plans for J.W.A. She's leaning against a bookshelf, flags from different struggles draping from the wall. 'I was going to ring up and vote for you to be part of the boy band.'

'Ha-ha,' I say. She doesn't join in with my ha-ha.

'What's your role in all of this?' a young man asks. He's sitting in an armchair. 'Are you part of building an anti-racist movement or are you just about books and selling and career and profile?'

'I don't think it's good for my career and profile that I'm seen to be in a rap band with the UPF, you know?'

'It's quirky,' the woman sneers. 'It's, you know, whatever.'

I explain that to write stories, I hang out with all sorts of people from all sides.

'They are arseholes!' she says. 'They are using you and your profile to try and humanise themselves!'

'You think there's no use in a writer —'

'Making them just seem like funny Aussie blokes?'

'Maybe it's helpful for people to know that dangerous people have charisma,' I blurt. 'That dangerous people get crowds not because they're cartoon villains, but because they use their charisma to get people on board.' I'm happy to back myself on this matter.

'But what are people to do with that information?' she complains. 'We have to have a collective response to this. We need to build a movement!'

I find out that the young man in the armchair has been seething about me – or at least something I wrote – long before J.W.A were trying to sign up Ice Berg Safran. He was not a fan of my article about the Brisbane Golden Dawn rally. He reflects on my story with a snort. He felt it was a smart-arsed effort to equate far-right violence with left-wing violence, when the two couldn't be more different. He says far-right violence is a form of 'structural violence' (that is, part of State, corporate and systemic violence), and left-wing violence isn't. And furthermore, my 'comedic' story contributed to this 'structural violence' by equating the two.

So the men who bashed the elderly Greek guy after the rally didn't engage in anything problematic, but the comedian on the scene who wrote about it did. In fact the comedian was the violent one.

The Sufi held a similar view in regard to the *Charlie Hebdo* attack. The psychopaths – the ones who should really take a good hard look at themselves and their actions – were the dead guys holding the pencils.

It occurs to me that Shermon quit the UPF in response to a piss-take. So for all three points of the triangle – the far right, the far left and radical Islam – piss-taking is a threat that needs to be kept at bay. People might start listening to the jokes.

Another thing occurs to me: What's wrong with interrogating violence, even if it's 'non-structural'?

I tell them I'm just interested in different things to them. 'I like looking at tangles,' I say.

'Like what?' the woman demands.

I remember the 'Talmudic son of a bitch' message from last night. 'Like that sometimes Muslims, who suffer Islamophobia, are anti-Semitic.'

Snort. Sneer. Like the Sufi, she argues there are power dynamics in play. There's not meaningful anti-Semitism these days, she advises, in the way there's meaningful Islamophobia. I tell her about the recent bashing of a local Jew by two men screaming in Arabic, and that the Jewish community centre in my neighbourhood is getting a $1.3million 'blast-proofing' security wall after a terrorist plot to blow it up.

Just as Santa has his Naughty and Nice list, Mrs Sneer and Mr Snort have their Structural Violence and Non-Structural Violence list. Alas for the bashed Jew and the community centre employees, they've only made it to the Non-Structural Violence list. That's the side of the ledger where the violence isn't worth interrogating.

The woman pushes a pamphlet at me. It's advertising the counter-protest to the Reclaim rally. It calls for people to show up at the steps of Parliament House. 'Are you going to promote us?'

I, of course, know something she doesn't: that the UPF won't be at the steps. They'll be an hour's drive away in Melton.

'How do you know they're going to be there?' I dangle. (I might as well tell her.)

'Reclaim called a rally,' she hisses.

'Are you sure they're going to be there?'

She groans, 'So what part are you going to play?' and rolls her eyes.

'I'm in the UPF rap band,' I squeak. 'You'll see me up there scratching records behind Ez-Erik and Dr Fash!'

The woman huffs off.

'There are no casual observers,' the young man in the armchair tells me.

'Deep, man. Real deep,' I sulk.

I head to the little bar area. The anarchist selling the beers wears a T-shirt saying 'Hello Titties', with Hello Kitty's cat head redesigned to look like breasts.

This is Ahmet the Turk's first visit to the Melbourne Anarchist Club. The thirty-year-old caught the footage of the UPF stamping in here 'as if they were fucking Brownshirts walking into a fucking Jewish school in Germany'. Beefy and bald, he says he's new to politics but when he saw 'these people attacked for essentially defending Muslims? I thought, You know what? We've got to show some solidarity. We need to tell them, "You are not alone." Just like how they've told us that we're not alone.'

So he called the club and offered to pull a team of Turks together. 'If you guys ever feel scared or frightened,' he told them, 'I can come down – my gang – we can sleep in the car, make sure no one comes in your place.'

He says he's torn over whether to bring Team Turk to the upcoming rally, because 'violence brings more violence', in his experience. 'Do you think it's making things worse?' he asks me. He's aware that Muslims have steered clear of the rallies so far.

I tell him it's a bit rich for someone to argue: There are these socialists and anarchists defending the Muslims, and the UPF attacking the Muslims, but hang on, the Muslims themselves shouldn't turn up.

His Turk gang numbers seven. They're all gym junkies. 'The guys I am going to be bringing haven't got an iota of radicalism in them, right?' He says it's important his guys are level-headed because, with text messaging, seven Muslims can draw in a thousand Muslims pretty quickly. 'But am I just making things worse?' he asks again. 'It's something that I have been thinking about every single day.'

I tell him I don't think bringing seven Turks to the rally is escalating things, although I pass on what I know about Blair. 'I've got it from the horse's mouth. Drama's good for his cause. He'll probably be pretty happy if things get inflamed.'

Ahmet worries about violence begetting violence because of how he feels when his wife is taunted over her hijab.

'I am too afraid to go out with my wife on Saturday and Sunday, bro.' At the places he'd like to go there are 'young scumbags'. 'If someone was drunk and stupid, saying something to my wife, bro, I don't know what's going to happen. And I don't want to go to jail, you know what I'm saying?' He says he holidays in Malaysia to avoid confrontations with bogans over his wife's hijab. 'It's horrible, because I'm a deep-down bogan, and I have a Mitsubishi Challenger with its long-range fuel tank and I want to take my wife out camping with me, but I can't.'

Ahmet the Turk slumps in his armchair. 'And here I am complaining about all my issues to you! But you're a Jewish guy, and you know, for Jews it never gets old. I remember a bloke – I think it may have been Melbourne Cup weekend or some shit like that, where an out-of-town country football club, they had their own bus and they leaned out in St Kilda, I think it was, and grabbed the bloke's Jewish hat and punched him. And I read the bloke left town. He got up and left! Where did he go? And that's fucked up. You know, I'd love to meet that bloke. I'd love to say, You know what, I've got your back, man. You know what I mean?'

I can only conclude that Ahmet is not yet familiar with the intricacies of structural versus non-structural violence.

Six degrees

Bill Leak has drawn a cartoon in *The Australian* of a drunk Aboriginal man that many have found offensive. I'm spooling through an article about it on a left-wing site called New Matilda. The article says how a while ago a newspaper published a cartoon that Jews deemed offensive. And according to New Matilda, powerful interests created hell for that newspaper, because that's what happens when you upset the Jews, while you can get away with insulting Aboriginal people.

Ah! I've become familiar with this parlour game. This is a left-wing version of Six Degrees of Kevin Bacon. In that game, movie fans find a way to link any random actor to Kevin Bacon: Brittany Murphy starred with Bruce Willis in *Sin City*, who starred with Brad Pitt in *12 Monkeys*, who starred with Kevin Bacon in *Sleepers*!

In this left-wing version – Six Degrees of Those Who Don't Eat Bacon – writers try their hand at linking everything back to the Jews or Israel. I think about Ralph always banging on about left-wing bigots. Maybe he's onto something after all.

The octopus

Okay, I was unknotting my back at the gym this morning. Rolling on a foam roller. Telling the trainer about my weekend and how the UPF are shifting the rally to Melton. And I go, 'The UPF are keeping shtoom till the last minute in the hope the socialists and anarchists don't show. So there are consequences if I squeal. Because just say I set off, as a result of my squealing, left-versus-UPF violence that otherwise wouldn't have happened. But then again, the UPF are heading to Melton because there's some mosque being planned, so they could bully the Muslims, so I could —'

'Just tell the fucking anti-racists.'

I first think he's being moral, but it's not that. My trainer also does graphic design, so he has a creative bent. He thinks my duplicity will be better for the book, because it will change events. 'You've become the puppetmaster,' he tells me.

And I stop rolling on the foam roller. I'm like, My God, the conspiracy theorists were right! It's exactly what they say: beware of the Jews, they play both sides – the communists and the capitalists. I am the devious Jew. The octopus on the world globe, stretching its tentacles – one touching the United Patriots Front, one touching No Room for Racism.

(I can deadlift 150 kilograms, by the way, which is two couches.)

I phone Jay, the No Room for Racism henchman. I pass on what Farma John whispered at the UPF barbeque.

'It was loose lips. Loose lips from the horse's mouth,' I tell him.

'Thank you,' Jay says. 'That's gold.'

The Return of the Gold Dinar

An excited Hamza pokes a USB stick into the big flat-screen TV in his lounge room. He wants to show me a new ISIS video. It opens with a swish logo sequence, like you get before a Lionsgate or DreamWorks film.

'As the winds of time swept their way through Medina,' the American-accented voice begins, 'they carried a call that marked the rise of history's most profound legacy.'

A battle scene, slick enough for a Russell Crowe film, plays out between ye olden day Muslims and infidels. These fighters morph into modern-day Islamic State soldiers and American soldiers. A ye olden day Muslim fires an arrow. Midair the arrow transforms into an aeroplane and smashes into the World Trade Center. 'The seeds of corruption were sown by America and cultivated by the Jews, heading a capitalist financial system of enslavement, underpinned by a piece of paper called the Federal Reserve dollar note.'

Dollar notes fan around a map of the world. This reminds me of those Occupy Wall Street videos that were flying around a few years ago. Also those Ron Paul ones. Also Scientology recruitment films.

Why's Hamza showing me this?

ISIS leader Abu Bakr al-Baghdadi mounts a podium. Now two men are kneeling in the sand, swordsmen raising their weapons above them. Now a man is thrown from a building. Now a spike is about to be driven into a hand. Mercifully – for me – at the moment of impact for each torture or execution, the screen snaps to black, like in a *Mission Impossible* trailer. Golden letters crash onto the screen: 'Return of the Gold Dinar'.

The Islamic State has got its act so together it's striking its own currency, the gold dinar. This is why Hamza is so excited. It's another sign, he explains, that we're edging closer to the Messianic age.

I spoke too soon about merciful cuts to black. The swords swoosh down, lopping off the heads of the kneeling men.

'Who are the dead guys?' I ask Hamza. 'Are they Muslims or are they —'

'Yeah, they were Muslims that died,' he explains. 'I wrote a piece in uni on the jihad media from the early '90s up until the 2000s, and the way it evolved.' Hamza starts discussing *The Return of the Gold Dinar*, wearing his arts student hat. 'One thing that stands out about this video is the use of English.' Hamza also appreciates 'the use of mixed media' (news footage and fictionalised battle scenes) and 'the cutting'.

Yes, the cutting, Hamza.

This is odd: Hamza's sister's boyfriend has a couple of kids. Twenty minutes ago the kids were stretched out on the floor watching cartoons. The sister and the boyfriend were here too. And they all just drifted out. I didn't notice them leaving. In this little house in Doncaster everyone quietly accommodates Hamza's ISISness.

'It wasn't as popular with the kids as that cartoon,' I tell Hamza.

'Ah, probably not.'

The boyfriend strolls back in and heads to the fridge. 'Well, what did you think?' he asks.

'Yeah, you know, it's definitely interesting,' I weasel.

'Cheesy, though, huh?'

I snigger nervously. Is attacking ISIS production values one of those no-nos, like drawing a picture of Mohammed?

'Can you say it's cheesy?' I ask Hamza.

'It is!' the boyfriend insists. 'It's very cheesy – the narration and all that stuff.'

'You look like you need a coffee, John,' is all Hamza will say.

As he brews it I tell him about a woman I met at the UPF and 19CC barbeque. 'She says, "This is really good for me because I'm homeless at the moment. My partner was beating me. I'm on people's couches." And she tells me about ice killing her town. She says, "I come to this group, and I just feel like they've got answers for how to fix up the community." So I tell this other woman at the anarchist club about her. Thinking she'll find it interesting because it shows how people you think are your enemy, sometimes they've got painful stories and you can understand them. But she didn't give a shit! She just said, "Well, fuck her. Why's she so stupid?"'

'Once you get deep enough into ideology,' Hamza says, 'you can start to lose a little bit of humanity.'

Is now the time to bring up what I really thought of *The Return of the Gold Dinar*? But before I can open my mouth he adds, 'I have seen that with a lot of lefties.'

Spewing

Three days before the Melton rally and it's all over the telly: 'Police have uncovered the infamous *Anarchist Cookbook* – a manual on how to make explosives and illicit drugs – along with five tasers at the home of a member of the United Patriots Front. Police found other material on hard drives relating to the making of explosives. The man has been charged with possessing a prohibited weapon.'

A cop pushes down the guy's head, easing him into the back of the police car. He is snaggle-toothed and ruddy. I remember him! He was shuffling around the UPF and 19CC barbeque. Farma John told me to chat to him. And I didn't, because I'd already blahed to

Blair and my brain was overloaded. Spewing.

I hit 'mute' on the news. Bookshelves line a whole wall in my lounge room. I wander over and pull a book from the top shelf. *The Anarchist Cookbook*. Thirteen years ago, a friend had scribbled inside it: 'John, I'm inscribing this book so I know you can't return it. And my inscription is – BE CAREFUL! As the warning on the back cover explains "this book is not for children or morons". So don't act moronic and blow yourself up. Happy Birthday! – Jeremy Weinstein.'

MELTON

Sunday rally

Two skinheads standing in the middle of the road lock eyeballs. They are a mirror reflection of each other. The socialists and anarchists circled around them, however, seem to know something I don't. That one is a Nazi and the other is an anti-Nazi.

'Fuck off,' screams the first skinhead. 'I'm a skinhead, you're a fucking disgrace.'

'You never asked for my political opinion,' counters his reflection.

'Your name is Angus,' throws in one of the socialists. 'You're a fucking Nazi. We all know this.'

'White laces, mate,' snaps the first skinhead, glancing down at Angus's shoes.

Not sure what that means, but this is the point of distinction. The first skinhead has black laces.

Trembling, Angus tells a local journo poking her dictaphone at him that he's nineteen and from a country town three hours' drive from here.

'Tell 'em what the white laces are about!' demands the first skinhead.

'Um,' begins Angus, 'so what happens is . . . there's an association with —'

'White means fucking white pride, you prick!' snaps the first skinhead.

'Well, that's the assumption, mate. However, people —'

'Are you a SHARP?' the first skinhead interrupts, referring to Skinheads Against Racial Prejudice.

'SHARP?' Angus sounds like a nervous politician buying time. 'No. I believe in the traditional skinheads who are apolitical. You know, in 1969, how you had the —'

'I know all about 1969, cunt!'

Angus ducks through the mob, past the police line to the far-right mob on the other side. An anarchist manages to poke Angus in the bottom with a flagpole, though.

Melton's been bubbling for two hours now. The 'patriots' skidded in in their utes an hour before the advertised time. They planted their flags in the grass right in front of the city council building. This council has approved the building of a mosque. Over one hundred cops in riot gear then jogged into place, sealing the 'patriots' off from the world. I can only see the tips of their flagpoles from where I stand on tippy-toes, here on the left-wing side. A couple of hundred have rocked up for the left, a couple of hundred for the right.

There was expansive space for rallying in Melbourne and Bendigo. This is not the case today. The socialists and anarchists are pushed up close to the police, confined to the same strip of grass as them. They can wander back, but they wander onto a road. (That's where the White Shoelace versus Black Shoelace battle went down.) Across the road, locals have gathered in a park to watch the circus that has rolled into town. Melton folks have also bundled together a little further up the road, near the shops.

Some left-wingers have brought a banner, FUCK OFF NAZI SCUM, that features a struck-out swastika and a middle finger. For some reason, this giant banner – this giant middle finger – is propped up to face the Melton folks up the road.

In fact, with the 'patriots' out of sight and inaccessible, Melton locals have become the proxy UPF for some of the anarchists and socialists. A few gangly anarchists with bandanas pulled over their faces chant at a man in double denim: 'Go home, Nazi! Go home!'

'I live here,' he says.

Now Double Denim is grumbling to the police. He complains that cops have hassled him for wearing a motorcycle helmet in the street, yet are letting these masked anarchists roam free. 'Why can't I do it?' he mopes.

The anarchists continue to berate him: 'Go home, Nazi! Go home!'

I tell Double Denim the 'patriots' are here to protest council approval of a mosque. He says he doesn't mind if a mosque is built here.

I pull on my sunnies. Why didn't I bring sunscreen? Why didn't I bring water?

Three kids on BMXs look on from the park. One of these BMX bandits, an eleven-year-old, is particularly feisty.

'Fuck you!' he shouts towards the crowd of socialists and anarchists; then, inexplicably, 'Rice Bubbles!'

'Why are you against those guys?' I ask.

'Because this is our country,' the kid cries. 'And they want to take our country. Fuck them!'

'But who's trying to take over Australia?' I ask.

'Dunno.'

'This is our country,' screams a female twenty-something. 'Fuck off to your own!'

I don't understand. She's telling a street full of white Australians to fuck off back to their own country. Are the white lefties proxies for Muslims and refugees? Or maybe she means she wants this foreign race of hipsters to fuck off back to their own country of inner-city Melbourne.

'Look at that guy. He's got goggles,' the BMX kid says of one such hipster. 'There's no oceans in Melton!' he screams at the man.

I spot Ahmet and his Seven Turks standing under trees near the police line. The bandanas pulled over their faces are theatrical – a couple feature skull jaws, others feature hot-rod flames. Tight T-shirts with anarchist slogans show off their gym bodies. People want photos with them, like they're characters at Disneyland.

Ahmet's here to protect the socialists and anarchists from the 'patriots', but that menace is already sealed behind the police line. Furthermore, Blair hasn't shown. He's decided to fly to Perth for that city's Reclaim Australia rally. (Today, Reclaimers are also hitting Canberra, Brisbane, Cairns, Sydney, Newcastle, Adelaide, Hobart,

Mildura, Esperance and Alice Springs.) So the only menace at this moment is an old woman.

'Scuse me, young man! Why do we cover our face? Are we ashamed to be who we are?'

Ahmet and the Seven Turks stare ahead, like Buckingham Palace guards when the tourists pull faces. But Ahmet's eyes, poking above the skull jaw, reveal he's upset. Like the socialists at the first Reclaim rally who weren't prepared for men in turbans, Ahmet wasn't expecting to face off a woman.

Mel the No Room for Racism matriarch is scuttling about, looking tense. Because I'm something approximating a journalist I need to ask a question, for prudence, even though I know the answer. And I'm right: Barbara, the Reclaim Australia founder, didn't follow through. She didn't publicly renounce Reclaim and there'll be no joint rally today.

The Reclaim side is peopled mostly by young men. Unlike the UPF's Bendigo family day, only a few 'mums and dads' are trickling in with picnic baskets. My theory? The wide coverage of that UPF guy's arrest for possessing a weapon telegraphed that this rally is radical. It's killed off the numbers.

A grandmother, a mother and a son gripping Aussie flags – and each other – push through the crowd of socialists and anarchists. This is the only way for them to reach the Reclaim side.

'Was this scarier than you thought it was going to be?' I shout.

'Yeah,' quivers mum.

'What did you think this was going to be?'

'I don't know. Not this.'

A Samoan teenager is wearing a hat that reads 'Samoan'. It's like he's in one of those political cartoons where everything's labelled so there's no confusion. He lives nearby and was pedalling past on his bike. Now he's come to the rescue of the family with the flags. He is pushing the anarchists away. 'I've got a mum, bro,' the Samoan screams at them. 'If you did that to my mum . . .'

A dad and his family stride through next. A big inflatable hand with an Aussie flag print is squeezed over his real hand. Anarchists dressed like ninjas swarm around.

'How you going today?' squawks one.

'Fucking excellent,' the dad snaps back.

'Go home, Nazi! Go home!'

One of the ninjas leaps and kung-fu chops the Aussie-flag inflatable hand. The hand hits the street. Four ninjas stomp on the hand and it pops. The dad darts off.

'Little faster, mate!' snickers one of the ninjas.

'You guys stay here,' Ahmet tells his Seven Turks. 'Relax.' He weaves through the ninjas, squats and picks up the deflated inflatable hand. He folds it and elbows through the mob. 'Listen, please,' he says, passing over the deflated hand to the dad. 'This was not appropriate to be taken off you. This is our flag too, you know what I'm saying? I'm not here about burning flags.'

The dad thanks this burly man hidden behind a skull-jaw bandana.

'I'm a Muslim,' Ahmet reveals.

The dad and his family look surprised.

Ahmet has more to say. 'My people are innocent of these crimes that ISIS done, man,' he begins. 'You know, every week we have a Muslim woman getting attacked on the streets. A woman! At least attack our men, you know? We know everyone's emotional. Everyone's scared. I promise these ISIS people will kill us before they kill you guys.' Ahmet looks over the police line to the tips of the UPF flags. 'You know, this isn't the answer. This is what they want us to do.'

'We just don't want them in the country to begin with!' the dad says of terrorists.

'We don't too!' insists Ahmet.

'Then why don't you get rid of them?'

Ahmet explains that before he was married he 'couldn't get a girl to text me back. You reckon I can get rid of terrorists?' Everyone laughs.

'Then why do you need to cover your face then?' asks the woman.

Ahmet says white supremacist groups take photos, and after the rallies harass the people in those photos. That's why they need the masks.

'There's too many people out there being racists!' responds the dad. So he doesn't think he's one of them. 'You know, it's silly. Why? Why?'

'Listen, if you find yourself stuck in the thick of it, you come next to any of us.' Ahmet motions to his Seven Turks. 'We'll protect you.'

Jesus! What was that? An explosion?

I dart up the street. Someone's thrown a slab of Jack Daniel's cans and the IED is now dribbling bourbon onto the street. Three shirtless Meltonite teens are facing off some ninjas. One of the Meltonites holds a BMX over his head. Is he going to chuck it at the ninjas?

I ask him what he's protesting about.

'Don't want to come over here in our country and respect the way we live? I reckon they should respect it. They expect us to go over there and respect them and the way they live. We respect their turf over there. They can respect ours.'

I'm confused as to who he's talking about. 'The Muslims or the protesters?' I ask.

He motions down the street to the protesters. 'The Muslims.'

As I leave, he's still holding the BMX over his head.

The No Room for Racism MC is a human beatboxer, pounding his mouth to 'You're the Voice'. The crowd dances and chuckles. This week John Farnham told Reclaim Australia to stop pumping out his songs at its rallies. The beatboxer wraps up his Farnsey and tells the crowd to huddle together. It's time to march up the street in solidarity with Muslims and refugees.

The folks at the front prop up high the giant banner, FUCK OFF NAZI SCUM with the big middle finger. But before a step can be taken an anxious bald man runs in front of the march.

'What is wrong with you?' he screams. 'Mohammed, *Alayhi salaam*, he promoted peace even in the time of war!'

He's like the guy blocking the tanks at Tiananmen Square. Mel rushes over to find out what's what. He says he's a local, a Muslim.

'This sign is not right!' he cries. 'Islam does not promote hate!'

'Can I just explain?' Mel says. 'It was a couple of people who made that banner. They don't represent all of us.' She says that for some people this rally is 'really personal. It's about attacks – physical attacks – on Muslims,' so the sign reflects that anger. She tries to upsell him to socialism. 'For other people it's more of a general problem. Like, why are people being divided, when it's actually the rich who are screwing us all over, do you know what I mean?'

'I get discriminated every fucking day! I get pulled over!' the man cries. 'You know what my name is?'

'No,' Mel says.

'My name is Jihad.'

'Oh.'

'I'm the one that got harassed all my life. Do you know the meaning of jihad?' He turns from Mel to the crowd. 'Who knows the definition of jihad?'

'Religious struggle, man,' offers a socialist wearing reindeer antlers for some reason.

'No, no, no!' Jihad responds. 'There's gonna come a time in this world when holding onto your faith is like holding onto a hot piece of coal. How long can you hold onto that hot piece of coal? That is jihad. Jihad is in every religion. It's the struggle to keep your faith.'

Hang on, isn't that what Reindeer Antlers said it meant? Regardless, Jihad goes on to say that jihad decidedly does not mean violence.

'What kills me,' he continues, 'before this rally, everyone in the community was getting along. Now this is what's going to cause conflict. Our Prophet, *Alayhi salaam*, when he talks about *ummah*, his community, He talks about Muslims, Christians, Jews, Buddha, everyone!'

The socialists and anarchists receive all the flak from locals who are annoyed by the rally, which seems unfair. They only rocked up because the far right rocked up. The Reclaimers are out of sight and out of mind, sealed off by the police. What would have happened if the layout was the other way around, the socialists and anarchists out of sight and the Reclaimers on the street? Would the various BMX enthusiasts be hassling them?

'You know what I reckon?' Mel tells Jihad. 'You should come to the next event with the biggest banner, that says what you want it to say.'

'I just had to say my two cents, because I don't agree with it.'

'Yeah, cool, thanks mate. Good on you.'

I, of course, am thoroughly delighted to have witnessed this. The Melton Muslim objecting to the rally defending Muslims, on scriptural grounds. Mel notices that I've been here to catch this scene. She looks thoroughly undelighted.

The socialists and anarchists march into town with their giant middle finger, and I head towards my car.

'I come to a peaceful domestic . . . domestic . . .'

I think this white guy wants to say 'demonstration' but he's too smashed, stumbling up the shopping strip.

I can't remember where I parked. A black guy – African, I reckon – happens to be walking a few metres ahead.

'I come to a peaceful domestic . . . a fucken protest,' the white guy slurs at the black guy. Both look to be in their early twenties. 'What happens, mate? You guys start fucken burning flags and shit.'

The black guy spins around and snaps, 'Have I talked to you?'

'You're involved with them!' He points to the protest in the distance, rolling up the main street.

'Involved with them?' The black guy loses it. 'WAS I WITH THEM?'

'Go take your diseases,' hisses the white guy, 'and get the fuck overseas.'

'Hey dude, calm down,' I say, jogging towards them. I've been watching from the road, but now I'm so close I can smell the perspiration.

The white guy ambles up the street and the black guy starts texting.

'This is my turf, motherfucker,' the white guy turns and snarls. 'I've been here since 1970, you dumb cunt. How long have you been here for?'

'It doesn't matter! I didn't even start it, you fucking idiot. You're the racist cunt!'

The white guy's a dot in the distance when an Islander, a friend of the black guy, arrives on foot. Now a red car skids up. 'Carl! Caaarl!' the white girl driving shouts to the black guy.

The Islander jumps into the back seat but the black guy, Carl, heads for the boot. He reaches in for something. I can't quite see it. Crowbar?

'Carl, you're a fucken idiot,' the white girl cries. 'Get in the fucken car!'

Carl puts down The Thing I Can't Quite See and slams the boot. I feel the knife in my pocket. I walk over to the red car and lean through the window. Carl's buckling up in the passenger seat.

'Sorry dude, I'll go tell him off,' I say, like a flimsy Oskar Schindler.

'Nah, you're all right, man,' Carl says.

'You were in the right!' I feel the urge to add.

The Islander in the backseat bends forward to Carl. 'Which one? Which one?'

'White shirt,' mutters Carl. 'Says "Independence".'

The car speeds off.

I catch my reflection rolling past the store windows: a pizza cafe, a sandwich bar, 'Job Prospects' and 'Proven Employment Solutions'. I turn the corner. Where *is* my car? I see the white guy who started the trouble, in his white shirt that says 'Independence'. He is sitting on the steps outside a sports bar, head collapsed in his hands. Six bouncers stand around him. They're telling him to calm down. Explaining he's too drunk to come inside.

Across the road from the sports bar I spot it. The parked red car. Carl and the Islander aren't inside it, though. They're strolling towards the white guy, hands in pockets, real casual.

The bouncers don't know the backstory between these guys. I'm the only one who knows that Carl and the Islander's casual stroll is a deception. That violence is brewing. I can stop this. I can warn the bouncers.

But I make another decision. I lean against the wall of the sports bar and just watch on. Carl hangs back a little. The Islander drifts over to the bouncers, leaps, and brings down his fist on the white guy.

Carl and the Islander dart off. The bouncers pull out their walkie-talkies as the white guy stumbles from the stairs with a bloodied face.

Deserved that.

I'm halfway back to Melbourne before it hits me. When push came to shove, I was down with a little non-structural violence.

FALLING APART

The other IDF

Avi has been punching out a weekly column for the *Times of Israel*. His latest responds to these rallies, headlined BURNING THE FLAG: A HATE CRIME EVERY TIME. He writes: '. . . there are two groups in this world that use a similar symbolic tactic at their "protests": the burning of flags. Those groups are Islamists and "peace activists". As a military man I find the act of burning a flag one of the most disgraceful.'

I type a text to Avi: 'I have you on tape saying you would have been happy to burn a Palestinian flag, for publicity for your Krav Maga gym, except your mum advised you against it.'

He types: 'I knew your tapes would come back to bite me one day.'

Now Avi's calling up. I'm stretched out on my couch. 'Listen, I've got a story you might be interested in,' he blurts. 'We're basically starting a new program to essentially recruit Australian Jews to the IDF.'

He means the real IDF – Israel Defense Forces – not his Individual Diet and Fitness workout classes. He says he'll train these Jews at his gym while sorting out the paperwork with the Israeli authorities. 'It's gonna cause a bit of a stink.'

The race war around the corner

A Muslim dude has rushed the grounds of one of the synagogues around the corner from my flat. (There are more synagogues than 7-Elevens in my part of town.)

The phone footage hits the websites and the nightly news: RACE ATTACK CAUGHT ON CAMERA. The Muslim dude's eyes are popping out of his face, and his fists are clenched by his sides. 'Go back to Israel!' he wails at the rabbi. 'Go back to Israel!'

'Nah, I'm from Australia!' huffs the oversized – both wide and tall – rabbi.

'You want to swear to Allah!' the Muslim yowls, pointing to the sky. 'You want to swear to Allah!'

The Muslim leaps for the rabbi's throat. The rabbi waves his hands around in a combination of a Jew talking with his hands and a karate chop. Now the rabbi uses his belly to topple the Muslim to the cement.

Two orthodox Jews spring in, each pinning one of the Muslim's hands to the ground with their feet.

'Do you really think you can rule this land?' the Muslim howls. 'Do you really think you can rule this land?'

Avi posts this under 'Respect to the rabbi for the perfect application of IDF Training techniques.'

I text Avi to fact-check that this rabbi had indeed taken his classes. Avi concedes he hasn't. The rabbi works for the kosher abattoir. That, Avi says, is why the rabbi had the muscle to flatten the Muslim.

Fortitude

Blair is lounging on a canvas chair in a backyard in Perth, scratching a dog. 'We were treated like kings,' he tells the camera. Neil is standing by, cross-armed, as is Dennis, the bloke with the Aryan daughters. 'And we all had a great day.'

This great day was the Perth Reclaim rally. That's where he – and other UPF leaders, I now see – ended up instead of Melton.

Blair makes an announcement that he is about to make an announcement.

'The UPF is forming its first political party, called Fortitude.'

So the ALA will not be the only brand-new party running on the anti-Islam ticket. To sign up the five hundred members needed to run at the federal election – which could be called at any time – the UPF will be holding a series of 'massive, huge' rallies. 'We come from the streets and we're going political. You just don't see that anymore. That's what makes us significant. We're going to be the most popular, most powerful political force in the country. Give us five years and I'll prove it.'

There's another matter at hand. Victoria's Labor premier, Daniel Andrews, sniped at the UPF through the television cameras after the Melton kerfuffle: 'If your views are not something that you're actually ashamed of, then why would you be covering your face?'

Blair is furious. Why attack only the 'patriots' for this? What about the socialists and the anarchists? He calls for a snap protest outside the premier's office this Saturday.

There's so much on the internet tonight. I'm tangled up in my doona. Blair's banging on, of course. 'I just saw a fucking TV ad for women encouraging adultery,' begins his Facebook post. 'AshleyMadison. com. "Life is short, have an affair." Lol. That putrid Marxist propaganda is ruthless. In my humble opinion adultery ought to be punished by death just like the good old days.'

So Hamza and Blair agree on the penalty for adultery. Both are pining for a past, half factual, half made up in their heads. For Blair, that's well before the White Australia policy was dumped. For Hamza? I don't know – before the Crusaders stormed in on their horses?

I follow far-right, far-left and radical Muslim folks on Facebook. A new conspiracy video contending Jews control the world rolls into my feed. And representatives from the three groups have shared it.

I click around. Donald Trump has squashed Jeb Bush, Carly Fiorina, and is now steamrolling towards the other Republican presidential candidates. 'Until we are able to determine and understand this problem,' he tells the crowd, 'our country cannot be the victim of horrendous attacks by people who only believe in jihad.'

He proposes a 'total and complete shutdown of Muslims entering the United States'.

No Room for Racism posts something I have to read twice: 'Listen, don't think for a moment that Trump is against Muslims, because he is not.' Strange position for a group that hits the streets to fight Islamophobia. 'He does business with all the rich ones and he is just using this issue to divide all non-rich people.'

Sometimes I forget that the No Room for Racism panda is Karl Marx with two black eyes.

Tradition

'I'm getting so tired of this.' The human beatboxer, who MCs the No Room for Racism rallies, is kicking his foot against the cement outside the premier's office. 'I got an audition for *Aladdin* on Tuesday and then I've got a screen test for the new Jessica Mauboy series. I've got other things I need to be doing, as you can imagine.'

'And then when Blair announces another snap rally . . .' I begin.

'Yeah, well it fucks up my sleeping first of all.'

There's no crowd here yet, left or right. It's an hour before the advertised time. Mel the matriarch and Mrs Sneer are spitballing, trying to guess from which direction the UPF will approach. The premier's office is tucked around the corner from the steps of Parliament House. The UPF could stomp in from that direction. Or from the gardens that roll out in front of the office.

Mrs Sneer says she's not comfortable with me listening in on their conversation. Fair enough. I am the Jewish octopus with a tentacle in each camp.

I wander over to the grown man in a business shirt and baseball cap leaning against a pillar. In so much as the anarchists have a CEO, he's the CEO. At the rallies he points his finger here and there, muttering into ears, and the little ninjas scuttle off on the mission.

The police scooped him up last weekend in Melton.

'Did you punch the horse?' I ask him.

'I didn't punch a fucking horse,' the CEO says. 'Nobody punched a horse. I made sure nobody punched a horse.'

'But were you the one who was arrested?'

'I was arrested for punching a horse,' he concedes. He also concedes, 'I was the lad who organised teams of three to push the horses.'

(These are polices horses, if that's not clear.)

'So the police just upsized it to punching a horse because they know it'll make you guys look bad?'

'They lie to the media,' explains the CEO. He's circumspect, though. 'We lie to the media. I don't hold lying . . . Like, I hate the police, but they use some of the same tactics we use against them.'

I tell him I was surprised by the No Room for Racism statement on Donald Trump.

'Why do you think the far left is involved in this campaign?' he asks, curious that I'm surprised.

'Because they oppose Islamophobia?' (Isn't that obvious?)

'That's an element – there's definitely that.'

The CEO sees my face scrunch up as I take this in. 'That's why I'm here,' he adds. He wants to make it clear he personally is here to fight Islamophobia.

What else is going on?

'There's also a perspective,' he says, 'that the current situation of capitalism is unstable. That, in crisis, the centre ground is discredited, and politics moves to the extremes.'

What he says reminds me of what Blair told me at the barbeque in Bendigo. For Blair, anti-Islam rhetoric draws a crowd, so he can then 'plant the seed of something a little bit more controversial'. The CEO explains that this is what the socialists and the anarchists do too. Although for them it's radical left-wing politics, not white nationalism. So while the two sides have been hitting the streets over Muslims for months, it hasn't really been about Muslims at all.

The CEO says socialists and anarchists are buzzing that Donald Trump and Bernie Sanders have broken into the mainstream. Blair was buzzing about this too. It's a sign that people are open to fringe ideas. A sign that the Messianic age is inching closer.

Western liberalism is crumbling, the three points of the triangle sense, now's the time to prepare for the takeover.

The No Room for Racism crowd begins to build. A black-stubbled young man, an organiser from one of the socialist groups, sits down next to me under a statue near the Parliament House steps. He has heard about the Muslim dude who tried to throttle the rabbi on the synagogue grounds. I ask him how come the story didn't make it to the No Room for Racism Facebook page, and other hard-left pages that monitor racist incidents in Australia.

He explains that a Muslim leaping at a rabbi screaming 'Allah!' is 'interpersonal violence', which isn't something these anti-racist groups cover. It's like if a guy pranged someone else's car and a fight broke out. I ask whether, when the Muslim shot the Jews at the Paris kosher deli, that too was 'interpersonal violence'. No, he says, that slid across to non-structural violence.

I look around at the placards the protesters here are holding up. I tell him the socialists should probably stop using the swastika with the red line struck through it. Someone might get the impression that they're against punching and shooting Jews.

It really is a neat trick. Anything you don't want to think about, just file under non-structural. I try to speak his language. I insist that religions are structures too. Forces that continue to shape the world as surely as capitalism and neoliberalism.

He looks at me like I'm batty.

The CEO of the anarchists fake-dawdles up the road behind Parliament House. I tag along. He doesn't want to draw attention to himself. He's on a mission to work out where the hell the UPF guys are. His side have kept their part of the deal. A hundred or so have shown up, ready to rumble. But where are Blair and co?

'You know what's in that synagogue?' I ask the CEO, pointing across the street to a white building with a blue Star of David above the door.

'What?'

'The rabbi Neil Erikson threatened.'

'Oh shit. Oh my god, and they're open today,' he says ominously, as a black-hatted man shuffles through the synagogue doorway.

We've almost full-circled before we spot the UPF blokes. They're hovering out the front of the Princess Theatre, across the road from Parliament House. *Fiddler on the Roof* is playing! Are there even twenty of them? One guy is resting a flagpole on each shoulder. There are too many flags for the number of attendees.

The CEO punches something into his phone. He salutes farewell, ducks across the road into a side street. Two ninjas are waiting.

'Good to see you, mate,' Blair says, striding over. The gym junkie seems to grow half a size larger each rally. 'You sunning your nose?'

My nose is still glowing like Rudolph's from the Melton rally last weekend. 'Yeah, being an Aryan, my Caucasian skin, sometimes . . .' I blabber out some smart-arsery then I cut to the point. 'There's a lot more of them than you today.'

'Yeah, I expected that,' Blair says.

His spin? The point of this rally is to draw out the mask-wearing lefties in droves. This exposes the premier as a hypocrite for only attacking the mask-wearing patriots. Thus the large crowd of lefties is a victory. That the UPF achieved this by exerting so little effort – with such a small crowd – is another victory.

Sure, Blair.

'Feel the person next to you! Feel the energy! Connect to it!' Blair roars into the microphone, wandering back and forth in front of the small gathering. There really is a fine line between being a Führer and being a busker. 'That's what a community is! That's what a nation is! That's our spirit! That's our tradition! Never forget who you are! Never forget where you come from! No matter what these people say, no matter what they do . . .'

Oh my god. Delight rushes over me. I cast my eyes up to the giant *Fiddler on the Roof* billboard. The musical that opens with Tevye, an orthodox Jew, walking out on stage as a mournful tune plays, and arguing the importance of tradition. And here is Blair clomping back and forth in front of the theatre, addressing the very same concern.

I reach for my pencil:

FIT BLAIR ON THE ROOF: A MUSICAL

A troubled man with a furrowed brow enters stage right. A mournful
tune plays. He turns to the audience.

~~TEVYE~~ BLAIR: ~~A fiddler on the roof~~ An air guitarist on the roof.
Sounds crazy, no?
But here in our little village of ~~Anatevka~~ Frankston,
you might say every one of us is ~~a fiddler~~ an air guitarist
on the roof.
Trying to scratch out ~~a pleasant, simple tune~~ 'Thunderstruck',
without breaking his neck.
Why do we stay up if it's so dangerous? Because ~~Anatevka~~
Frankston is our home. And how do we keep our balance?
That I can tell you in one word:
Tradition! We've kept our traditions for many years.
We always keep our heads ~~covered~~ burqa-free
and always wear a ~~little prayer shawl~~ flag cape.
This shows our devotion to ~~God~~ God knows.
And because of tradition everyone knows who he is!

A chorus line of dancing ~~Orthodox Jews,~~ Shermon, Neil and Ralph
burst onto stage.

CHORUS: Tradition! Tradition! Tradition!

I slip away from the Princess Theatre, past the UPF, the police
horses and the chanting anarchists. I duck around the corner to

Rabbi Gutnick's synagogue.

The rabbi is up in the loft, rabbiting to a young man. Rabbi Gutnick has had the same great idea as Blair – a podcast. The young man apparently has the technical nous to pull it together and they're discussing recording dates.

Rabbi Gutnick tells me to take a seat at the small table. I cut to the chase: 'Blair – he's the UPF guy – was giving this full-on speech, just around the corner. I look up and there's this huge *Fiddler on the Roof* sign. And I thought, Why does Tevye get to crap on about tradition and his people and how important his family customs are, and his distinct culture? Why does Tevye get to do it but Blair isn't allowed to do it?'

Rabbi Gutnick puffs up his cheeks and breathes out. 'Because Tevye isn't abusing other people,' he explains.

'I guess so.' I add, 'But we go around saying, "We're the chosen few," so why can't white people?'

The rabbi winces. 'Are you able to differentiate in your head the way Judaism defines itself as the chosen people and people that believe that they are somehow a superior race?'

'No, not entirely.'

'The chosenness – in all the teachings that I've learned, there's always been impelling responsibility saying, "You are chosen for something, therefore you need to do something in the world, you need to create." It's giving you a mission! A purpose! Never does the chosenness ever lead to: "Because you are chosen, therefore you have to rob people or protest at some parliament —"'

'What about when the Jews left Egypt?' I say. 'And God said to them, "Now take the gold from the Egyptians."'

'That was in the article I sent you!' Rabbi Gutnick complains. 'You wouldn't have known that without the article.'

I haggle. I tell him I'm not ragging on the Jews per se. That I've travelled the world for work, and black Americans, folks in Togo, families in Japan – I've gotten the sense most people think they're the chosen.

'Judaism would say that's a hundred per cent right. There is something unique about everyone. Otherwise they wouldn't be here.'

'Can white Australians have a sense of there's something —'

'Absolutely.'

'What are white Australians chosen to do?'

'Dunno.'

As I exit the synagogue out to the street Rabbi Gutnick has one more thing he wants me to know. The Jews only stole from the Egyptians the gold that was rightfully theirs, and only because God told them to.

The wine bar sits next to the Princess Theatre and across the road from Parliament House. I stare out the window.

'You will always lose in Melbourne!' sing the anarchists and socialists on the steps. 'You will always lose in Melbourne!' The hippies and ninjas are pushing their hands to the sky, pulsating as one, like they're the cast of *Hair* waiting to move into the Princess Theatre. One young skinhead (non-Nazi variety) performs a backflip!

The No Room for Racism crowd is much smaller than at my first Reclaim rally. And today was a flop for the 'patriots'. Blair looked frazzled. Like he knew he had screwed up by calling this snap rally. He looked weak.

This wine bar was shuttered during that previous rally, for fear the race war would come smashing through its window. Like the other shops along this strip, today it's open for business.

Last year's boy-band phenomenon will still be touring, but performing to smaller rooms. That's the vibe of today.

CRONULLA

Cronulla is a riot

The first time I chatted to Nicholas Folkes I was trying to figure out how he could run a party against Asian immigration while being married to an Asian immigrant. Now he has willed into reality that he is the 'official organiser' of the 'Cronulla Riot 10th Anniversary'. You can order from his Party for Freedom website a commemorative glass platter or a 'Sydney is Fun, Cronulla is a Riot' T-shirt.

Blair is not happy and has pulled the plug on his own involvement. 'Apparently a lot of you seem to think the Cronulla rally is a fantastic idea and that I am weak for not supporting it.' Big orange earmuffs are wrapped around his neck. Blair is taking a break from his carpentry job to film this. 'The organisers for this rally are selling T-shirts with "riots" written on the back. Do you really think that is the best way to get our message across? I think it's a good way to make you look like a fucking idiot, to be honest. You are just making a complete mockery of patriotism and yourselves. Say what you want about me, I don't care. Someone's got to tell it to you like it is.'

Shermon, in contrast, is peppy. 'We are going to return to where it all started,' he gloats. He sees the suburb of Cronulla as 'the very motherland of anti-Islam', because of the 2005 riots.

But I'm watching a doco filmed at the time of the 2005 riots, and the white Aussies aren't talking about Islam. The text messages flashing up on the Nokia phones read: 'Help support Leb and Wog bashing day . . . bring your mates.'

'Fuck off wogs, fuck off wogs, fuck off wogs,' shout the whiteys at the train station. So does that mean Ralph Cerminara, with his Italian father, wouldn't have been welcome then? The fright-word of the shock jock Alan Jones isn't 'Muslims', it's 'men of Middle Eastern appearance'.

A surfie dude does air concerns about Islamic courts, although he has trouble pronouncing 'Isla . . . la . . . mic'.

Now, in this old doco, Muslims are gathering at a mosque, plotting to fight back. So the riots must have been about Islam to some extent. Back at the beach, a Croatian is nose to nose with a skip. The Croatian has come down to fight the wogs, but the skip is informing him that, as a Croatian, he is a wog himself.

So, for the folks in the decade-old doco, religion is jumbled up with ethnicity, which is jumbled up with race. Everyone seems confused. And ten years later?

'G'day, patriots,' Shermon greets us from his bedroom in a new Facebook video. Channel 7 has been shadowing him and his anti-Islam mates for a current affairs special. 'Do you know what they've done?' Shermon reveals how a sympathetic producer called him today. 'Even though they've interviewed Daniel Nalliah, they've removed him and his interview completely from the segment.' The producer's boss at the network thought that including a black guy who's on the anti-Islam side would make the story too confusing for their audience.

Cronulla tenth anniversary memorial day

Nicholas Folkes lives in the inner west, ten minutes' drive from the Sydney CBD. A black coffin leans against a wall in his hallway. Stencilled on the lid in white paint: MULTICULTURALISM. I step over his Eurasian kid, who's snoring in a sleeping-bag on the floor of the lounge room.

'Sorry? You joking,' he croaks into the phone to his mate Josh. 'Somebody slashed all my car tyres?' Nicholas tells Josh that the saboteurs are trying to foil his efforts to get to Cronulla Beach today. He tells him not to worry, they'll take the van instead.

He glances over to the kitchen, which runs off the lounge room. His wife, who I find out is Japanese, is pressing oranges into a juicer. 'Just be careful,' he warns her. 'If you go outside to have a smoke or whatever, just be careful.'

His wife is wearing scrubs. 'Do you ever get hassled?' I ask. 'Do people at your work know you're married to Nick?'

'No!' Nicholas and she burst out laughing. In fact, at her last shift at the hospital Nick popped up on a telly, in a news report. She looked around at the nurses and nobody had the faintest.

'She's not even my Facebook friend.'

Nicholas has loaded up the meat for today's barbie and is now reversing out from in front of the butcher's shop, Josh riding shotgun. I'm squeezed in the back of the van, between flags and megaphones and eskies of pork sausages. His other mates are reversing out in a flatbed truck, a pig strapped to the back.

'The lefties are going to go apeshit when they see us with a pig on the spit!' Nicholas predicts. Not the Muslims, I note, the lefties.

Josh holds up his phone so Nicholas can spit out a Facebook video rant while driving.

'The lefties this morning, they slashed four of me car tyres. They thought they could stop us!' He shifts to a faster lane. 'The thing is, you need to come down. Remember those men that stood up ten years ago and protected their suburb!' The rioters are the Anzacs to Nick.

Josh spools through text messages. 'Gangs are coming out of western Sydney,' he tells Nicholas. 'There's a meeting at ten o'clock this morning with Antifa, Socialist Alliance, and some of the Islamic groups.'

I'm spooling myself back here. Shermon's just posted on Facebook: 'Good luck to everyone in Cronulla today. I've been stopped from leaving town to attend. I cannot even enter Cronulla or I'll be arrested and jailed on site.'

Fearing a riot, the cops, the local council, and a Muslim

community leader have tried to stop today's rally. Nicholas and Shermon were the only two defendants named in the court papers. (Why Shermon, out of all the 'patriots'? I don't know.) The courts have banned Nicholas and his party from running the event itself, but legally it's hard to stop a random mob from rocking up to a beach. Nicholas and his mates plan to be part of that random mob.

'What a load of BS,' a commenter throws back at Shermon. 'Nicholas is on his way there now. You're a coward.'

I hope Ralph hasn't pulled out too. I want to see that man. I want to tell him about my stroll down the streets of Lakemba. Nicholas reckons he'll show.

'Ralph,' Nicholas says. 'He's a lovely guy, but once he gets the goon juice into him, he turns into a fucking spastic.'

'Now we're driving through the streets of Cronulla,' I report to my dictaphone over the wind gushing through the windows. 'We've passed by some concrete trucks. Working on the weekend. Good work ethic. You think this looks a bit like Surfers Paradise?' I ask Nicholas.

'Yeah, but twenty years ago,' he shouts from the front. 'It's sort of just really relaxed and it's the way Australia should be.'

Nicholas pulls over to the side of a busy road and heads to the rear of his van. He pulls out a black burqa from the boot. 'I need to go incognito,' he explains. 'Just so we get in. Because if I dress up in this, I'm not going to get attacked by the anarchists.'

How did he come across this burqa?

'It's made by a patriot in country Victoria,' he says. 'But I've got some authentic garb that I bought online.'

He owns more than one?

'Are you trans-Muslim?' I ask, but he doesn't hear me over the traffic.

Back in the van, Nicholas turns the keys in the ignition. 'I tell you what, I don't really want to bloody drive in this because it doesn't give you much visual.' He fidgets with the eye-slit on his burqa. 'All right. Let's go. Magic.'

An Aboriginal man with one arm confronts Josh in the carpark at Cronulla Beach. Josh is brandishing an Australian flag.

The Aboriginal man points at the Union Jack. 'This isn't the Union Jack's place to tell anybody to be in this continent!' He says that white Australians don't own the land, so they can't tell Muslims they're not welcome.

Josh waves his hand in front of his own nose, implying the Aboriginal man reeks of alcohol. He doesn't. 'What *doooo* you drink?' he snarls.

Hmm. So much for the insistence by the 'patriots' that they have no beef with Aboriginal people, and that their grievance isn't about 'race'.

'You're here to start trouble,' Josh declares. He clicks his fingers at a nearby policeman. 'Get rid of him!'

A policeman wanders over and shoos the Aboriginal man away.

Journos have figured out that the person floating through the carpark in a burqa is in fact Nicholas, the organiser of today's event. (I didn't tell them.) Most huddle around him, although one, a female journo, is gathering vox pops from passers-by in the carpark. She approaches the Aboriginal man and asks what he thinks about the fact that Nicholas – a non-Muslim and a man – is wandering around in a burqa. The Aboriginal man motions at the riot police in the corner of the carpark. Seeing they're wearing balaclavas, he reasons with the journo, why can't this guy wear a burqa?

The cops have allowed the anti-Islam crowd a large patch of grass, down a dip that runs alongside the beach. Every time I stick my ear into a conversation, the people are muttering that they expected a bigger turnout. This vast grassy area is rubbing everyone's face in it – only about a hundred folks have shown up.

Nicholas's mates have driven their small flatbed truck down into the dip and are lifting off the pig.

The UPF may be a no-show, but a knock-off of the UPF has turned up. They've named their gang after the postcode of their suburb. These boys are younger than the stars of the UPF and are wearing new flannel shirts with the sleeves cut off neatly, matching mirror sunglasses, and what look like brand-new akubras. To my mind, they've crossed the line into dress-ups. Although all our clothes are dress-ups, I suppose. Regardless, they've triggered a memory of when I was fourteen and tried being a goth for a weekend.

Pastor Daniel has shown up and is sitting on a plastic chair. There's the Half-Jewess in a wig, a big hat and big sunglasses. She says she can't risk appearing on someone's Facebook feed or she'll get fired from work. And . . . huh! There's Ralph. In a flag cape, no less. He's deep in the mob that has gathered around the fire above which twirls the pig. I slide through the mob. Ralph catches me out of the corner of his eye and drifts away before I can reach him. He's trying to make out his escape has nothing to do with me. I approach him from another angle. Once again he drifts away.

I look over at the flatbed truck. I elbow through the crowd and climb onto the back. 'Ralph!' I call down.

Ralph and others turn their heads up to me.

'Safran, how are you?' Ralph says, faking normality.

'Good to see you. Not too bad.' I cut to the point. 'I did what you said. I went to Lakemba and wore my Jewish skullcap!'

He glances around, trying to telegraph that I'm mad.

'Anyway, I spent over an hour there.' I pull at the top of my pants. 'I even had some *Fiddler on the Roof* tassels on. No one cared. No one *caaared* about me!'

Ralph looks around at his mates again and snorts. 'Where's the footage, mate? Where's the footage?'

I tell him there's no footage. 'I went there by myself.'

'I'd need to see footage to believe it, all right? I wouldn't believe it until I see it.'

Ralph returns to drinking and chatting with his friends.

Nicholas and his mates didn't think through the pig-on-the-spit idea. It takes between seven and twenty-four hours to roast one, a bloke informs them. Isn't that something you should know if you're 'strayan? The crowd tucks into the pork sausages instead. Nicholas was worried there wouldn't be enough. There are.

I glance around. Pastor Daniel is picking something from his teeth. A kilted man gripping bagpipes circles a patch of grass, not even blowing his instrument, just fingering the holes. This is the sequel to the great race riots of 2005?

Lacking any other avenues to explore, I start to feel out if any of the bald people here are skinheads. But they're all just bald. Rumours flitter around that the anarchists are about to spring out from the beach, or charge from over the hill, but despite what the T-shirt promised, Cronulla will not be a riot today. Nicholas's mates reload the barely warmed pig onto the back of the truck.

I share a taxi with the Half-Jewess and Ralph. I'm being dropped off first – there's one more man I want to visit today. Ralph's being a piece of shit. He's talking to us but clearly hoping the Muslim driver is listening in – 'Lots of terrorism these days, guys' – that sort of thing. By the time I get out of the taxi I feel like a piece of shit myself.

Shape-shifting lizard

I'm back in front of Jim Saleam's roller door, the one that had been kicked in by anarchists. Jim, my chief suspect in the affair of the anti-Asian posters in Redfern, has advertised that today he'll deliver an 'urgent address' on 'the 2005 Cronulla Civil Uprising'. Jim is not a fan of Nicholas. He's one of the people who think Nick's too soft on the Jews.

I stroll down the laneway that runs along the side of the build-ing. Jim opens the door.

'G'day, I'm John. I'm a writer.'

'You missed the speech, but if you want to come in and do an interview . . .'

Jim is certainly friendlier this time. We walk through to his gloomy and cluttered office. I get to see the bashed-in roller door from the other side. It's blocking out most of the sunlight. He offers me a chair and takes a seat behind the desk. Jim is sixty years old and his office is tactile in its fascism. Where the new kids have Facebook posts he has old photocopied newsletters piled up everywhere. It's like walking into a vinyl record shop. Weathered protest posters from the 1970s lie around.

A bulky young man enters. Jim signals that everything is cool. And the bulky young man just stands behind me.

Jim has been in this game a while. Twenty-five years ago he was sentenced to three and a half years' jail. He had provided a shotgun to two skinheads who fired into the home of the African National Congress representative in Australia.

'This thing I'm writing is for a book. Do you mind if I use a dictaphone?'

'No, you —' Jim stops. He squints. 'So, you remind me of someone.'

'Ah, yes. Who's that?' I breathe in the musty air.

'Mr Safran.'

It hits me that I've grown a beard since last time. And I'm wearing sunglasses. I didn't pull on the sunnies to hide myself, it's just hot as hell outside. Goosebumps pop up on my arms.

'What's wrong with Mr Safran?'

'I don't talk to Mr Safran.'

'Oh really? What did he do?'

He squints extra tightly. 'You see, you look remarkably like him. One of his incarnations. If you are him I can't talk to you.' And he looks up at the bulky young man. 'Quite honestly, I can't pick him. It's been a while. I mean, since I've seen him.' He turns back to me. 'I think you gave your name to me before as Dave.'

'No, no, no. I gave my name as John.' So he definitely only invited me in on a misunderstanding. This stuffy air, my day in the heat, this off-kilter conversation, I'm feeling half in a dream. 'So why can't you talk to John Safran? What did he ever do to you?'

'You look remarkably like him. You remind me of him deeply. I know John is a bit of a chameleon character and he looks like one thing one day and one thing the next. I know that, but I can't really talk to him.'

'Okay.' I don't know what else to say. 'Fair enough.'

We walk back out through the door to the laneway. The sunlight hits me again. Jim says, 'I wish you well and I bear you no personal —'

'What did John Safran ever do? That's what I don't understand.'

'It's just his particular writing style is not edifying to me. It's more the way he perceives his political opponents. I think that he perceives me in a particular way.'

'Oh really? How does he perceive you that is wrong?'

'I think he perceives me as something out of a Nazi comedy routine.' Jim stares through my sunglasses. 'And he is pretty wrong.'

Today's 'urgent address' on what Jim calls the 'Cronulla Leb Riot' is not the first time he's concerned himself with the Lebanese community. His website is bursting with attacks. 'Sydneysiders deserve a "Great Leb Roundup". Who needs them? . . . Lebs have snubbed Australian assimilation . . . their patriarchal sons roam like alpha males, terrorising blonde women . . . bad attitude, bad haircuts, bad garlic breath, bathed in aftershave, dog neck chained, and flinging spastic cramped finger motions . . .'

So as the tenth anniversary of 'Leb and Wog Bashing Day' is winding up, it would be remiss of me not to pass this on. Jim Saleam grew up in Maryborough, Queensland, along the Mary River.

The old people there remember Jim and his parents and grand-parents. Jim denies this, but those old people recall: the Saleams were Lebanese immigrants. So I have to push back on that thing you said, Jim. You kind of are like something out of a Nazi comedy routine.

THE HOLY LAND

IDF update

I contact Avi: 'How's the army recruiting going?' I'm being a smart-arse. As if he's followed through on his plan to train local Jews for the Israel Defense Forces.

'Good. I've had two join the IDF.'

'No way!'

They joined the real IDF? Not his Individual Dietary Fitness version?

'Yeah. Why is that so surprising?'

'Because it's a big thing to organise people to join a foreign army. It's not like holding one of your rubber-knife workshops.'

'Mate, if people were allowed to join as non-Jews I'd have at least four times that joining. I get about one application a week. But most are not Jewish.'

I tell him he needs to be to be careful when people phone him up to join the IDF. 'The dude just wants to lose weight but in a wacky mix-up you've got him on a plane to the Golan Heights.'

Avi tells me he joined the Israel Defense Forces when he was nineteen, a little over a decade ago.

'And you were on heroin?'

'Where are you getting your sources?' he asks.

'You told me last time.'

'I was a heroin addict.'

The army didn't know this. He filled out the enlistment forms while in rehab in Australia.

'I was fucking 50 kilos. I was a bag of bones. I was the lightest in my unit. They used to always put me on a stretcher because it was easier to carry me. At the end of the army I was almost the heaviest in my unit. I gained 25 kilos.'

I tell Avi that Blair and his fellow white nationalists ask why the Jews are allowed an 'ethno-state' but they aren't.

Avi thinks Jewish nationalism and white Australian nationalism differ. Here in Australia, white people are not the original owners of the land, Aboriginal people are. Over in Israel, he contends, Jews are the original owners of the land. There are ancient Jewish symbols carved in caves, he says, as surely as you'll find Aboriginal symbols carved in rocks here. And when you're the original owners you get to say what's what.

Avi moves on to a story. He has doubt in his voice now, something I haven't heard before. He tells me about his cousin, a settler in the West Bank. 'He's a fucking nutcase. Right when I got to Israel I went to his farm. He would go into a Palestinian village on a horse, with no weapons, no fucking nothing. And then he would go to a kid, "Do you want to ride on the horse?" So the kid would jump on. And then my cousin, he would start making the horse jump up, and it's got no saddle or anything. And the kid's bouncing on the back. And my cousin would be laughing. And I go, "What are you fucking laughing about?" He goes, "Do you see what I'm doing? I'm making the horse jump so it knocks the kid's balls in." "But it's a little kid, what are you doing?" And he goes, "This little kid now, he's going to be a terrorist soon."'

The paradox

There's a secret Palestinian in my very Jewish street.

'I don't really feel comfortable telling people,' Del says, pulling on a cigarette behind the kosher bakery. 'If it ever comes up, with customers asking me what my background is, I always just say I'm a bit of this and that, and I'm a bit Italian, and then just leave it at that.'

Del worked in a boutique in the street before moving to the bakery. 'It just feels like I ended up here accidentally, not having any idea what kind of area this was. Then realising, just going, Oh, God. Then I did this thing where I was, Oh, okay, maybe this is really good, that I'm building relationships with people who are Jewish, because there's always fear of the unknown. Then I have this weird Jewish fetishism. Even with comedy and stuff, I'm obsessed with Woody Allen. I just find Jewish people fascinating.'

I want to know what Del makes of Avi's stance that Jews are the aborigines of Israel. 'Don't some Palestinians still have the keys to their houses?' I say. 'And it's like, I'm going to get back the house one day, that I was kicked out of in one of the wars.'

'The only thing I know is that my grandmother, she had a house in Haifa when she was growing up and that got bulldozed. But there's no key.'

The family moved to Jerusalem. Years later, when Del's father was sixteen, soldiers pulled him over and made him march back home, a gun to his back. 'And my aunt said when he got home he was crying. Like he's sensitive, but he's really proud to be macho. And then I think the next day he was like, I'm leaving the country. He couldn't handle the fact it was allowed for someone to have that much power over him, a stranger. It's just not fair. Even if the Jews were the first people there, there are Arabs who made it their home and they had families for generations.'

There's no shortage of bakery or boutique jobs closer to Del's home. She admits it's odd that a Palestinian travels across town each day, but she likes the vibe of the Jewish street, where people 'squawk and get to the point'. She says other Palestinian Australians have complicated feelings too. 'They say, "Look at the Jews, look how they stick together. Let's learn from them." It's a weird paradox of anger and admiration.'

Del tells me her aunty is trapped in a paradox of her own. She's convinced that her doctor, who is Jewish, is trying to poison her. 'She's going on and on and on. And I'm like, "Why do you see him if you think he's poisoning you?" And she goes, "Jews are the best doctors."'

Play dates

I called Hamza to ask his view on the Jews being the aborigines of Israel, but he just started ranting about the Palestinians being the most incompetent Muslims in the world. He said I should head to an Australian Hizb-ut-Tahrir conference and see their buffoonery for myself. The radical group, founded by Palestinians, is banned in places like Germany, China and Russia. Its aim is to establish the Islamic State, although it doesn't accept the authority of ISIS's current leader, Abu Bakr al-Baghdadi.

At the conference a sheikh sneers about 'Australian values' from the podium. What is so la-di-da about 'Australian values', he argues, that anyone would want to take them on board? I imagine a leftie sitting here: 'Preach it, brother!' (in fact a socialist was handing out pamphlets outside this community centre) then wincing as the sheikh continues. He had been asked to appear in a photo with a gay community leader. This is the abhorrent 'Australian value' that has been on the sheikh's mind.

I end up nibbling cake in the corner with a young bearded man named Sabbir. I show him a picture I just found on the internet. Hindu Indians have set up an altar with incense. Where there would usually be a picture of Ganesha or Vishnu, there sits a photo of Donald Trump.

'Bloody hell!' says Sabbir. We giggle and a woman (I can only see one pink finger, nothing else) blows a 'Shush!' from beneath her niqab.

He is more interested in my snaps of the UPF and No Room for Racism rally outside the premier's office. Sabbir studies at Sydney University and says conversations with his left-wing friends are 'riddled with tension'. Apart from differences of opinion on things like homosexuality, 'there's tensions that haven't even been discussed. Islam's take on economics might make a lot of lefties uncomfortable. We don't have a gripe against ownership of capital. These aren't things that make Muslims go, "Upset the established order! Take the means of production from the bourgeois!"'

I can't get Sabbir worked up about the UPF, who he thinks are 'the convenient bigots to point at and be like, "They're the problem." There's nothing the UPF could do that compares with the kinds of atrocities Israel commits, which Australia has a cosy relationship with.'

I pick up a Hizb-ut-Tahrir pamphlet on the way out: 'How To Deal With Spies – The paranoia and manufactured threat surrounding Muslims has been accompanied by an upsurge in the activity of Australia's spy agencies, most prominently ASIO. This includes both overt and covert attempts to elicit information from people and in some cases entrap them.'

That explains why people I chatted to at the conference today kept glancing at my iPhone, presumably suspicious that I was recording. This iPhone eyeballing happened at the Lakemba mosque too.

Walking to the train station I wikipedia Abu Bakr al-Baghdadi, the man Hizb-ut-Tahrir refuse to accept as Islamic State's leader.

I discover he's only one year older than me. I'm hit with that melancholy you get when you realise someone around your age has achieved so much more than you and you mightn't ever catch up.

After that feeling subsides I start to wonder what Hamza's problem with Hizb-ut-Tahrir is anyway.

'They're pussies,' Hamza tells me. He's pacing in his lounge room, agitated, while I look on from the couch. 'They were founded specifically with the goal of re-establishing the caliphate. Now the caliphate has been established, they're the first ones to reject it.'

'Oh, because they don't accept what's-his-name?'

'He fulfils all of the requirements!' Hamza stabs his finger in the air. He thinks what's-his-name meets the conditions set out in scripture. 'Where are you guys?' By 'you guys', he means members of Hizb-ut-Tahrir. 'What have you done? You're experts of Sitting Around Drinking Coffee.'

The pug trots into the room and starts licking my sneaker.

'They've done nothing! They love to stand around in their fancy suits, living in the West, drinking coffee, having sweets. They love their sweets. Guaranteed, you want to know the best sweets places to go to in a city, ask the members of Hizb-ut-Tahrir. Because that's all they do around the city. Eat sweets!'

'They did have good cakes there, that's true.'

'They love their sweets. They love everything except fighting for Islam. They will never do that.'

Hamza says a man from Hizb-ut-Tahrir asked him to speak at the conference. 'I said, "I'm not going to that conference." He was like, "I understand. You're under pressure from the government." I said, "No, I'm not under pressure from the government. I just don't want to go!"'

I tell him I'll probably catch up with the Hizb-ut-Tahrir guys again.

'Say to them, "Why are you guys such pussies? How come your leader has been to Syria three times yet he's never raised weapons?" Do it in your best John Safran confrontational voice.'

Hamza sure is fiery today, furious even. He tells me his buddy, the World of Warcraft gnome, called up a radio station this week after Malcolm Turnbull sniped, 'If you don't love the country then leave it.' The gnome told the talkback host, 'I'm one of those on a no-fly list and I want to leave.' Hamza explains, 'He was just trying to point out that a lot of us don't love it, and want to leave it but you won't let us, Malcolm.'

The pug yawns.

We return to the dining table where our Qur'ans lie open. I point my finger at a passage about the mushrikun, believers in multiple gods.

I read aloud: '"To those of the mushrikun, with whom you made a treaty," blah, blah, blah, "when the sacred month has passed, then kill them."'

I look up to Hamza. 'So that means you can go kill the Hindus?'

He nods.

Something's bothering Hamza. His cheeks are pinking up. He's looking furious again.

'And mind you, if you ever do read anything to a Muslim, don't skip over it by saying "blah, blah, blah". They might take offence at that.'

This is a delicate relationship we have.

Hamza turns the page of his Qur'an. 'The Bible has bad parts too, but we've learnt to pretend they're not there.' He says people are hoping that Muslims will pretend some parts of the Qur'an aren't there either. 'There's that hope that there will be that reformation in Islam.'

The federal attorney-general said this week that he wants to introduce a new criminal offence: 'advocacy of genocide'. He was reacting to a Hizb-ut-Tahrir leader who cried at a rally, 'Judgement Day will not come until the Muslims fight the Jews. Tomorrow you Jews will see what will become of you – an eye for an eye, blood for blood, destruction for destruction.'

'They're passing laws that do almost criminalise using the Qur'an to preach,' Hamza says of the proposed law. And with this, Hamza says what the attorney-general doesn't. And what writers in the newspapers don't, through lack of knowledge or because it's just too awkward. The Hizb-ut-Tahrir man didn't pluck those words from thin air.

'No one has been prosecuted yet for quoting a verse of the Qur'an,' Hamza says. 'But if they come out and say, "We want to ban the Qur'an altogether"? Man, go for it. Maybe that will wake the Muslims up, and they can go home.' Home being the Islamic State.

I tell Hamza about the latest rallies. 'We have this strange sort of . . . like we see eye to eye,' he says of the UPF. 'We agree on refugees. We don't want them coming here and we want every Muslim to leave Australia. Both of us are saying that. We're not friends, but we agree.'

I tell him what the left-wing folks at rallies say about why people want to fight for ISIS. 'Because Muslims feel oppressed in Austra—'

'I'm sick of hearing that. Look. I can go around here.' He motions out the front window of his unit, looking out on the street. 'I don't have problems. I know that if I want to live for material purposes and I want to live a good worldly life, I would stay here. A lot of people ask why are Muslims not attacking Australia yet? Why haven't we seen —' He interrupts himself, perhaps recalling the Lindt Café siege or the worker killed at the Parramatta police station. 'Look, it's

not as if it hasn't happened, but nothing large has happened. I tell
you, at least from ones that I know, they would say, "Look, we've got
problems with the Australian government. But the Australian people, most of them are pretty cool." They don't want to harm them.
They want to harm Australian soldiers. They want to harm police-
men. They want to harm politicians. That's why the average people
are fine. Most Australians are very easygoing. It's hard to have any
problems with them.'

Because I'm something approximating a journalist I bring up
'Unemployment in La—'

'John,' he moans. 'Let me count every single person I know who
has left. None of them are unemployed. None. Not a single one.
Some of them were the most wealthiest of all. This is a purely religious thing. These people want to go there to be part of the land of
the Muslims. On top of this, they also want to fight to strengthen
the State. On top of this, they want to die to establish the State.'
Hamza heads to the kitchen. 'Again, since I've seen you, I've had,
I think, three people I know die in Iraq or Syria.'

Every time I come over for a play date, Hamza drops a line that
snaps me wide awake.

FARMER JOHN

Undercover brother

I push through the door of the spray tan salon. My month-old beard is bushy and strong. This morning I caught a cab from my flat to the costume shop. I was just browsing for Coke bottle glasses to make my eyes look different, but when I told the dude behind the counter the plan he thought the beard and glasses weren't enough to de-Safran me. The plan is to sneak into an Australian Liberty Alliance meeting this evening and find out if Debbie Robinson is a Jewess, leading a secret Jewish group plotting a war against Muslims. I told him about the characters who rock up to these things: the Blairs, the bikies, the gronks, the Farma Johns. The dude liked the sound of Farma John, so he did me up in this akubra, these mirror glasses, this flannel shirt and jeans.

Okay, I'm stripping that all off here at the spray tan salon, to get rid of my signature pastiness. A woman hands me a paper G-string.

By late afternoon I've landed in Sydney for the ALA meeting. I've hooked up with my friend Soph. She's cocooned in a fur coat and wearing earrings that dangle like chandeliers. I asked her to dress as a wealthy Jewess and she's gone the full yenta. (Soph is actually a Jewess.) I adjust my akubra hat and admire my bronzed forearms as we wait in Soph's apartment.

Not long before kick-off time, her phone buzzes. It's the ALA text message revealing the secret location. The meeting will be held in a hotel conference room in the CBD. We must arrive by seven pm. Security will be tight. Must bring driver's licence or passport.

I can't whip out my own ID tonight so instead I'm Joseph Inkerman. I pull my fake New South Wales driver's licence from my pocket and pass it over to Soph. I lied to a prop maker. I told him I was shooting a police drama and needed the licence for a scene where a cop pulls me over.

Soph looks nervous. The licence seems fine to my Melbourne eyes, but the texture just doesn't feel right to her. The prop man pressed up three licences, each a different thickness. Soph rubs her fingertips over them and is unimpressed by all.

We jump into a cab.

The cab slows down in front of the hotel. Oh my god, that's Ralph loitering. My Farmer Joseph Inkerman disguise better work.

I tell the cabbie to keep driving and Soph and I hop out a block up from the hotel.

Why's Soph coming? I want her to confront Debbie Robinson, so Debbie will have less wiggle room. She can't claim she won't answer because it's Safran the Public Nuisance Loon throwing her the question.

Ralph watches the farmer and the mink-coated lady drift down the street. He's suspicious of us. But he's also eyeing other folks and he's suspicious of them too. By the time we pass him he's moved on to other things, blabbing to some bloke. I've gotten away with it. Ralph doesn't know it's me.

A line stretches through the hotel lobby. At the front of the line stands a security guard, gripping a metal-detector wand and letting people through a door to a little room. And in that little room – is it? I squint. Yes, it is: Debbie Robinson, pacing.

Soph and I join the line in the lobby. The sun is beaming through big glass windows, so it's not weird that I'm behind mirror sunglasses. I also don't stand out because, as I predicted, oddities are everywhere. A man in a too-tight leather vest and red bow tie. A millennial with molehills of dandruff atop his shoulders.

The line creeps along. Two men are twanging that they like Donald Trump because he doesn't give a faaark about political correctness.

We reach the front and the security guard waves his wand over Soph's fur coat. No beep. He waves the wand over me. No beep. The guard ushers us through the door into the little room. I see that it leads to a bigger room, and at the door of this bigger room stands Debbie Robinson, welcoming each attendee. Before we can go in there, we have to head to the table in this little room. A man in a suit sits with a biro, checking off names. I pull my fake licence from my flannel shirt pocket and rub it between my fingertips. Soph points to our names on the list. The man ticks us off. He doesn't ask for our IDs. Don't know why.

We're now far from the glassy entrance of the hotel, so it doesn't make immediate sense that I'm wearing mirror sunglasses. Or an akubra hat. But I've locked into my brain that this is what Farma John might well wear if he were here, so I hold my nerve. Soph and I walk fake-confidently over to Debbie.

'Helloooo,' gushes Soph, like they catch up for coffee each Wednesday.

'Helloooo,' returns Debbie.

I hold out my hand, nod, and offer the softest of grunts. My lisp is my fingerprint. Can't risk opening my mouth. Debbie narrows her eyes.

'Hello,' she says, with almost a question mark at the end.

In the conference room Angry Anderson – the Rose Tattoo singer, in case you know of another one – leans his bald head towards the microphone on the podium and snarls a welcome. He will be MCing tonight. Angry explains that he'll be running for the senate for Australian Liberty Alliance. Malcolm Turnbull hasn't called the election yet, but everyone thinks it'll happen any day now.

Soph and I tuck ourselves into one of the rows of seats. Not too far to the back. That might make us look like we've got something to hide. Not too far to the front, because we do have something to hide. Over a hundred folks have shown up. The crowd isn't the Pastor Daniel rainbow coalition. Nearly all are white and middle-aged or beyond. Christ, that's me too.

My mirror glasses and akubra have been noticed. Angry Anderson, glancing over, makes a crack about watching out for the person next to you. He or she might have come along to spy. I think he thinks I might be a socialist ratbag. As opposed to thinking I'm that TV prankster.

He introduces a senate candidate with blond hair and reads through her bio. At the bit where it mentions she's married, he adds that he hopes she has a sister.

The senate candidate takes the microphone. It's Islam this, Islam that for half an hour. Then Angry returns and takes another swipe. He says if you want to look inconspicuous you don't wear a hat and sunglasses indoors at night. I call Angry's bluff and just sit there with my arms folded. The ALA director, the man who blocked me from the Parliament House lawn in Perth, wanders over. He takes a squiz at me and moves along.

Question time! Angry says this Q&A will be better than the ABC's *Q&A*. I elbow Soph and she saunters in her fur coat towards the microphone set up in the aisle. She's number four in a short queue. A half-dozen senate candidates smile out the front, fielding the friendly questions. Angry's checking out the blond candidate's legs.

It's Soph's turn. She leans into the microphone. 'Hello, thank you for tonight,' she begins. We've workshopped her question: 'I'm interested in some of your other policies. Such as your foreign policy towards Israel, which I really like as my family has a Jewish background. I was just wondering, Debbie, if you or any other directors of the party . . . what your religious background is, and if any of you are Jewish?'

Debbie's smiley face twists sour. 'Well, I'm . . .' she starts, and stops. 'I don't think that's relevant. We're a secular party. It's not relevant whether we're Jewish, Christian, no matter what we are.'

'Sorry, I didn't mean to insult you.'

'You didn't insult me —'

'I just don't think the question was answered, so —'

'I just don't think it's relevant! I don't think it really matters. In this particular country it doesn't matter where you come from.'

One of the male senate candidates chimes in: 'Religion doesn't come into play in this party.'

Religion doesn't come into play in this anti-Islam party?

Debbie says the time for questions is over. Soph falls into a conversation with one of the candidates by a big glass bowl of mints and I wait out the front of the hotel, the night air goosebumping my tanned forearms. My head's starting to itch from the akubra.

Debbie and her entourage file out, wheeling overnight bags. A bouncer in a suit is guarding their mini-van.

'G'day,' I say to Debbie as she passes. 'I'm pretty confused about why, if a whole party's got to do with religious background, you won't talk about your religious background.'

'This has nothing to do with religiousness!'

I walk after her. 'But it's got to do with Islam.'

'It's done, it's done, it's done for the night,' utters the bouncer, pushing himself between Debbie and me.

'It's no one's business!' shouts Debbie.

'But . . . if . . .' I struggle. 'Then why is being Musli—'

'It's done, mate, it's done.'

Debbie is about to climb in the van, but halts. She turns and stands on her tippy-toes to see over the bouncer. 'John Safran?'

I remove my mirror sunglasses. 'Yes.'

'The person who was stalking people in Perth! I know all about you. Keep away or I will get the police and have you arrested.'

'Thank you,' says the bouncer. 'Goodbye.'

As the van drives off I see a man down the end of the road under a streetlight. It's Ralph, squinting at me.

Back at my hotel I've been punished by God for buying carbs after the ALA meeting. I put the beef pastry in the oven here and it burnt and set off the alarm, and then two employees ran up. That *whoosh* sound, that's the blades on the industrial fan they brought up. And they're telling me the fire department has to come now, because that's the regulation.

Anyway, that's not what I wanted to tell you. While that's all been happening, a random has shot through a message: 'Hi John, I just noticed Ralph Cerminara released a video of you. That guy's a real scumbag.'

I head for Ralph's Left Wing Bigots Exposed. Ralph has written above a video: 'As promised, left wing bigot reporter and supporter of Islam John Safran.'

I click 'play'. There I am, sitting on a carpet. It's that lounge room at the UPF afterparty in Bendigo, following the huge rally. Ralph has blurred everyone out except for me.

Twangs a man in the blur, 'Smoke a joint. Get into it.'

Adds a woman, 'Suck it in.'

I draw back on the cigarette.

'Take a couple of puffs.'

A hand reaches in from the blur and passes me a bag of grass. I twitch the bag in my hands.

Ralph has typed under the video: 'Smoking pot. Your busted bigot.'

The footage hasn't been shot incidentally. Ralph passed me the joint and bag of grass so he could film me handling them. Wily goy.

I spool up his Facebook page and see he's been teasing this for a while: 'EXPOSED: Tonight we'll reveal a left wing reporter taking drugs and handling drugs. Yes, we have the video. This is going to be huge.'

Online, the left and right are united. The first comment under the video: 'Worst. Exposé. Ever. Who gives a fuck if Safran smoked a joint?' Meanwhile over at an anarchist page: 'Oh, the shock! Oh, the horror!'

Ralph starts arguing with his followers that this exposé shows I'm not of sound enough mind to discuss political matters. But everyone just starts chatting about the time I drank peyote on television.

Ralph battles on. He insists this proves I'm 'unwashed' and 'filthy' and 'like a bogan'.

Ralph, you idiot. So you know, for next time, when someone like me drifts into your circle, if you want to psych him out and damage his brand, go with the opposite: he's pretentious, he's a latte swiller, that sort of thing.

I love this bogan rebrand.

A new comment shoots through on Left Wing Bigots Exposed: 'I don't smoke but I could not give a toss if others do. Father Bob won't be impressed, though.'

THE MAGICAL KINGDOM

Tell me how you really feel

'We, French-Muslims, are ready to assume our responsibilities.' Dozens of celebrities and academics have written a letter to a Paris newspaper. The signatories say that local Muslim communities must work harder to stop the extremists in their midst, and to honour those killed the letter lists all the recent terrorist attacks in France.

Except one.

The one at the kosher deli.

'You are ready to assume your responsibilities,' writes a French Jewish leader in reply, 'but you are off to a bad start. You need to understand that these anti-Semitic attacks were committed against Jews, who were targeted for being Jewish. In any case we'll always be here to remind you.'

Those signatories aren't the only Muslims who believe in Jewish exceptionalism. From France to my home town:

I've seen the face of this famous-enough Muslim, an anti-racism activist, on all sorts of posters. MCing events in support of Muslims, Aboriginal Australians, immigrants and refugees. But I see today he's busy on Facebook, tormenting a family of Israeli immigrants (so, to be clear, Australians) who run the cafe around the corner from my flat. A Muslim friend of his wandered in for a snack a few hours ago and spotted an item on the menu: 'Israeli breakfast'. Finding out that the family running the cafe are Israeli, she lashed out at them, freaking out everyone in the cafe, and now the famous-enough Muslim is lashing out too, 'exposing' this family for being Israeli.

I'd thought that 'immigrants are welcome' – that's what's chanted at the rallies that the famous-enough Muslim MCs. His Facebook fans pile on: Jews are stingy, so no doubt this Israeli breakfast is the stingiest breakfast ever. That sort of thing. Both the famous-enough Muslim and his fans seem to think this cafe is part of some larger plot.

Maybe I'm missing something, so I walk around the corner and ask the dude behind the counter about the cafe. It's just a small business – Australian, run by the children of Israeli immigrants. The Israeli breakfast is soft-toasted challah (the braided bread Jews eat on the Sabbath) spread with hummus and avocado and poached eggs.

The next time I see the famous-enough Muslim, he's bellowing into a microphone on the steps of Parliament House about racist Australia.

First night of Chanukah

Christ, it's only been three weeks since the Paris massacre, after which Melbourne Jewish organisers cancelled Chanukah in the Park, fearing terrorism. The organisers have now reversed the decision but relocated the event behind walls, so folks can be frisked at the gates.

They have piggybacked on an existing event at a local racetrack: a two-week-long Santa's Magical Kingdom fair. As a rabbi put it in the *Jewish News*, for one night only his group will be 'transforming Santa's Magical Kingdom into a Chanukah Magical Kingdom! We're redoing it and taking over! It's beyond massive.' The rabbi assures the Jews they won't even know it's a Santa Magical Kingdom.

And now Soph and I pull through the entrance at the racecourse carpark. Soph's wrapped in the fur coat she wore to the ALA meeting. I had thought that was a one-night-only disguise but apparently it's her new look. Three teenagers in skullcaps and 'Chanukah Security' T-shirts watch the cars roll in. ISIS may have defeated the Kurdish fighters, but are they prepared for the three weedy Jews with bumfluff on their faces?

At the gates of the racecourse stand two more pencil-necked Chanukah Security kids. They ask me which night of the eight nights of Chanukah this is. Good grief. They're doing a lame version of the Israeli airport interrogation, where soldiers quiz people on Jewish matters to catch out terrorists posing as Jews.

'Goddamn let me in!' I snap. They let me in. I'm a bit on edge tonight. I can't stop thinking about the Israeli Breakfast Incident and that famous-enough Muslim.

The racecourse grounds are alive. Under the night sky, folks are gliding past fairy-floss machines and popping balls into the mouths at the Laughing Clown stall. I spot my friend's travel-agent mum. She's been dark on me ever since I revealed, in small talk at a funeral, that I book my flights on the web these days.

A man dressed as a dreidl hands me a jam doughnut. He whispers that he's an actor, if I ever need an actor for one of my shows.

Soph and I wander into the big top. Set up all around is a massive gingerbread and lollipop town. Bright lights flash, organ music grinds.

Something is off, though. And it takes a minute for my eyes to figure it out. Dotted throughout the candy-coloured wonderland are ominous black shapes. Shapes that remind me of the leaked photos of the hooded prisoners in Abu Ghraib, Iraq.

Good Lord! They're the Christmas trees! The Jews have thrown black sacks over all the Christmas trees.

I twirl around. There's more than just that. What appears to be a dozen Muslim women in burqas are gathered by a sled in the snow. I tilt my head down. Elves' boots are poking out from the black sacks. The Jews have burqa'd Santa's elves.

Soph taps me on the shoulder and points up. A huge black shape nearly reaches the top of this big top. The Jews have burqa'd the giant centrepiece Santa. When I squint I can make out the tip of his red cap.

We burst out laughing and can't stop. We stumble through the tents and the outdoor exhibits, tears in our eyes. Elves are out, the rabbinical organisers have decreed, but reindeer are allowable. No black sacks for the reindeer. I pull on Soph's coat and impersonate a wheezy New York rabbi handing down this decision: 'How are reindeers Christmassy? Were there not two reindeer on the ark?'

Soph folds over, howling.

Imagine the front page of the *Herald Sun* – the local Murdoch tabloid – had Australian Muslims taken over Santa's Magical Kingdom and blackened out all things Christmas. Creeping sharia! War on Christmas! In fact things are more stark than that. The *Herald Sun* is sponsoring tonight, handing out free papers to us Jews.

I noticed something else when I was up in Sydney for the Cronulla anniversary pig-spit. In Martin Place, not far from the Lindt Café, stood a giant candelabrum – a Chanukah menorah. Imagine the meltdown had that been, I don't know, a giant Muslim prayer rug? A giant Mecca compass?

That's the analysis of the situation I'm meant to give, isn't it? The docile one. The one that would earn me a round of applause and a pat on the head on *Q&A*.

But there's another way to look at the situation, isn't there? How about this. When the hostage pressed the black flag against the window at the Lindt Café, there was Arabic lettering on it, not Hebrew. Maybe that's why the Martin Place passers-by don't mind a Chanukah menorah.

What is wrong with me? We've been driven behind walls because Muslim terrorists target Jewish events, and I've twisted it into a story of 'Jewish privilege' over the poor Muslims? We were happy out in the public park last year.

In fact, isn't this turn of events just like Houellebecq said it would be in his novel? Little incremental changes to make way for the new way?

Fuck you, famous-enough Muslim. (I'm still stewing over him.

Is that what's behind my bitterness tonight?) I thought you and your pals only had a problem with Jews in Israel. Seems like you've got a problem with Jews who've left Israel too. Side note: Did it occur to you that leaving Israel to set up in Australia is reverse Zionism? Although I guess the family who runs the cafe will never erase the stain of being descendants of apes and swine. That will follow them everywhere. But hey, maybe I'm looking at this the wrong way. Maybe I should drop in on Mrs Sneer and Mr Snort at the Melbourne Anarchist Club and they can explain to me how spreading avocado over soft-toasted challah is in fact structural violence. Hang on – of course, how could I miss it? There was hummus mixed in there too! Cultural appropriation! Oh, the humiliation! Yes, Muslim buddies, I've read your complaints about the Jews 'stealing' hummus. Hey, friendly reminder, you ripped off all our Torah stories for your Qur'an. Hashtag CulturalAppropriation. Hashtag IslamIsIggyAzalea.

I look over to the racetrack. A rabbi is gliding up into the air on a cherry picker to light the candles on the huge menorah. He sings the prayer and adds a little sermon, telling us we Jews are the canaries in the coalmine.

We've escaped the racecourse and have already gulped two cocktails each at the bar down my street. Now Soph has pulled a bottle of Japanese whiskey from her fur coat. She's pouring shots for the bar staff and they're playing along with the fun, although their eyes are darting around, looking out for the boss – presumably this is a fireable offence. We wobble out the door. Wobble past the shoe repair under the bridge, my grandparents' old shop.

Now, ten minutes later, I'm pacing in my lounge room. Soph has sunk into a big red chair. The Houellebecq book is on the coffee table. So is Pastor Daniel's *Worship Under the Sword*. And the one about the Warsaw Ghetto Uprising, and others.

I pull out my dictaphone. I tell Soph to ask me about the books. I need to get this down.

'Okay,' she slurs as I hit 'record'. 'What are you reading?'

'*Flags Over the Warsaw Ghetto: The Untold Story of the Warsaw Ghetto Uprising.*' I pick it up.

'Do you like it?'

'I think it's radicalising me,' I tell her and the dictaphone. 'I'm reading and I start thinking, Fuck, like I owe it to the Jews, and the Jews should really stick together and not trust anyone. Because in it, the sort of poncier Jews in the Warsaw Ghetto, they were like, "Don't worry, the Polish underground will help us" – the non-Jewish ones. And they just don't. And you think, you've got to stick up for yourself.'

Soph's drinking from the whiskey bottle but looking at me closely.

'It seems,' I say, 'like these hardline right-winger Jews who were more mercenary – if the softer, poncier Jews had gone along with them, they might have been in a better position.'

'To do what, though?'

'To fight back against the Nazis! Yeah, but it's more like looking at how this projects onto the future. Don't let this fucking happen again. I know it's far lower-stakes, but when a Muslim attacks a rabbi on the synagogue grounds, it's like the socialists at the rallies, they look away because, oh, it's a bit awkward.'

I stare at the burning building on the book's cover. 'And you also think, Why did they choose to get on the trains? All five hundred thousand of them. It's embarrassing.' I fling the book back on the coffee table with the others. The truth of what I've just said hits me. All these books *have* been radicalising me, while I've been whining about the Torah and the Qur'an.

The Socialist Children's Union

It's good to get smashed on Japanese whiskey once in a while. I didn't connect the dots before tonight. Why the socialists drive me crazy with their theories on different categories of violence and which ones are important and which ones aren't. I've been hanging with the local socialists but my connections run deeper than that. My grandparents were proper high-stakes socialists in Poland before the war. Part of the Bund, who were the opponents of the Zionists. The Bund thought you should be able to live as a Jew in Poland or anywhere in the world. The Zionists said the Jews needed a homeland to be safe. The Bund was very popular – it ran schools and everything – until the Holocaust.

My grandparents fled the Nazis (my mother was born mid-journey, in Uzbekistan) and they arrived in Australia on a boat.

'Well, that didn't work out,' most of the Bund folks thought of their ideology, reflecting on the concentration camps. So they dumped socialism and turned Zionist. Except for a tiny band of Jews, including my grandparents. These Jews continued the socialist dream. They set up a Bund in Melbourne, with a youth division, the

Socialist Children's Union (Sotsyalistishe Kinder Farband, or SKIF).

I remember the derision from my friend George Weinberg when I headed off to SKIF meetings and summer camps. He echoed the wider Jewish community's sneer. Even after the Holocaust you morons don't think we need Israel? A backup plan, somewhere we can flee? And lately, reading those books and attending the rallies, I can't get it out of my head: what if the sneerers were right and my grandparents wrong?

Wait till Ralph finds out I grew up in the Socialist Children's Union. Surely an update for Left Wing Bigots Exposed.

THE HUSTINGS

The election

Malcolm Turnbull walks to the podium. 'The governor-general has accepted my advice to dissolve both houses of parliament effective tomorrow morning. And call an election for both houses.' The prime minister blinks from the camera flashes.

Three years ago – the last time Australia voted – there was no Australian Liberty Alliance (Q Society), Fortitude (UPF), nor other anti-Islam parties like Love Australia or Leave.

Malcolm Turnbull makes less of a hoo-ha about Muslims than his predecessor, Tony Abbott. So one line of thinking is that Liberal voters seething about Islam will jump to one of the minor parties. Maybe one of these radicals will get into the senate.

Two nights after the prime minister's announcement, Pastor
Daniel, who is running for the senate along with other members
of his party, has posted a photo on his Facebook page. The pastor
sits in a restaurant, smiling, next to fellow senate hopeful Pauline
Hanson. Written underneath: 'Tonight national president of Rise
Up Australia Party Daniel Nalliah met with One Nation's Pauline
Hanson for discussions. Stay tuned for more news leading into the
upcoming federal election.'

Pauline's grinning so widely her eyes have stretched and she
looks kind of Asian.

As well as a wooden cross as tall as himself, and an Australian
flag, there's now a VOTE RISE UP banner taking up space in Pastor
Daniel's office.

'I'm so old,' I tell the pastor from across his desk, 'I remember
with my own eyes and ears that last time around Pauline Hanson
was worried about Asian people. She wasn't worried about Muslims.'

'Actually, I was not in the country at that time.' Pauline served
federal parliament from 1996 to '98. Pastor Daniel was arriving as an
immigrant just as she was leaving office. 'But that's what I'm understanding too.'

Pastor Daniel tells me he has been 'educating her on the teachings of Islam' for a while. Guiding her through the Qur'an. As with
the Chinese in Mildura, he got there before anyone else did.

So he's responsible for the Pauline reboot? Easing her from the
Asian peril to the Muslim peril?

'Today in society you've got to be absolutely duh if you don't know Islam is a problem,' he says.

'Does she still have a problem with Asian immigrants?'

Pastor Daniel motions to the Facebook photo on his laptop: Pauline and him grinning in the restaurant. 'If that's the case, I don't think she'll be sitting next to me.'

On the way out of Pastor Daniel's office, I spot Rosalie Crestani. The whitey who thanked the traditional owners of the land at my first Reclaim rally is now unfurling a banner in Rise Up Australia's campaign office, upstairs at the church.

'We're in a spiritual war,' she says of this election. Rosalie is running for the senate too. 'I'd tell you more but you'll think I'm nuts.'

I tell her if that's the case I definitely want to hear it.

'God has got a special calling for Australia in the End Times,' she reveals. 'I believe we are in the End Times. We are coming to a very crucial time in human history.'

So, like everyone from the anarchists' CEO to Hamza, she's convinced we're on the cusp of something new.

'Wow. Why Australia specifically?'

'Just looking at some of the prophecies that have been spoken. We have been called the Great South Land of the Holy Spirit.' I find out that some believe, based on the writings of an old Portuguese explorer, that the Messianic age will play out in Australia. 'Now, I'm not a theologian, but Daniel Nalliah is meant to be part of that plan.'

I glance through the pastor's window on my way out. He's alone, praying on his knees, face tilted up to God. Or just the grey ceiling of his office, depending whether you think Rosalie is nuts or not.

I stride towards Pauline Hanson, who is meeting and greeting voters at the entrance of an Adelaide shopping centre.

'I wasn't going to do the interview with you,' she twangs. 'Did you get my message that I wasn't going to do it?'

I babble out some weasel then cut to the point. That she fought against immigration from Asia in the '90s, but is now political buddies with Pastor Daniel who immigrated from Asia in the '90s. 'Please explain.'

'Was that my immigration policy?' she snarks. 'You're incorrect.'

'You weren't against Asian immigration?' I squeak in disbelief.

'No.'

'Oh my god.' I don't quite know what to say. 'You do know there were cameras back then?'

'I never did —'

'There must have been a bit of miscommunication. Because I was there first time around and there was definitely —'

'The media never got it right.' She pouts. 'I am sick of the misperception!'

How has she spun things around so she's the victim in all this?

I stand my ground and insist that if she's not against Asian immigration now, she must have changed her mind on the matter. 'How do I know I'm not going to bump into you in fifteen years' time and you're going to be —'

'Wearing a burqa?'

'Yeah, and you're going to have some excuse abou—'

'It won't happen,' she promises. 'I will never wear a burqa!' She turns and walks through the shopping centre doors.

I'm left there thinking about what Aboriginal people say – that

Australians have wilfully erased from their memories what has happened in the past. Add another thing to the list. As well as no white invasion in 1788, Pauline Hanson wasn't against Asian immigration in the 1990s.

I wander through the shopping centre myself and chat to shoppers who say they will vote One Nation. I ask them about Pauline's spiky views on religion and race. They all ease, straight away, into something else – Pauline's struggle as a regular Australian and how much they admire that. More fat for my theory: Australia doesn't do radical, and for this anti-Islam thing to work it's going to have to seem as normal as a trip to the beach.

As well as remembering Pauline Hanson the first time around, I remember the late 1980s. The artists formerly ahead of the curve, like Prince and Michael Jackson, feared a new sound, hip-hop, was taking over. So they'd crowbar a rap interlude into their remixes. These rap interludes couldn't help but sound like cynical efforts to stay in the game.

Pauline Hanson's not the only superstar of old crowbarring anti-Islam into the remix. Reverend Fred Nile, founder of the Christian Democratic Party, is touring the country to promote candidates running in the election. This reverend lives in my head as a faint childhood memory, along with Ossie Ostrich and icy-poles from the milk bar. He would pop up on the news as a fuddy-duddy.

'There is no liberalism or modernism in our party,' he croaks this evening from a town hall podium in Melbourne's inner north. He promises that his party will oppose government programs that push 'the ridiculous idea that gender is fluid'. He had seen on television a mum laying out 'a girl's dress and a boy's uniform, saying to her son, 'Which one will you wear today?''

He's speaking to an audience notable for its lack of Anglo-Saxons. Instead there are Egyptian, Syrian and other Middle Eastern and African Christians.

'It may sound strange,' the reverend tells me later as we tuck into the night's dinner. 'I get on better with the ethnic people than I do with a lot of the white people.'

'Why is that?'

'I don't know. I just seem to be able to relate to them and I'm more popular. I get invited to all their churches, whereas I think the strict Anglicans and Baptists are a little bit weary of Fred.'

I tell him I've noticed that white Christians weasel. They won't cough up why they believe what they believe. So there'll be a white guy from the Christian lobby on *Q&A* and he'll recast his religious belief as something other than religious. He'll say his problem with gay marriage is that it 'breaks with Australian tradition'. Meanwhile Pastor Daniel's new immigrants don't give a hoot. They just don't get that you're not meant to say that you think homosexuality is wrong because the Bible says so.

Reverend Fred Nile agrees that immigrants, like the ones in this room, are the best foot soldiers for his brand of hardline Christianity. They're replenishing the troops as white Australians give up the faith, or become those sappy PC Christians who substitute climate change for the Devil.

Bolstering his Christian army isn't something new for Fred. 'When the war came to a conclusion in Vietnam I set up a special committee to help bring Vietnamese refugees to Australia. Most of them were Catholic.'

'Was that important?'

'It made me much more sympathetic than if they were Hindus.'

He clicks out a throat lozenge from a packet and says that without the immigrant vote, he doubts he'd still be in parliament to fight his war against gay rights.

Strange, I think to myself, how immigration and multiculturalism are seen as victories for the left.

Like Pauline Hanson, Reverend Fred Nile has only recently rejigged his shtick to include concern over Islam. 'No Halal Tax On Easter Eggs!' reads one of his press releases.

'I do attend all the Islamic events,' he tells me. 'They invite me as a member of parliament. My wife, Silvana, it's always nice how well she gets along with all the young Muslim women.' Reverend Fred Nile looks nervous for the first time. 'I probably shouldn't be telling you this.' As with Blair, it won't be good for business if it gets out that he's not a heartfelt Islamophobe.

Reverend Fred Nile says there may be tensions now, but he can envisage a future where Christians and Muslims come together and march against the homosexuals.

I told the reverend that Pastor Daniel doesn't weasel like his Caucasian counterparts, but it's still easy to misunderstand why, ultimately, the pastor has a problem with mosques and the Qur'an. It's not to do with terrorism. As revealed in his trial for religious vilification, he thinks Islam is satanic, on a par with witchcraft. A secular dude might be fine with Islam if terrorism dried up. But this would not placate Pastor Daniel. The Qur'an, to him, is a spiritual danger.

People, peaceful and decent, will end up in hell if they follow it. And that's why he must fight Islam.

Pastor Daniel and Hamza might be on the sharp end of things, but their extremeness flushes out the mindset of the devout: magical thinking, seeing patterns in the world, a sense that there are no coincidences, a determination that friends and strangers must be saved, karma and providence. I read a poll that ranked countries by how important their people consider religion to be. Australia lay near the bottom of the list. At the top of the list were countries like the Philippines, India, and Muslim lands – countries from where our new immigrants are coming. I don't know if terrorists are crossing our borders, but magical thinkers – pixies – certainly are. This is why Australia will change. I know this because I'm a pixie myself. I just crossed over to your side momentarily to warn you.

There's one more party I need to drop in on, the just launched Australian Muslim Party. There's a particular policy I'm interested in. But first I stop off for a coffee.

'What's the go with the beard?' a Muslim dude asks me in a cafe in Lakemba. (Second visit and still no beating, Ralph.) 'Is it a religious thing? A Jewish thing?'

'Nah, it's just a beard.' (My disguise beard has become just a beard.)

We've been chatting about how he thought I was an atheist. 'My friends think you're funny, but we thought you were atheist. You mock God and you do it for fun.'

'In Judaism you're allowed to.'

'Yeah, we are not allowed to,' he says, a little mopey.

I tell him what I read in a book by an Australian Muslim, Hanifa Deen. She lists the different levels of offensiveness. I tell him her impression of how Muslims judge offence. 'She says, "Oh, on the lower end, there are things like calling someone a raghead on the train. Right up to the highest end, which would be insulting the Prophet." To me, that list is the wrong way around. Maybe that's the Clash of Civilisations.'

The dude warns me not to do a show in Syria. 'There's no trial there, you understand? They don't trial you.'

'Worse than a bad review.'

Soon I'm out of the cafe and trotting up a staircase to the offices of a new political force. The young, sharply dressed man, Diaa Mohamed, runs the Australian Muslim Party, which plans to run in the election. The offices are freshly painted and relentlessly bright white. In the Ikea picture frames on the wall, Diaa has kept the photos that came with the frames. Which is okay with the roses, but weird with the stock-photography families.

'There's a Christian party – Christian Democratic Party. We go off the similar idea as Fred Nile and what he's doing,' Diaa explains.

We sit down at the Ikea boardroom table and I ask, 'What is the Australian Muslim Party's public television policy? Would it allow religious satire on the ABC and SBS?'

'I don't mind anyone criticising Islam as a religion,' Diaa says. 'As long as it's not offensive.'

'Like the *Charlie Hebdo* guys —'

'That's offensive. They knew what they were doing, and they did it on purpose to get a reaction, and they got a reaction. It was a big reaction, and I'm not saying I agree with it, but they knew what they were doing. They were trying to incite or provoke. Why are you trying to do that? I don't understand. What are you getting out of it?'

'One of the *Charlie Hebdo* cartoons was making fun of imams —'

'One of them was drawing a picture depicting the Prophet Mohammed, which they know we don't allow.'

I tell him what I read in Hanifa Deen's book, and that I think the list is the wrong way around. 'It's unacceptable to say something bigoted to someone on a train,' I tell him. 'It seems like a lesser thing to be insulting an idea in a book.'

'If someone swore to your mum on the train, what would your reaction be? You'd go, "I might get angry, I might get physical. There might be a fight." We love the Prophet Mohammed much, much, much more than we love our mothers, or fathers, or kids. That's why it's the most offensive.'

Muslims believe that Moses and Jesus Christ were also prophets. So they too are not to be insulted. Diaa spins this as evidence of his dedication to multiculturalism. See, the Jewish and Christian prophets would be protected too.

'Let's not talk about Islam,' I say. 'Let's talk about the Torah. There's a law where you can stone the homosexuals. You can kill a witch! Isn't it inconsistent to say, We, as religious people, should be allowed to express these offensive things, but you're not allowed to be offensive in response?'

'I don't think the Qur'an has anything offensive in it.'

'What about the talking tree?' I say of the hadith. '"Hey, there's a Jew behind me. Come and kill him." As a comedian, and as a Jew, why wouldn't it just be totally acceptable – the most normal thing in the world – for me to make fun of that?'

Diaa strokes his beardless chin. 'Are you killing him because he's a Jew? Or are you killing him because you're fighting a Jew? See the difference?'

I don't understand what this means. But it's his explanation for why the passage isn't offensive and therefore not deserving of ridicule. I try again. 'But am I allowed to say that it is ridiculous, and Mohammed is ridiculous for coming up with this?'

'No. You can't say Mohammed is ridiculous. You say, "What he said, it sounds ridiculous, and I don't believe it." There's no need to insult the person.'

'He started it.'

Diaa looks at me firmly. 'Like I said, we love Mohammed more than we love our family.'

'I was watching this – there's this Jewish comedian, Mel Brooks. And in one of his sketches he's Moses.' Diaa looks unimpressed. 'He holds up three tablets and goes, "My people, these are the Fifteen Commandments," and then he accidently smashes one of the tablets and he goes, "My people, here are the Ten Commandments."'

Diaa's nostrils start flaring.

'And I just think, religion's really potent and tense and it's probably healthy that Mel Brooks is —'

'Nah, I don't think so,' Diaa rules.

Diaa's not the only Australian with an opinion on who should be able to say what and when. Dvir Abramovich, chairman of a local Jewish group, the Anti-Defamation Commission, is presently denouncing a play written by a Palestinian Australian, Samah Sabawi, saying that the love story set in Gaza should not be taught in high schools. More outrageously, Dvir once denounced *John Safran's Race Relations*.

Avi is inserting himself in the free speech debate too. He has written a column supporting Pauline Hanson's desire to, if elected, overturn racial vilification legislation. Avi explains that he wants unfettered freedom to pay out on Muslims.

Now Avi's buzzing in my pocket. 'Do you think the Jews are going to turn on me?' he types. 'Because I've publicly supported Pauline Hanson?'

'Yes.'

'Yay!'

'Jews like that legislation, so they can go after Holocaust deniers.'

'Can't have it both ways.'

Avi says the sacred cow of the Jews would be open to attack in his free speech utopia. 'Let the Holocaust deniers say what they want!' he preaches to his online followers soon after our conversation. 'Let the Islam preachers say what they want!'

WHERE THE WILD THINGS ARE

Life of Pie

'The black is Islamic State. The green are the rebels. The red is the Syrian government. Yellow are the Kurds. Which makes it all quite confusing.'

Hamza is taking me through a map on his laptop.

'Why is the Iraqi government so bad at defending themselves?' I ask.

'Well, if you were paying attention to the song . . .'

I laugh. Not entirely sure why. He's just shown me a new ISIS music video on the TV. Funky graphics, bloody faces, jeeps skidding through sand. 'For the sake of Allah we will march to the gates / Of the paradise where our maidens await.'

Now Hamza continues: 'You would see how they sang, "We have men who love death just as you love your life."' He turns from the laptop on the dining table to me. 'I mean, would you want to die for no reason?' he asks. 'Like, let's just say tomorrow Israel calls you up and says, "John, we need you. We need you to defend Israel against the Islamic State." Honestly, would you go?'

'Uh . . . I'm not sure . . . I don't . . . But I'm too old.'

'I mean, you can live a comfortable life in Australia, why would you want to go there?'

'Yeah.'

'You wouldn't go, would you?'

'I see what you mean,' is all I'll say.

'So you can understand, therefore, why you've got ones who are fighting because they're either forced to, they're paid to. Then you've got people who, you know, martyrdom is actually their aim.'

The pug stares at me through the doorway.

'I remember there was a Russian general,' Hamza goes on, 'who said, "How can you defeat an enemy who looks down the barrel of your rifle and sees paradise?"' Hamza turns to his sister, who has wandered in from the kitchen. 'Did you put the shepherd's pie in yet?'

'No,' she says. 'I'm just waiting for the oven to preheat.'

'Okay.'

'You can't have the pie,' his sister says.

'Why not?'

'It's not halal meat.'

'Oh.'

She points towards his belly, hidden under his thawb. 'Remember, you're on your diet and you're going to have something else.'

'Oh yeah.'

Hamza is turning tubby, something well hidden by his Muslim muu-muu. But I'm not one to talk. Jim Saleam commented on his website after my visit: 'he's put on a bit of weight'. Wanting to take a swipe at another of his enemies, he attributed this to 'the ABC Christmas function'. Ralph, take a tip from Jim next time you want to take me down. I don't care if you call me a bigot, just don't call me fat.

J-Safe

'I'm at the shule around the corner,' Soph texts me. (Shule means synagogue.) 'A congregant stabbed another congregant!!! I'm texting from the bathroom. The police are here.'

The story has gone international by the next day. The *Times of Israel* reports: 'Man stabbed in synagogue over reported herring dispute.' (Nibbles are sometimes provided after a synagogue service.) Soph saw nothing, but the *Times of Israel* quotes a bystander: 'The man who was stabbed did not want to pass some herring to the other, who got angry, picked up a knife and stabbed him.'

But it is not Jew-on-Jew crime that has been weighing down this town. A gang called Apex, heavy in African immigrants, has been rolling through, carjacking and burgling houses for weeks.

Some young local Jews are pulling together a vigilante patrol. Their plan is to drive around the streets and keep the town safe. They're discussing it all on a private Facebook group:

'OK Guys. Right now we have two-man patrols going. Mendel and I do Sunday night. David and Manny do Tuesday night. You have until Sunday to find a partner and notify the group. Times and routes will be refined as we get more info. I want action and results. This group is not for pikers. It's for winners and winners get shit done. I don't care who your partner is. It can be your spouse or your mum. You need a partner. It's for safety. In the IDF and the police you get a partner. You build an organic relationship. I'm not here to hold your hand or make you feel good.'

Amazingly, Avi isn't behind this, although he can see he has missed an opportunity. He quickly concocts a competing Jew patrol, and a few days later *The Age* is reporting on Avi's new project, J-Safe. At this stage still only a Facebook page, J-Safe hopes to 'protect the Jewish community in Melbourne's south east' by providing a forum for locals to 'warn others about crime in real time'.

The local Jewish opera singer stops me outside the petrol station down my street. He's the one who told me to see Avi about the Q Society.

'Have you heard of Apex?' he asks. I can barely hear him because men and machines are ripping apart the petrol station to make way for apartments. He says his friend had a run-in with the Apex gang two weeks ago. 'They came out of this jeep and they had baseball bats and they pinned him down and started smashing the ground with the bat, and they demanded his credit card and passwords.' Something else is weighing on his mind. 'You could say these guys are African. But let's face it. It's Islam.'

I walk away from the noise and call Avi from outside a cake shop. I tell him what the opera singer said.

'No, he's an idiot,' Avi declares. 'He's wrong. They're South

Sudanese. They're actually Christian. Mate, I would be right onto it if they were Muslims.'

Of that I have no doubt. (By the way, he claims he now has three more Jews interested in his Israel Defense Forces training program.)

Avi might think the Jewish opera singer is fearmongering, but others are pointing that accusation at Avi himself. A Jewish security group, with trained volunteers, has been running for years in this town, so why is Avi setting up this renegade J-Safe?

George Weinberg is one of the trained volunteers. I call and ask what he thinks about Avi's new online group.

'I just think it should be called what it is. Which is: I-want-to-drum-up-some-business-for-my-martial-arts-gym-so-let-me-get-mental-and-drive-everybody-insane-so-that-Jews-are-too-scared-to-leave-their-house-at-night-and-I-can-put-the-third-level-on-my-house.com.au.'

The peacenik

Oh my god, good news. Although I'm scared to say it out loud in case I jinx it. The opera singer has sent me a text.

'Miriam from Q Society wants to meet with you.'

Is the opera singer in the Q society? Or does he just know of them? Of course I will meet her.

'What does Miriam do there?' I type.

'Founder.'

I don't understand. Did the opera singer mention my name to her? Or was it the other way around? And why now? After they stonewalled me at the Perth press conference, and my fight with

Debbie Robinson outside the ALA meeting, did the news of me not spread over their network? But I know from working at the ABC that the left hand doesn't always know what the right hand is up to. Miriam sounds like a Jewish name.

The opera singer says that Miriam will meet me in two days' time at a Middle Eastern cafe one suburb up.

Miriam, in her sixties, lights a cigarette. So that's why she wanted this outside table, despite the chill in the air. The bookshop next to the cafe is closing up for the evening; a man is carrying a sandwich board in from the street.

'I know you want to get inside,' she says of the Q Society. 'I don't know what you want to ask.'

I tell her I haven't plotted out exactly what I want to discuss. 'I'm not that clever.'

'Yes you are,' she says. 'You are a clever boy. You don't need to worry about that. If you're your father's son, you're very clever.'

It's hard to suppress my surprise. My dad knows the head of this secretive group I've been trying to infiltrate? 'Do you know my father?'

'Many years ago,' she says. 'He was quirky. I mean, if I remember rightly, he studied Russian when nobody else studied Russian.'

She draws back on her cigarette. 'I identify with you. I don't know everything about you, but whatever I've seen . . . I feel very akin in your journey, even though I did it thirty years before you. I didn't record it the same way that you do.'

She asks me with whom I've been speaking for my book. I tell her all sorts of folks, Muslim and non-Muslim.

'You know how Eskimos have ten words for white?' she says. 'Jews have about seven or eight words for joy? Muslims have about seven words for deception. When you speak to a Muslim you need to be conscious of that, even though they will say, "I don't know what you're talking about."'

Twilight begins settling in.

'I was a real peacenik,' she says, calmly stirring her coffee. 'I was very dedicated to love and harmony. I took it really seriously. I have travelled the world, from Sweden to India to Southeast Asia to Israel, right? I've been on your trip. Believe me. I've *om*ed. I've vomited. I went looking for God. I was so committed to peace and seeing that linking force – that we could live in a peaceful world. I even wrote a master's thesis on it. That was when you were a toddler. It's outdated now. My new information that I've learned – I sort of feel embarrassed. It doesn't hold. We need new paradigms. We have got to be cautious.'

So how did the Q Society begin? I ask her.

'It's no secret. We'd meet in a pub in Kew.' Kew is a leafy suburb in east Melbourne. 'Maybe 2009, 2010. I can't remember times. Everything is sort of tsemisht.' She squints. 'Do you speak Yiddish?'

'A bisl.' That's my joke. 'Bisl' means 'a bit', but I don't know much Yiddish beyond that word. 'Everything is sort of tsemisht' means 'everything is sort of mixed up'. Perfect.

The Q Society is so named 'because we met in Kew'. That's not a particularly Jewish suburb, I think to myself. For others in the group the Q stood for questions or Qur'an. 'Everybody made up their own shtick about it.'

The members knew each other before their pub days. But not

in real life. They met in anti-Islam forums on the internet. 'We said, "It's not time to be keyboard warriors anymore. It's time to educate."' They invited local speakers to the pub, then international speakers to other venues. And word spread around. They started as ten people and grew until there were chapters in other states. 'That's how the Q Society was born.'

The group expanded its aims. 'After a while, we'd write letters to the politicians, talk to the politicians. They give you lip-service, but they haven't got time to study Islam. They haven't got time to really see the truth.' So the Q Society 'launched Australian Liberty Alliance. We thought, We have got to create our own political party.'

'Is everyone in it Jewish?' I ask over the rattle of a tram.

'Are you a fool?'

'What?'

'Are you mad? Sorry, Jews? Jews are running from this! Jews do this moral equivalence.' She says Jews tell her that if halal is banned, kosher will be next. And they ask her how they can rise against Muslim immigration when they were immigrants themselves. 'If only Jews *would* be there. Then we would have a greater force and have much more money.' Like her enemies, she thinks the Jews are good with money. 'It's not a Jewish organisation. I wish more than anything it was. I wish more Jews would wake up. I'm a pariah. I've lost half of my Jewish friends.'

'How come they don't just accept that you're in the —'

'They're scared. They think I'm some sort of extremist. I'm not. I'm so mild.'

I realise now I can ask a certain question and it'll sound perfectly natural. 'What about Debbie Robinson? She's Jewish?'

'No,' Miriam says, adding, 'why is she Jewish?' Then she rattles off the company line I heard at the ALA meeting. The Q Society is a secular organisation. The religion of its members doesn't come up. In fact, she's never asked Debbie about hers, so she really doesn't know.

I laugh, remembering the last book I wrote, about a true crime. Each time I thought I'd secured the unquestionable truth from someone, that person would take a breath and add a qualifier. And I'd no longer hold the unquestionable truth.

I tell her that Neil Erikson had said the function he attended was like a Jewish wedding.

'How can you tell they're a Jew? Is it written on your forehead?' Miriam says that neo-Nazis (and John Safrans) conjure up conspiracies because the Q Society supports the Jewish state. 'We promote Israel because Israel is the first stop. Israel is the canary in the mine. Whatever will happen in Israel will happen further afield, down the line.'

She insists she has thoroughly investigated Islam. Even pulled on a burqa, 'just to know what it's like'. She recommends I try one myself. 'You've got to dress up in a burqa and run though the streets. It's fun.'

'Where'd you get your burqa from?'

'I had it made. Couture.' She says she didn't want to hand over money to a Muslim shop.

'How old were you?'

'Only five years ago. I wanted to prove to myself . . . A lot of women say they get harassed when they wear a burqa. But no one harassed me at all. No one even looked at me. They served me in the pub.'

She tells me I can borrow hers. 'It's a very interesting experience. It's extremely powerful being under a burqa.'

'Why is it powerful?'

'You can see everybody. They can't see who you are. It's an incredible thing. I'd hate to wear it all the time and eat spaghetti. That would be a nightmare, eating spaghetti with a burqa.'

Miriam asks me not to judge the Q Society. 'I'm telling you, there's a calibre of people there, you wouldn't believe it. We've got a lot of avant-garde people there. I hope you understand that. It's not some rabble-rousing group. I've never belonged to a group. Ask your dad. He'll tell you I was a big rebel.'

She lights her third cigarette. The tip glows in the night.

'I'll tell you something. It's not just that I've been on a similar journey. But knowing your parents and your grandparents, it makes me feel familiar with you, to be honest.'

'Borscht is for me,' my dad says to the waitress. A new Polish cafe has opened down my street.

My dad remembers Miriam and her family. When his father died – my dad was twenty-three at the time – he stood with the mourners around the grave. 'Miriam's mother had arrived late and then she abused me for not having given more specific directions in the funeral notice. That was the sort of woman she was.'

He recalls an earlier incident. When he was in grade three he was over at Miriam's house for a birthday party. 'I can remember all the parents were there, sitting right in a circle, and there would have been around a dozen kids there. We were all Jewish. And every child had to get up and either recite a poem or sing a song. This was out of the blue. What happened . . . the effect was so dramatic. I still remember it today. After every child, there was polite applause from the parents. Then I sang my song. There was a stunned silence and a look of horror. I said to my parents, "What is wrong? What happened?" They said, "Don't you worry." The following week at school I was sent out to Jewish religious instruction.' His parents weren't aware that class existed. 'I'd been going to the general Christian one and that's where I'd picked up my favourite song, which was "Away in a manger, no crib for a bed, the little Lord Jesus lays down his sweet head. I love the Lord Jesus . . ."'

I chuckle and slurp my chicken soup.

My dad says he wanted to return to the Christian class because that class was calm and orderly, while in the Jewish class the kids 'would virtually be swinging from the rafters like monkeys'. But he wasn't allowed back. He was stuck with the monkeys now.

The tinnie

My friend Mads is half Greek, half Welsh. Her brother spent a summer as a passionate Greek nationalist, Greek flag up on his bedroom wall. Then he just went back to being himself.

Mads elbows me as I'm driving. She's been spooling through her phone. She tells me the situation is pull-overable and I pull over the car. She pushes the phone in my face:

'Islamic preacher Musa Cerantonio among five arrested over alleged plan to join Islamic State.'

The police claim Musa and his mates drove to Bendigo, purchased a second-hand boat – seven metres long and thirty years old – and towed it 2800 kilometres to Far North Queensland. That's where the cops jumped them. 'It is believed police had been monitoring the men for weeks.' The police say Musa and co planned to pull the boat into the ocean and sail to Indonesia, then continue on somehow and join an Islamic State-linked terrorist group.

What a vivid scene – had they pulled it off. A little boat, lit by moonlight, bobbing through an impossibly vast sea. Musa out the front like Max in *Where the Wild Things Are*.

Back on earth: plotting to fight for ISIS can get you life in prison, the story says.

As the day rolls on, the story captures the imagination of Australia.

Musa and co are labelled the 'tinnie jihadists'. People are taking the piss, that the men thought they'd survive the boat trip.

I was used to the ABC hassling me for info about the mysterious jihadi. (I was pretty much the only journo he'd talk to.) But today commercial radio also came calling. One radio host left a voicemail message, speaking of Musa and co as if they were loveable larrikins, little Aussie battlers – punching above their weight.

I remember when I was hanging out with Musa over a year ago. We had wandered into the garage at his mum's house, hunting for a collection of cassettes: the Qur'an in audiobook. He wanted me to listen to them while driving. Boxes were piled all over. 'The problem is, I can't entirely remember where I put them.'

Magpies were screeching in the backyard.

'Here's a lot of CDs,' Musa said, digging through a box.

I poked my nose in another box and saw something familiar.

I had a very similar box stored away in a cupboard at home.

'*Mad* magazines,' I said. 'Are they yours?'

'Oh, yeah. I used to love *Mad* magazine as a kid.'

I had stumbled across my first *Mad* in grade six, at a school fete or something. I remember hyperventilating with laughter in a booth at a restaurant as my family chewed on their food. The mocking of the pompous, the ripping apart of the ridiculous ways humans think and act.

How could anyone who grew up with *Mad* magazine think ISIS is a good idea?

And then there I was sitting in the lounge room watching him and his brother spit lines at each other from Monty Python. Musa had grown up with them too. I had left his house concluding that, despite his solid sarcastic education, the Qur'an had won over *The Life of Brian*. But maybe I was wrong.

As the day wraps up, the deputy prime minister, Barnaby Joyce, is asked about Musa's alleged plot to escape Australia in a tinnie to fight for ISIS. 'It's like a Monty Python movie, he sneers. 'And it's come to an end. Welcome to the constabulary, you clowns.'

The news story said police are combing through Musa's computer and phone. And that they had been watching his house. Not to make this all about me, but have I been monitored? Are there long-lens photos of me walking past the ceramic owls in his mum's front garden? And my WhatsApp conversations with Musa – is an ASIO spook spooling through them right now? As I am:

'How'd the sacrifice go?' I'd typed, wanting an update on the Eid sacrifice. The one the organiser had barred me from attending.

'We're here now,' Musa typed back from the park. He then sent a photo of a sheep, its throat slit. A blood-covered knife lay by its side, in a patch of blood-smeared grass. 'That's not my one. I haven't done it yet.'

'Are you nervous?'

'Nah. Just waiting my turn.'

Then twelve minutes later: 'All done.'

The courtroom is spilling out into the foyer. I've only managed to hustle my way in by flapping my journalist union card. Beards, beards, everywhere beards. Young Muslim men in beanies and parkas. Thick necks and shorn heads, north, south, east and west. An oil painting of a distinguished white gentleman from a bygone age looks down on the court.

The magistrate is bristling. The young men in the front row, here to support Musa and his Mus'keteers, refused to stand as she entered the court. Musa's lawyer is trying to smooth things over. 'They stand for no one other than Allah, that's the basics of it, your honour.'

The magistrate seethes. She lectures the young Muslims on respect, for several minutes, but then carries on. They win.

The Mus'keteers file in, early twenties to early thirties. They are sealed behind glass that runs along one side of the courtroom. Musa looks . . . Well, he's taking this seriously. And he's standing up. Apart from Musa, I'm familiar only with Shayden Thorne. He joined Musa and me for dinner one night.

This is early days. Today only the charge – 'prepare to enter, or for another person to enter, a foreign country with an intention to engage in a hostile activity' – will be read out.

Shayden Thorne asks if he can have his glasses, currently in a drawer at home, delivered to his cell. The magistrate nods.

'I think your honour should be alerted that Mr Thorne is an indigenous person,' says the lawyer. 'That's usually recorded, your honour.'

'Absolutely.'

Another of the men asks if he can have his antidepressants delivered to his cell. They help ease his anxiety. The magistrate wants him to visit a psychiatric nurse.

No one asks for bail. The magistrate tells the lawyer and the men that they'll be returning to court in four months' time. (That won't be the trial, just some more pre-whatever. The trial is who-knows-when.)

The Mus'keteers file out.

A hijab-clad woman standing in the wind outside the court says hello. 'I recognised your face.'

'I was just in court,' I say.

'Yeah, I know. My husband's one of the men.'

'Oh really?' What do I say? 'It's pretty crazy,' I manage, and think about their road trip from Melbourne to Far North Queensland.

'My husband goes camping and fishing all the time.'

Lost in translation

On the Friday before the election, Pastor Daniel and his political team are handing out pamphlets along a suburban shopping strip.

A shopper accepts one. '"Keep Australia Australian" means what?' she asks.

'Everyone that comes in assimilates into Aus—'

'No thanks, I'm not a racist.' She hands the pamphlet back.

Another shopper, after chatting with a Rise Up Australia member, holds up the pamphlet to me. 'That confuses me.' She points at the section explaining that 'multicultural' is bad, but 'multiethnic' and 'multiracial' are good. 'What's the difference?' she asks.

I've noticed that this scene – far left, far right – has as much specialty lingo as the Dungeons & Dragons scene. Antifa? Cultural Marxists? Structural versus non-structural violence? Multiracial versus multicultural? And the role-players forget that outsiders have no idea what they're banging on about.

Australia remixed

The senate ballot paper unrolls in the booth like a Torah scroll. Printed above the boxes are the party logos. But above the Australian Liberty Alliance candidates there is no logo. I can only assume it didn't have its shit together to send in the artwork on time.

To be fair, it has its shit together better than the UPF. Those guys failed to sign up the five hundred members needed to get their party, Fortitude, on the ballot. (I saw Blair last week screaming through a megaphone at a rally, 'I hate politics! You've been wasting your vote for seventy years or longer! This is where our fight is! This is politics now!')

And it has its shit together better than the Australian Muslim Party, which also failed to sign up five hundred. (And Diaa Mohamed, the dude I met, has been charged over an alleged fraud racket. 'The charge stems from cocaine allegedly found at Mr Mohamed's home during a search warrant,' reports the *Sydney Morning Herald*.)

I number the boxes.

By morning Pauline Hanson has declared victory. She has won a senate seat. And soon after that her party claims three more. The no-logo situation was indeed an omen: Australian Liberty Alliance comes up short. Pastor Daniel, the man who steered Pauline through the Qur'an, is also unsuccessful.

'Pauline Hanson is not a welcome presence on the Australian political scene,' said Malcolm Turnbull before the election, when he was throwing iftar dinners and his stock was high. But with his party just scraping through to victory, he's crowbarring something new into the remix.

'I respect her,' Malcolm says now. 'Half a million Australians voted for her.'

A fortnight later Pauline sits on the panel on *Q&A*.

'I do not believe that Islam is compatible with our culture and our way of life,' she begins with confidence. 'I am concerned for every one of you here in this audience tonight and everyone at home, because I want safety on our streets.'

I gulp. A few months ago an ABC radio host announced that he would not give airtime to extremist groups like the UPF or Reclaim Australia. That style of talk was for Facebook pages and the dark corners of the net, he said, not for prime time.

'This hatred wasn't created by me,' Pauline continues. 'It is under the belief of Islam. Read the Qur'an and what the Qur'an preaches.'

A month ago Australian Liberty Alliance had its advertising rejected by Murdoch newspapers. Its sharp talking points went too far for the mainstream.

'Islam does not separate itself from political ideology,' Pauline goes on. 'Whereas Christianity, under the Westminster system, does separate the rule of law.'

The Facebook talking points from the outlier groups are now on the telly. And in the senate.

She rolls into something that sounds pure Pastor Daniel. We are not a multicultural country, 'we are a multiracial nation'.

Pastor Daniel Nalliah, Ralph Cerminara, Blair Cottrell, Shermon Burgess and Debbie Robinson were all just a bit *too* strange to be elected, it seems. Nonetheless their ways have broken through, been laundered into the mainstream through this ordinary Australian.

'Now One Nation is filling that void, you will see a dramatic decline in support for grass roots patriot groups. This is not a bad thing. This is what we wanted since the Lindt Café siege and we finally achieved it! It took thousands of Patriots rallying to get media to mention Islam, now it only takes Pauline to open her mouth. My advice to Patriots thinking the loss of support is a bad thing? It is the exact opposite. It's a good thing. So relax, enjoy the success and support Pauline.' So writes Neil Erikson on Facebook.

Another incident had gone down on that *Q&A* episode. A man in the audience confronted Pauline, asking what she would do about Islamophobia. 'Only recently, after your rhetoric has come onboard the media, I get called a Muslim pig because of you.'

The man becomes an instant hero on Twitter and in the following morning's think pieces. Then someone finds a post on the man's Facebook page: 'May Allah curse the Jews pigs.'

Jewish community groups complain. 'Will the ABC now do the right thing,' asks the head of one, 'and share the findings of the disclosure with the one million viewers of *Q&A*.'

I watch the show next week. It does not.

Beer o'clock

I still feel shit about something, even though it's been months since it happened. That taxi ride with Ralph and the Half-Jewess, after the Cronulla pig-spit. Ralph was babbling about terrorism in the back seat, hoping the Muslim driver would overhear. And I let him get away with it.

I can't track down the driver, but I can track down Ralph to confront him about the matter. So I'm back in Sydney. The Half-Jewess is sipping a beer opposite me at this bar. She says Ralph will rock up soon.

The Half-Jewess has decided the UPF might be anti-Semitic after all. 'You think there were warning signs on that?' she asks.

I tell her yes, there were warnings. That Blair Cottrell wanted a picture of Hitler hung in every classroom is one that comes to mind. And that he wanted *Mein Kampf* put on the school curriculum is another.'

She says Ralph is good guy, though. But I push back, reminding her of the taxi ride. 'He was being a dick,' I say. 'The taxi driver had done nothing. He was just existing while being visually Muslim.'

'The thing you have to remember,' the Half-Jewess explains, 'is that everyone that puts their face out there to criticise radical Islam, they get death threats. They're making a big sacrifice for everyone else. And I don't think we need to get bogged down in small things – someone having a bit of a go at someone during the daytime, talking about someone.'

Ah. Now I understand. Non-structural being a dick.

Ralph wanders into the bar, an Australian-flag T-shirt pulled over his belly. Amazingly, he falls into a fight with someone on his way from the door to our table. A young olive-skinned man with a beard springs up from his stool one table from us. What's going on?

'This guy,' he points at Ralph, eyeing the Australian flag on his belly, 'gave me this hating look, as if I'm a Muslim.' He explains that he's not Muslim, he's Greek-Irish.

'Are you telepathic or something?' snaps Ralph.

'I just saw your dirty look when you walked in, sniggering at me.'

'No, that's my face.'

I'm delighted, thoroughly, to be catching this. It'll make it harder for Ralph to deny my charge that he was being Islamophobic towards the taxi driver. He's somehow managed to be Islamophobic towards someone who's not even Muslim. 'Ralph,' I say, 'he's —'

'I look at everyone,' Ralph sneers. 'I'm ex-army. So I analyse anyone. I sit with my back to the wall.'

Greek-Irish isn't buying it. He says a few years ago he was a hipster with a beard but now he gets greasies from those who take him for a Muslim. 'I feel judged for the way I look and that means whoever created the judgement is racist.'

Ralph posits that the Greek-Irish is the real racist for assuming his stare was racist.

I shift my stool a little so it's me and Greek-Irish versus Ralph. 'Ralph —' I try again.

'You don't know anything about me,' Ralph tells Greek-Irish. He insists that, far from being a racist, he fights racism, even if it means confronting those 'on my own team'. He says he heard that an anti-Semite spoke at a Reclaim rally in Perth. So Ralph called up the man. 'We had a 45-minute conversation, which I recorded. He actually comes out, he goes, "If we got rid of all those Jews in America and got rid of Israel, then everything would be solved."'

Greek-Irish looks at Ralph. 'I agree with him.'

Oh.

'Have you heard of Oded Yinon's plan?' Greek-Irish asks. (I haven't.) 'He wrote it in 1982. A documented plan of how Israel needs to cause a disruption to gain their "rightful inheritance". From Egypt to Euphrates. American Jews adopted it in 2006.'

I start biting my lip and shift my stool away from Greek-Irish. He notices the big-screen TV hanging on the wall of the bar. Some soldiers are crawling through the sand as a newsfeed scrolls below. He thrusts his hands towards the screen. 'All of this is playing out exactly to that plan. Why has ISIS never attacked Israel? Never once! ISIS is a puppet tool of Israel!'

My arm tenses up and I gulp down the last of my gin. A little dribbles onto my fat gut. I tell Ralph and the Half-Jewess I'm leaving.

'You're John Safran!' Greek-Irish says as I pass. 'You're a funny bugger!'

I don't reply.

I sit on the bench outside the bar and wait for an Uber. Spooling through the news on my phone. Belgian authorities have completed their investigation of a terrorist attack in early 2016. CCTV footage, they say, shows a man at Brussels airport standing among dozens of high school students, readying to activate his bomb. Then he spots a new target. 'The attacker seemed to rush towards two Orthodox Jews. He really, clearly wanted to kill a Jew.' From Brussels to Adelaide: a counter-terrorism squad has swooped in on a man after discovering a series of videos he allegedly filmed, along with Jewish-conspiracy literature. 'The videos provide explicit verbal instructions, as well as physical demonstrations with weapons as to how to kill Jewish people,' the police prosecutor has told the South Australian court.

'It's funny,' a neighbour of the man has told the *Advertiser* journalist. 'He's a Muslim but he's always at Dan Murphy's.'

I poke around. The ABC has reported the story too, but – well, well, well – it's chosen to whitewash the context of this anti-Semitic crime. In contrast to *The Advertiser*, it's carefully omitted all parts of the story that tell you an alleged radical Muslim was behind it. For all the ABC readers know, a neo-Nazi was just busted.

Safran, take a goddamn hint and get the goddamn message. You have to look out for yourself. These people – you know, like whoever decided to whitewash that story – will not be hiding you under the floorboards when the shit goes down. You need the Jews.

There's another news story. Ice addicts have been attacking ambos, and in a *Herald Sun* article, Avi has managed to insert himself into the drama as a self-defence expert.

I call him up. 'How do I join IDF?' I ask.

'Join IDF?' Avi says. There's silence. 'Which one?'

Palms are sweaty

I bounce up the steps of IDF Training in Caulfield, in my new sneakers and tracksuit. It's a quarter to seven in the morning.

'What the fuck is that?' Avi asks as I step through the door, onto a foam floor encircled by gym equipment.

'Nothing, my dictaphone. I always travel with it in case I need to interview someone.'

'John, I thought our whole relationship was an interview, an ongoing interview.'

Two guys are stretching, two are slouching on equipment, waiting for Avi, who has just pulled a couple of dumbbells from the rack, to begin the class.

I tell Avi he's getting a bad name around town. Jews were gossiping about him at the annual interfaith friendship walk, which I slunk along to yesterday. They thought his trashing of Waleed Aly, his support of Pauline Hanson and other antics were 'bad for the Jews', inviting attention, and therefore a danger to our community.

'Jews are the most insecure fucking people in the fucking world,' Avi says. 'Swear to God, it's lucky I was born a Jew. Otherwise I would be the biggest anti-Semite.'

'It's not Jews, it's just people,' one of the stretching guys throws in.

'Oh, shut up, Frenchy.'

I find out that Frenchy, a bearded French man, is the only non-Jew in the class.

'He's always gotta make everyone equal,' Avi complains. 'He doesn't realise there are groups in society that are worse than others. Like, French are all the way down at the fucking bottom.'

'There are shit people in every group,' Frenchy says. 'Look at you.'

We hit the machines.

'Who do we hate the most?' Avi asks.

'The French!' shouts Sammy, a young guy who's bicep-curling, seemingly wanting Avi's approval.

'Really?' says Avi, pointing to Frenchy. 'I like his Frenchship.'

Sammy gives it another go. 'The Iranians!'

'I think the Jews of Caulfield, they're the top of my list,' says Avi.

'Jews from Jerusalem,' Sammy counters.

'Why Jews from Jerusalem?' Avi asks, now very serious.

'They just suck. I lived there for over a year. All those fucking headbanger religos.'

Up and down, up and down, religious Jews nod while praying – I'm guessing that's what Sammy means by headbanger.

'My first military confrontation in the army, I was deployed against eight hundred thousand religos rioting.'

So Sammy has served in the IDF. 'Why were you deployed there?' I ask. The religious Jews, Sammy explains, didn't want to serve in the army and were protesting laws that would require them to do so.

'That's Sammy's claim to fame,' Avi snorts. 'He beat up defence-less civilians.'

'They weren't defenceless,' Sammy says, putting down the weights, 'they had God on their side apparently.'

I'm confused. I thought Avi supported the IDF. But maybe not if they're attacking religious Jews.

'I had fun,' Sammy goes on. 'I got to beat the fuck out of reli-gious people, with a licence.'

Avi's becoming uncomfortable with this talk. 'Ah, Frenchy,'

he deflects. 'Because France is so good?' Avi tries a French accent. 'Francé is so awésomé, thàt's why I'm in Austràlià now.'

'You hear me say "France is so awesome"?' Frenchy whines, stepping away from the shoulder-press.

Avi says France is going to hell because of Muslim immigration.

Frenchy says that in the past, new arrivals took a little bit of time settling in to France, and Muslims are merely the latest version of this immigrant story.

'Frenchy and his fucking airy-fairy loveheart story,' says Avi.

'I'm sorry I'm not giving you the easy answer. You want easy answers to complex problems. I'm sorry, my friend.'

Avi tells Frenchy that he's sick of terrorists doing 'a Jewish chaser' after every big attack. Terrorists raid the *Charlie Hebdo* building, then do 'a Jewish chaser' at the kosher deli. Terrorists go on a rampage in Mumbai and then do 'a Jewish chaser' at a Jewish community centre.

'I'm sorry, Avi, but who are the first victims of Islamic terrorism? Muslims.'

'Oh . . . oh . . . oh!' Avi convulses. 'You fucking left cunt. You keep bringing that shit up. "Let them kill me because they kill themselves." What a fucking stupid ideology. Shut the fuck up.'

Frenchy tells Avi that if he wants to help quell terrorism he should tell Israel to pull out of Palestinian land.

Avi slides up real close. 'What land is the Palestinian land?'

'When Israel was given back to the Jews after the world war, there were certain borders tha—'

'We have something called the Bible, which is the oldest recorded precedent.'

'If you go back that way it's endless,' Frenchy complains. 'How many thousands of years are you going back? If that was the case I would say the Kingdom of France used to stretch down to Germany.'

'I believe the Torah is a great source to understand history.'

'It's just stories written down,' Sammy butts in. 'How do you know it happened?'

'Because three religions that hate each other all are claiming these same stories are true.'

'So you think the twelve plagues came and saved the Jews from the fucking pharaohs?'

Avi grew up in a family of seventeen kids (I remember many of them beetling about Yeshivah College at lunchtime). He has the voice of someone who had to figure out how to cut through the competition at the dinner table. 'In history,' he annunciates, 'at that time, we – the Jews – were in Egypt.'

Then he realises that we've been talking, not training, for a while. 'Right, we're going to do the rear delts.'

Frenchy looks at the clock on the wall. 'We've got no time, mate.' He pulls on his jacket and reaches for his helmet.

'Cos you spent too much time arguing with the facts,' Avi says.

'See you guys later, have a good one,' Frenchy tells us.

'All right,' says Avi. 'Don't fall off your motorbike.'

Sammy's leaning against the bench-press, snickering with a bloke about last night's leaked audio of Donald Trump. Thinking he was off mic, Trump had told a reporter that women melt when you're rich and powerful, you can even 'grab 'em by the pussy' and they don't mind. Everyone is saying, on Twitter and in the news, he's well and truly screwed up this time. He'll never be president now.

Avi marches up to Sammy. 'You just said something against Trump?'

'I'm just saying,' Sammy pleads, 'I'm just saying, it's pretty funny.'

'No, no, don't mention him. Unless you are saying something nice about him, don't talk, okay? Do I go around talking about your God?'

'I don't have a God,' snaps Sammy. He heads out after Frenchy, but not before looking down at my dictaphone. 'I fucking did not have a good workout. Thank you, John.'

Avi told me he's busting to put $500 down on Trump winning the election in a few weeks. I told him a Trump victory would be good for the book.

What an arc! From the back of the ute at my first Reclaim rally, all the way to the White House. There's two-bit Blair and Shermon on that ute babbling to their little rabble. Then the far-right movement grows, then explodes into the Bendigo Gazebo Spectacular. But then, as fast as it rose it whimpers out, Blair clomping in front of the Princess Theatre to a piddling circle of mates. Can it get any worse for the movement? Yes it can. Cut to Cronulla Beach, the tenth anniversary. An underwhelming turnout watches a barely warm pig rotate on a spit. You can stick a fork in the movement because, unlike the pig, it's done. This book, it seems, will cover the rise and fall of Reclaim, a blip in Australian history.

Plot twist: a rumble is felt through the ground and a red-haired monster galumphs over the hill and takes out a senate seat. Pauline wins. Reclaim wasn't a blip after all, it was a foreshadowing. Then some clown over in the US – they say he's in cahoots with white nationalists – clobbers Jeb and Ted and Marco. So Pauline is a fore-shadowing too? Of something that's bigger than just Australia?

I stare at a headline on my Facebook feed: 'The Huffington Post Pollster presidential election forecast gives Hillary Clinton a 97.5% chance of winning.'

So what's good for the book won't be happening. Oh well, them's the breaks.

WELCOME, PRESIDENT TRUMP

Plot twist II: Trump wins

'The Trump presidency is probably the greatest demonstration of the fact we are moving into a new age.' Blair is addressing his Facebook troops, gum trees bent behind him, a grey sky hanging overhead. 'Up until now, regular people, working-class people, they have voted for who they are told to vote for. This time, the masses of the working-class people voted in spite of the mainstream media corporations. It's never happened before in human history.'

Talk of class and media manipulation might sound a little left-wing, but he soon shifts gears.

'First thing,' he advises Donald Trump, 'is a security agency must be set up, for the purposes of identifying the hostile people in places

of influence, in media, governments, education. Compiling information on these people, finding out who they are, prosecuting them or
physically extracting them from their positions of influence.' Blair
warms to his theme. 'You cannot heal a body if, in the major organs
of that body, you are going to permit cancer and disease to exist.
There must be a healthy, national, strong, moral, patriotic education
system once more. Not social sciences, not theories on gender, not
convincing children to be transvestites.' Blair shoos a fly from his
nose. 'Focus on educating the next generation. Don't worry about
existing leftists. Let them run around the streets setting fire to trash
cans. Let them grow old and die off and they will be forgotten.'

Last season, Blair spotted Reclaim and anti-Islam and saw an
opening to smuggle in white nationalism. Now he sees another
opportunity. Blair is hosting a Celebrate Trump rally this Sunday,
outside Parliament House in Melbourne. But it didn't begin life as
Blair's rally.

Trump has attracted fans worldwide who occupy that murky
space between trolling and believing. Rebelling against a culture
of safe spaces, microaggressions and hectoring political correctness. Wearing 'Make America Great Again' caps largely because it
annoys the right people.

A young dude has written a private message, which is circulating
online. It's about the Celebrate Trump rally Facebook page. 'I know
the guy that started it. He did it as a joke. It's just another memeing
kid. He was fucking around.' He explains that Blair and other 'patriots' latched on. The young dude says of his friend, 'I'm not sure if
he'll be there, because it may have been taken from him.'

Election debrief

I slide past the JERRY SEINFELD LIVE tour poster stuck to the wall of the building opposite IDF Training, and now I'm trotting up the stair of the gym, and god, I can even hear Avi talking shit from down here.

I step inside and Avi has Sammy backed against one of the mirrored walls.

'Bernie Sanders is a total fuckwit,' Avi blares. 'Would he drop fucking dead? He's the worst fucking Jew. If he dies of a heart attack I hope nobody takes his organs, because he'll fuck up the next person.'

'Can't you run out of breath yet?' Sammy asks.

'No.'

'I'm just pointing out that he's a politician that's kept his line the whole time. Done.'

'He's a piece-of-shit socialist and I hope he drops dead. I hope they don't give him a Jewish burial.'

'I was hanging out with the socialists last night,' I tell them. 'They're all excited.'

'Because they think the revolution is coming now?' asks Sammy.

'Yeah, it's like if Trump can be elected, that means Bernie Sanders probably could have. Everyone's fed up with the system. They said Trump asked the right questions – about lost jobs and Wall Street – but gave the wrong answers.'

Avi's public support of Trump has been noticed. He reads out one message posted on his Facebook page: '"I'll be sure not to send my kids to your gym in case your racist bigotry right wing hatred filters down to them. Also I want to make sure other parents . . ."' She's a Bialik mum,' Avi says, Bialik being a local Jewish school. 'I love how my newsfeed is full of crying lefties. Get used to it, folks, welcome President Trump.'

We get in one round on the machines before Sammy and Avi fall into another screaming match. This one is about Bernie Sanders' policy on Jewish settlements in the West Bank, and which Israeli troops should be stationed where in the Holy Land.

'You know what I read?' I butt in from the cable-pull.

Avi turns and snaps, 'What did you read, fucking John, you and your fucking books?'

'Listen, you two might have been in the army, but I read a book. This fucking book said Jewish settlers once lived on a plot of land in Egypt. And the Egyptian government told the Israeli government to pull these settlers out, as part of a peace deal.'

'And they got pulled out,' Avi says.

So he knows about this. 'The difference between them and the West Bank settlers,' I go on, 'was they weren't touched in the head by God as much. They took the land as opportunists. They weren't there because they thought they were helping to bring on the Messiah.'

'They got relocated,' Avi says. 'They got their houses paid for. They got an upgrade, basically.' He asks me what my point is.

I think about all the people I've been hanging with over the year, Pastor Daniel, Hamza, and the rest. 'It's hard to cut a deal with people who think that what they're doing will bring on the Messiah.'

Celebrate Trump rally

The waiters have begun packing up the outdoor tables, across the road from Parliament House in Melbourne.

'Is there time for another coffee?' I ask the woman scooping up the salt and pepper shakers from my table.

'Yeah, absolutely time for another coffee.'

'When's the race war starting?'

'We have been told to get everything in at around eleven-thirty, so I guess about midday. They're saying it's Trump people and anti-Trump people. It's the same people that come every time, it's just a different pretend cause.'

I look up to the Princess Theatre. The *Fiddler on the Roof* billboard has been taken down, replaced with one promoting a new musical, *The Book of Mormon*. I think about penning another parody. If only there was a word that sounded similar to Mormon that was applicable to Blair.

'Let's bunch it up, guys. Come in. Everyone bunch it up.'

This is not something you have to say when there are enough people at your rally. Fifty or so folks follow Blair's instructions and bunch it up on the road.

A man beams next to three little girls. The girls' home-made banner, spinning Hillary Clinton's insult, reads: ADORABLE DEPLORABLES.

A young guy thrusts over his head a portrait of Donald Trump dressed as a Roman soldier with laser beams firing from his eyes. TRUMP GOD EMPEROR is printed beneath.

'Free Harambe!' shouts his friend, marching back and forth with a picture of Harambe the gorilla.

The folks in the crowd, like those two guys, look more like meme-ing kids than the 'patriots' who have rocked up to the previous rallies.

'This is Sampson.' Big Blair motions a teenager to the micro-phone. 'He's the one who organised this.'

'I just like Trump,' mutters the teen. 'I'm just liking all his ideas and, I mean, you can't really go wrong with him.'

'Can't hear ya!' shouts a bloke.

'Everything he's doing, it's good for the world, he's gonna be good for Australia. So, ah, it's good all round.'

Blair now brings a man to the microphone who I know to be a new UPF leader, although Blair doesn't reveal he's from the UPF. I scan the street. Blair and his buddies haven't brought along the UPF flags and signs today. This new UPF leader speaks of crony capitalism and other political matters, but the memeing kids only light up when he complains about political correctness. This grievance is the connective tissue between the two groups. Having drawn them in with this, the leader goes for the upsell.

'Now, Donald Trump, he didn't need to run for president,' he begins. 'He's a man who's a billionaire already, has everything in the world, even a hot wife. The man does it because he is a nationalist. He loves his country, just as we love ours, and what we are seeing today in this year is a revolution in the spirit of our people.'

The words 'Islam' and 'Muslim' aren't mentioned in any of the speeches.

A journo from a major network scrunches her brow and asks the guy with the TRUMP GOD EMPEROR poster if he is part of this thing called the alt-right. And what exactly, she goes on, is the alt-right anyway?

These oddball interests of mine now have to be everyone's interests. In 2013 I interviewed Richard Spencer, a founder of the white nationalist alt-right. His movement felt as marginal and esoteric as a secret society that believed aliens built Stonehenge. Now the alt-right has made it to the White House. Trump's chief strategist, Steve Bannon, says he's a fellow travellor of the movement. Forget 2013, this stuff was obscure three weeks ago.

Blair rolls over to me, pointing a video camera.

'Shalom,' I say.

'How you doing? How's the book coming?'

'Pretty good.'

'What prompted you to attend this extravagant event today?'

'You know, extra chapter.'

Next morning I open my laptop and see that Blair has juxtaposed a picture of me laughing with a picture of a stereotypical rabbi, laughing and rubbing his hands. (A screenshot Blair's taken from an anti-Semitic Arab film, incidentally.) Blair complains that I 'excel in making everything serious into a laughing matter'.

Another person in this story unhappy with my sarcastic ways. But I'm not budging. I might see tangles everywhere, but on this one matter I'm not confused at all. The clowning must go on.

I pull up a recent news item in *The Independent*: 'North Korea bans sarcasm,' reads the headline. Dictator Kim Jong-un has circulated an edict on the matter. Apparently he got wind of the fact that people were employing sarcasm to say the things you'd get a bullet for if you said them straight out.

Karma police

Sammy's flashing around his phone at training this morning. He's showing us an article from a 2001 edition of *Dolly* magazine, where a twenty-year-old Sammy sits with a beautiful girl. The article is about men and women who are best friends but don't want to sleep with each other.

On any other day, I'd want to find out what chain of events led to Sammy featuring in *Dolly*, but Avi's got a more interesting story to tell. He's leaning on the mirrored wall next to me as I do cable-crossover chest flies.

'They called me on Saturday morning, this Shabbos,' Avi says. He's talking about the Australian Federal Police. 'They go, "Do you have a few minutes? Can we come over?" I'm like, "I've got to go to synagogue. Can it wait till tomorrow and I'll come to you?" To be honest, I was thinking in my head, If it's a threat, if they're alerting me to a threat, I don't really want my wife to hear it.'

Avi turns to the class and shouts, 'Switch!' Sammy and Frenchy switch machines.

'She would freak out,' Avi goes on. 'All night I'm thinking, Fuck. Which motherfucker is threatening me now?'

He met with the AFP officers the next day. But, he discovered, there hadn't been a threat made against him. The officers had called him in because they were concerned that he, Avi Yemini, was becoming the threat.

Some people had alerted the AFP to his program, training locals for the Israeli Defense Forces. Turns out there are laws against recruiting for foreign armies, even for allied countries like Israel. The officers told him his operation was too amateur at this stage to warrant an arrest but, 'They're saying if I go up a notch . . . basically, what they're warning me is, if the Israeli government turns to me and says, "Can you start recruiting for us," and I did that, that's when I've crossed the line.'

Avi says to the class, 'Charged with recruiting foreign fighters? Fuck, that would be so great.'

Sammy suggests he could fake emails from the Israeli government and forward those to the AFP.

I pipe in: 'The AFP will be asking you how come this email is from IsraeliGov43@hotmail.com.'

The class cracks up.

'No,' adds Avi, 'from BenjaminNetanyahu@gmail.com!' and we all crack up again.

(Later I realise I could have smashed it out of the park with BenjaminNetanyahu@yahoo.com.)

Walking down the stairs with Sammy I ask about the *Dolly* article. Did he really not want to sleep with his best friend, the beautiful girl in the photo? He says he actually did want to sleep with her.

Avi's pulling on his rowing machine, I'm pulling on mine. I'm shocked by his latest news this morning.

'I just needed to get that off my chest,' Avi says. 'And I thought Joh—'

'You're going to be in such trouble.'

'Everyone's going to go psycho. As soon as I drop it to the *Jewish News*, shit's going to hit the fan.'

'So, who reached out for who?' I ask. 'They reached out for you?'

'I can't remember who started it.'

Avi stood up for Pauline Hanson on his Facebook page, and one thing led to another, and now, Avi says, he'll be bringing Pauline and her fellow One Nation senator Malcolm Roberts to town, to address Jews at a town hall meeting.

'This is the format. I was going to introduce them both, welcome everyone, blah blah, talk about whatever bullshit, that's my skill. They each will make their speech, and – stop laughing.'

'Sorry.'

'Topics they're going to cover are "the difference between the current problematic Islamic immigration and the successful post-Holocaust Jewish immigration —".'

I wince so hard I nearly topple off the rowing machine. 'Jesus fucking Christ. Who organised these questions? You or them?'

'This is me.'

'What does your wife think about all this?'

'She'll probably hear about it on Facebook.'

'Your Asian wife who Pauline would have been against in the nineties.'

'Like I've said to you many times before, you can't judge a politician on their past policies, otherwise there's no one left. It's what you stand for now. She loves Asians.'

'There will be protests too, won't there?'

'There'll for sure be protests. You think the world's gonna turn on me?'

I tell him no doubt.

Avi pulls faster. 'I think maybe she's the Moshiah.' Moshiah is the Hebrew word for Messiah.

'Pauline, why?' I ask, matching his speed.

Avi thinks. 'Well, the Moshiah comes on a cloud. There's no arguing she's in the clouds.'

'Yeah.'

'What other signs do we have? She's got to be a descendant of King David. I reckon King David was a redhead.' Avi digs deeper. 'What other signs are you looking for? Do the gematria of "Pauline". Yeah?'

Gematria is the numerology practised by Kabbalah rabbis. Letters of the Hebrew alphabet are assigned numbers, and words with matching values are seen as connected. 'I bet you it's going to come to "King Moshiah" or something.'

Avi's thinking about the Moshiah but I have another Jewish tale in mind. 'You know the story of the golem?' I say of the mud creature brought to life by a rabbi to protect his city from anti-Semites. In the story it all backfires on the Jews; the rabbi can't keep the golem under control. 'How do you know you're not building a golem that comes back and destroys the city?'

'I can't complain if it does,' Avi says. 'The city needs a bit of destroying. I hope it takes out Yeshivah first.'

Final pocket hums

'Hi John my name is Imaad and I'm a mate of Musa Cerantonio,' reads the message on my phone. 'I visited him this morning and he asked me to message you. He says he would like you to visit him if possible. He says he would like to discuss how your book is going amongst other things. He's currently at the Assessment Prison in the city on Spencer St.'

There's a prison in the Melbourne CBD?

I call up Musa's brother Nick. He says I should pop on over because Musa is scheduled to ring home today.

I jump in my car. Musa's not the only Footscray fameball. A graffiti artist has hit world headlines for painting a huge Hillary Clinton in a bikini on the side of a local shop. The furious council demanded he paint over it. And today I drive past his response: the artist has daubed a black burqa over Hillary, her eyes poking through the eye-slit.

I sit on the couch that Australian Federal Police officers have sat on since I was last here.

'If he gets convicted he's gonna be in prison for a while,' Nick says, perched on the armrest of the other couch in the lounge room. Musa was meant to call at midday and it's already twelve-fifteen.

'Wow. Like ten years? Twenty years?'

'I don't know but it seems like they would try to make an example out of him, more than the other guys.'

Nick and his mum are cleaners in the same medical clinic, and both were at work when they got the news.

'It was near the end of my shift and someone came in, like: "Your mum. She's crying." I'm like, Oh shit! I'm walking slowly, thinking, What could have happened, is someone dead or something? Like, fuck! And then when I get there, she's bawling her eyes out: "I just got a call from the police. Robert's been arrested." (Nick and his mum will only call Musa Robert, his name before his conversion to Islam.) So we have to go to the boss, "We're going home. Our house is being searched by the police."'

I look at the owl clock on the wall. It's half past twelve.

'We drive up and see these two massive black cars out the front of the house.' Nick motions to the dining table. 'And we had to sit at the table for a bunch of hours while they go through everything. We did our statements and that kind of stuff. They didn't really find anything. They had to take my laptop, and that was a pain in the arse.'

What if the Australian Federal Police took my laptop? Surely I could explain away the ISIS literature, like I could *The Anarchist Cookbook* on my shelf ? I wonder how many laptop jihadis, busted for downloading ISIS material, were just playing with fire or goofing around, or doing whatever I was doing when I tried being a goth for a weekend when I was fourteen.

A week later, Nick continues, he was home sick, delirious with flu-like symptoms. 'And there was banging on the door. "Police, open up!" And I'm like, Oh fuck! I go to the front door and there's nobody there. I'm thinking I'm hearing stuff. I'm thinking I must have PTSD from the previous week. I must be way sicker than I thought.'

He wasn't hallucinating, though. Soon officers were spilling into the backyard and bashing on the back door. This time ASIO had come with the AFP.

'And they took all kinds of silly stuff. They took my son's toy gun, the AK-47.'

I remember Musa firing a toy gun in this very room. He pulled the spongy tips from the bullets to reveal the sharp metal tips beneath. He said he couldn't believe a manufacturer would be so irresponsible.

The owl clock strikes one.

Nick says of the raiding officers, 'The whole time they were very polite. They were like, "You don't have to stay here, you're not in trouble." I said, "I'm not going anywhere, I'm sick as a dog!" Some of them were the same from last week, so you chat with them again.

The whole time I'm cracking jokes, which I thought were good jokes, and you don't get any reaction. When you talk to them they're like all smiles, but when you crack a joke they are like very serious. They are the police.'

When he says this it reminds me of the other Nick in this tale. Nicholas Folkes likes cracking jokes too. He reckons what he does, dressing up in a burqa, is 'like *The Chaser*'.

The clock strikes half past one. No phone call. Nick says this simply hasn't happened before. 'Actually, he calls home too much.'

In fact, jokers are everywhere. A psychologist, a Palestinian Australian, who has spoken with Musa, pulled a Hulk mask over her hijab at the supermarket this week. I saw it online. 'Have you ever seen a Hijabi Hulk?' she asks the camera. 'Am I scary enough? What if I said, "AAAAARRRRGGG"?' Some Muslims criticise her online and she responds, 'I blame John Safran. I've been watching a number of his videos lately.'

The clock strikes two. I shrug at Nick and he shrugs back. We wander to my car. I drive away from Musa's home to mine. Although that won't be his home for the foreseeable future.

Sitting on my balcony I fill out a prison visitation form. A few days after I've sent it off Nick shoots me a text: 'Robert's lawyer will be contacting you soon about whether or not they will add you to his visitors list. Just a heads up. Adios.'

The word comes through. The prison will not allow Musa to see me. Nick tells me more. The prison will not allow Musa to phone me. And Musa wrote me a letter but the prison won't let it through.

Almost twenty years ago, I was one of eight youngsters racing around the world shooting short documentaries for a television show. It was the first time I'd been on television. One week I streaked through Jerusalem, one week I weaselled my way into a baptism in a lake. And one week I showed viewers how to break into Disneyland through a hole in a fence along a highway.

But I can't scale a prison wall. This is getting out of hand.

I reach for my pencil.

Acknowledgements

Thank you Ben Ball, Meredith Rose and Penguin; Sophie Braham, Noah Erlich, Scarlett Jae Nohay and Abigail Ulman; Peter Grace and Andy Fleming; Laura Waters, John Godfrey, Princess Pictures, and SBS; Ben Naparstek and *Good Weekend*; Hannah Stenning and news.com.au; Kevin Whyte, Georgina Ogilvie and Token; Madeleine Parry, Elle Marsh and Hannah Moore. Plus all who appear in this book and helped me along the way. On occasion, names and identifying information have been altered.